9/11 and the
Visual Culture of Disaster

INDIANA UNIVERSITY PRESS

Bloomington & Indianapolis

9/11

and the
Visual Culture
of Disaster

THOMAS STUBBLEFIELD

This book is a publication of

INDIANA UNIVERSITY PRESS
Office of Scholarly Publishing
Herman B Wells Library 350
1320 East 10th Street
Bloomington, Indiana 47405 USA

iupress.indiana.edu

Telephone 800-842-6796
Fax 812-855-7931

© 2015 by Thomas Stubblefield

∞ The paper used in this publication
meets the minimum requirements of
the American National Standard for
Information Sciences–Permanence of
Paper for Printed Library Materials,
ANSI Z39.48–1992.

Manufactured in the
United States of America

Library of Congress
Cataloging-in-Publication Data

Stubblefield, Thomas.
   9/11 and the visual culture of disaster /
Thomas Stubblefield.
      pages cm
   Includes bibliographical references and
index.
   ISBN 978-0-253-01549-5 (cloth : alk.
paper) – ISBN 978-0-253-01556-3 (pbk. :
alk. paper) – ISBN 978-0-253-01563-1
(ebook) 1. September 11 Terrorist
Attacks, 2001 – Influence. 2. September 11
Terrorist Attacks, 2001, in mass media. 3.
September 11 Terrorist Attacks, 2001, in
art. 4. Emptiness (Philosophy) I. Title.
   HV6432.7.S78 2014
   973.931 – dc23
                                    2014029044

1 2 3 4 5   20 19 18 17 16 15

FOR C. D. S.

Contents

Acknowledgments

As pieces of this book have passed through so many skilled and caring hands over the past decade, it is impossible to faithfully represent the full catalog of those who have helped bring it into being. What I offer here represents only a small sampling of the many individuals who have participated in the ongoing conversation.

I initially began to wrestle with issues surrounding the visual culture of 9/11 in 2004 while pursuing my master's degree in art history at the University of Illinois, Chicago. Throughout these early investigations, I was encouraged and inspired by Bob Bruegmann, Peter Hales, Hannah Higgins, and Woodman Taylor. Together, they not only pushed me to clarify and develop my ideas further, but introduced the possibility of my one day turning this project into a book. For that, I am eternally grateful. Several years later, the project was given new life at the Visual Studies Program at the University of California, Irvine. Anyone familiar with the unique interdisciplinary spirit of the program will immediately see its influence on my methodology and overall approach to visual culture. It is hard to imagine having the same opportunity to pursue these questions across such a disparate field of media at any other program at the time.

I would like to thank Peter Krapp, who was (and remains) extraordinarily giving of his time. Peter can always be counted on for a relevant source or thought-provoking question. Additionally, Cécile Whiting offered tireless and timely feedback throughout. I am also grateful to Martin Schwab, who had the uncanny ability to force me to revisit the assumptions of my argument with a single well-placed question. Mark

Poster too proved an invaluable resource, particularly with regard to helping me to build the theoretical toolbox that this project necessitated. I will never read Foucault without thinking of him. In addition, my interaction with colleagues in the program was critical in helping me to sculpt my ideas into the form that they would eventually take. For this, I thank Chris Balaschak, Kim Beil, Mark Cunningham, Douglas Hodapp, Ari Laskin, Tim Seiber, Sami Siegelbaum, Nicole Woods-Beckton, and Ken Yoshida. It is also important to acknowledge the generosity of the University of California, Irvine, in this endeavor. The Chancellor's Fellowship, numerous traveling grants from the International Center for Writing and Translation and the School of the Humanities, and a Summer Dissertation Research Fellowship allowed me to dedicate myself more fully to this project and are in no small part responsible for its success.

This project has come to full fruition while I have been working as professor in the Art History Department at the University of Massachusetts, Dartmouth. Throughout the endless revisions, I have benefited tremendously from the guidance and support of Anna Dempsey, Memory Holloway, Pamela Karimi, Hallie Meredith, Erin Sassin, and Michael Taylor. Allison Cywin and Charlene Ryder helped enormously in the endless hunt to procure images and essays. In addition, I am indebted to the students of the College of Visual and Performing Arts at UMD, especially those in two classes, The Visual Culture of Disaster and Theory of Photography, who kept me on my toes and forced me to keep my ideas fresh and relevant.

I also want to thank Indiana University Press for its diligence and commitment to this project. In particular, I would like to express my gratitude to my editor, Raina Polivka, who believed in the book from the beginning and worked tirelessly to bring it into being. Jenna Whittaker deserves ample credit for somehow ensuring that everything moved forward while at the same time always looking over my materials with a conscientious and critical eye. Eric Levy provided the fine-tooth comb and meticulous scrutiny that was needed to my whip my prose into shape. I am also very appreciative of the insightful suggestions and comments of the outside readers. Additionally, I want to acknowledge Tom Gunning, who fielded my questions about the representation of falling bodies in early film with characteristic expertise and generosity.

Finally, I want to thank Barbara, Dave, David, and Trisha Stubble-field for their unwavering support, Hayden, Zoey, and Damien for interjecting some much-needed perspective throughout, and Karen, whose gentle nature and wild optimism make all things appear obtainable.

9/11 and the
Visual Culture of Disaster

I don't know what we'll see when the smoke
clears . . . but I fear it may be nothing.

LYNNE SHARON SCHWARTZ,
The Writing on the Wall

Introduction

The collision of the jet passenger planes with the Twin Towers, their subsequent collapse into nothingness, the ominous absence within the smoke-filled skyline, the busy streets of Manhattan turned disaster movie – these scenes were images as much or more than actual events.[1] The hard truth of this realization came less than a week after the attacks when Karlheinz Stockhausen described the disaster as "the greatest work of art that is possible in the whole cosmos" and once again on the eve of the one-year anniversary of 9/11 when Damien Hirst expressed his admiration for the terrorists' ability to create such a "visually stunning" piece of art.[2] With the remains of the dead still being sifted out of the rubble at Ground Zero and the *Tribute in Light* beaming into the night sky as a daily reminder of the horrific events of the day, it was all but impossible to see through the callousness and publicity-driven nature of these remarks at the time. Eventually, however, as references to the Hollywood disaster movie and the rhetoric of the sublime reverberated throughout popular discourse, the realization set in that the eerily photogenic quality of the event was not a coincidence. Rather, as Stockhausen and Hirst suggest, the attack was aimed at and made for the image.

As a result, the disaster appeared tailor-made for a familiar postmodern discourse. In a discussion with Jürgen Habermas held only days after the attack, Jacques Derrida catalyzed this response by noting that the shared interest of "maximum media coverage" between the perpetrators and victims of 9/11 reflected a pervasive desire to "spectacularize the event."[3] Not long after, Samuel Weber diagnosed the "theatricaliza-

0.1. Paul Fusco, *Tribute in Light,* 2002. By permission of Magnum Photos.

tion" of the attack and subsequent retaliation as an escalation in war-as-spectacle, one which shifted the stakes of the conflict from a specific geographical space or national identity to the media itself.[4] Summarizing what has since become a refrain within the scholarship of 9/11, Katalin Orbán describes the disaster as a "constitutively visual event that can (and did) become a real time global media spectacle, where maximum exposure, rather than concealment, ensures terror's success as an act of communication."[5]

While acknowledging the primacy of the image to the event, the enduring association of the disaster with spectacle served to obscure the fact that the experience of 9/11 and its aftermath was one in which absence, erasure, and invisibility dominated the frame in equal measure. Following the logic of implosion rather than explosion, the World Trade Center withheld its contents from view as it fell; its stories "pancaked" on top of one another rather than turning themselves inside out. With the vast majority of the dead dying behind the curtain wall of the towers' facades, "the most photographed disaster in history" failed to yield a single noteworthy image of carnage.[6] This absence within the spectacular image of the event was carried over into the visual culture that followed. Indeed, from the phantom presence of the *Tribute in Light* to Art Spiegelman's nearly blank *New Yorker* cover to the erasure of the Twin Towers from television shows and feature films to the monumental voids of Michael Arad's 9/11 memorial, the empty image came to function in the aftermath as a kind of visual shorthand for the events of that day.

In addition to the prevalence of absence as a visual motif, the wake of 9/11 also saw an existential absence of images, which shaped the discourse and memory of the event in powerful ways. While Hollywood's unofficial ban on representations of the disaster is perhaps the most well-known example of this phenomenon, the art world would also reproduce this invisibility through a disconcerting reticence which has only recently been rescinded. More overt instances of negation were on display outside of the museum as works such as Eric Fischl's *Tumbling Woman* and Sharon Paz's *Falling* were quickly removed after backlash from the media and residents of New York. These localized instances of censorship echo the resurgence of iconoclasm on the global stage as spectacular images of erasure (the dynamiting of the Bamiyan Buddha, the strategic falling of the statue of Saddam Hussein in Firdos Square by the U.S. military, and even the destruction of the World Trade Center itself) were utilized as weapons in the larger battle for and within the image. Whether through the presentation of absence within the frame or through the eradication of images at the hands of censorship or iconoclasm, everywhere the image seemed to echo the empty hole in the Manhattan skyline.

This book centers on the paradox of the visual culture of 9/11, which both foregrounds the image and the visual experience in general and at the same time steeps the events of that day in absence, erasure, and invisibility. While invisibility is conventionally perceived in terms of the substrate or precession of a sign, Jacques Rancière suggests a less neutral status by insisting that absence be understood as a product of the image's coming into being. For this reason, analysis must begin not with the familiar historical question of what kinds of events elude representation, but rather, "Under what conditions might it be said that certain events cannot be represented?"[7] Following this logic, a central

0.2. Sharon Paz, *Falling*, 2001. Window Project, Jamaica Center for the Arts, New York.

thesis of this project is that media and the images they produce articulate not only presence but also the conditions of their own invisibility. In certain cases, they even actively structure their own disappearance. As such, absence functions not as negativity but as a particular mode of presence which shapes experience and official histories in often dramatic fashion.

Pursuing these configurations of invisibility and erasure across the media of photography, film, monuments, graphic novels, and digital media reveals these spaces to be a site of conflict in the wake of the disaster. From the deployment of the codified trope of the "unrepresentable" in the 9/11 monument to the unique mode of vision offered to the analog photographer, the presence of absence proves capable of reaffirming national identity and even implicitly laying the groundwork for the impending invasions of Iraq and Afghanistan. At the same time, these configurations offer an outside to the dominant image of the event by conjuring conflicting relations of spectatorship, as in the recurring image of the empty city in post-9/11 popular culture, or unraveling the stability of subjectivity via the curious descent of the anonymous falling body in Richard Drew's iconic photograph.

This activation of absence and the tenuous relation to narratives of power that it charted rendered the inner workings of the image temporarily accessible, albeit in often convoluted and/or muted form. Indeed, 9/11 and its wake not only confirmed a formative role of the invisible in spectacular relations, its mutually constitutive relation to the visible, and its openness to reconfiguration via violence, but also placed the reconstitution of this interrelation on display within the visual record itself. As theorist Marie-José Mondzain explains, while the millennial celebration "marked a dominance of the visible and its industries . . . on 11 September 2001, the empire of the visible, the servant of all modern forms of the combined powers of economics and icons, suffered its greatest blow. . . . The visible entered a crisis."[8] Symptomatic of this crisis was the advent of a "visual fast" in which the excess of the visible temporarily gave way to a regime of absence, invisibility, and erasure. This period of iconoclasm, marked by both an absence of the visual and a pervasive visual absence, spanned roughly from the end of live coverage of the event to the eventual waning of the taboo against representation, which began to take shape across multiple media in 2006. In this window of time, the reconfiguration of spectacle was made visible in the "aftermedia" of the event, those modes of representation (primarily photography, film, and graphic novels, but also mixed media and sculpture) not involved or only indirectly involved in the live presentation of the event.

Representative of this phenomenon is the dilemma that faced Hollywood in the aftermath of 9/11. Because of its extended temporal gap between production and exhibition, commercial cinema in the wake of the disaster was confronted with a host of issues regarding representation that the instantaneity of television news and the internet excused them from. Nowhere is this more apparent than in the handful of films and television shows that contained images of the towers and which were scheduled to be released in the weeks that followed 9/11. Literally overnight, the establishing shots and backgrounds of previously benign scenes became loaded with an unforeseeable significance that made many within the film industry timid about their release. With the removal of the entirety of the New York context still beyond the reach of technology or at least the budget of most dramas and comedies, those films which contained such images were left with a missing signified that seemed as unrepresentable as it was inescapable. With the exception of a few films, the overwhelming response to this dilemma was to digitally remove the towers from the New York skyline. The official explanation for this erasure in films such as *Serendipity, Zoolander, People I Know, Spider-Man,* and others was summarized by Columbia Pictures chair Amy Pascal, who claimed that "the sudden appearance of the World Trade Center in a film is a reminder of the pain and suffering moviegoers are trying to forget."[9] Yet, as these missing scenes were quickly made available online, this "removal" was inevitably incomplete and partial.

While not subject to the same regulation and social taboos as the film industry, the art world tended to internalize the invisibility of the disaster, producing what can only be called a deafening silence in the aftermath of 9/11. Aside from a handful of isolated pieces by Thomas Ruff, Eric Fischl, Carolee Schneeman, Tom Friedman, Thomas Hirschhorn, and Luc Tymans, one is hard pressed to find work that grapples with this monumental event, despite its explicitly visual nature.[10] As MOCA's

0.3. "September 11" show at MoMA PS1, September 11, 2011–January 9, 2012. © Matthew Septimus. Courtesy of MoMA PS1.

chief curator Paul Schimmel explains, this lack of engagement on the part of artists has been reproduced by the institutions of art, which as a whole have all but ignored the subject.[11] Interestingly, the first forays into grappling with this event have almost unanimously relied upon excessively indirect, even cryptic connections. The long awaited "September 11" show at the Museum of Modern Art's PS1 gallery in New York crystallized this logic. Only a single work from the show (Ellsworth Kelly's collage that reimagines Ground Zero as a monochromatic swath of green) directly engages with the event, while the majority not only eschew direct reference but were in fact produced before the disaster occurred. According to curator Peter Eleey, as 9/11 was "made to be used," the banishing of its image from the exhibition serves as a symbolic refusal of the logic of terrorism.

While it is easy to dismiss this reliance upon anachronism as a failure to fully engage with the event, as, for example, critic Hal Foster does, taken in the context of the visual culture of 9/11 as a whole this curatorial strategy might actually reflect something larger about the role of the image in the aftermath. If one can put aside Eleey's rather idealist if not naive assertions regarding the ability of the museum to somehow disentangle the event from the spectacle of the image, this strategy comes to articulate a powerful vision in which 9/11 serves as its own structuring absence within the visual record of the event and its aftermath.[12] From this standpoint, absence reflects not so much the shortcomings of a politically cautious curator or cultural institution, or the incomprehensibility of the Modernist tradition of the sublime, but rather the power of the missing *as image* within a new regime of the visual. This activated status of absence is made possible by recent revisions to the spectacle at the hands of both new media and the increasingly modulated and diffuse forces of late capitalism which undergird them.

POST-SPECTACLE, NEGATIVITY, AND DISASTER

Confronted by both an urgency to make sense of an incomprehensible event and an undeniable affinity between the disaster and familiar discourses of postmodernism and trauma studies, scholarship in the aftermath largely approached September 11 as an illustration of existing theoretical tropes. However, the critical distance of the last decade allows for a more radical and singular method. This entails reversing the causal relations between theory and event so that the disaster is recast as a constellation of immanence which one does not so much bring theory to, but rather allows to disclose new concepts and modes of analysis.[13] This strategy serves to disentangle the visual culture of 9/11 from some of its early conceptual framings and, in the process, resuscitates difficult, ongoing questions regarding the new modes of seeing and representing that the disaster made possible as well as the correlative methods and theories needed to accommodate these assemblages. One such place for reappraisal is the apparent conflict between the visual excess of the disaster and its penchant for images of absence, which from this perspective appears not as an impasse or even an opposition, but rather as an origin or locus for this productive relation.[14] Presenting an image of disaster in which the mutual exclusivity of the visible and its other no longer hold, the visual culture of 9/11 articulates a "spectacle of absence," a fluid constellation in which antispectacular forces do not simply coexist with the dominant image of the event, but exert a formative influence upon and at times even comprise it.

In this environment, the binaries of what might be called "first wave spectacle theory" (Debord's *Society of the Spectacle,* Lefebvre's "spectacle of the street," T. J. Clark's "hierarchy of representations," and, to some degree, Douglas Kellner's "megaspectacles" and "interactive spectacles") inadvertently end up naturalizing and/or pacifying the blank image. At the root of this operation is the inverse relation which theories of spectacle often posit between appearance and invisibility. Exemplifying the latter, Guy Debord describes the violence of spectacle as inseparable from an essential negativity:

> Considered in its own terms, the spectacle is affirmation of appearance and affirmation of all human life, namely social life, as mere appearance. But the critique which reaches the truth of the spectacle exposes it as the visible negation of life, as a negation of life which has become visible.[15]

While suggesting that the invisibility of "life" might be resurrected via critique, Debord nonetheless portrays the invisible's relation to the spectacle as simply the placeholder for that which is sacrificed to the image and as such inevitably represents loss, expenditure, and death. Yet even this presence of absence is concealed in the spectacle. After all, in order for the image to take the place of life it must not simply negate its outside, but negate its own negation. In this way, all aspects of life and indeed reality itself collapse into the image. The discourse of spectacle therefore subjects the invisible to a dual erasure which renders it not only inactive relative to the presence of the visible, but absent at the level of experience. In the context of the disaster, this dynamic led to the recurring association of the presence of absence within the visual record of 9/11 with a failure of representation, the collapse of the dominant image, and, in turn, a new vulnerability in Empire.[16] These formations appeared as hiccups or glitches within the mode of representation or, equally unsatisfying, outright reversals in the power relationships of an otherwise impenetrable spectacle. Approaching these phenomena in terms of a twenty-first-century media ecology suggests that these instances of absence might instead operate as specific constellations within a larger regime of flux and flow rather than as simple negations or noise within the "dominant image."

As operations of the spectacle increasingly move from temporal to spatial registers, representational images to presignifying flux, and material commodities to immaterial becoming, the solidity with which theory once invested this critical rubric of spectacle has broken down in the last several decades. In "Eclipse of the Spectacle," Jonathan Crary chronicles the ways in which Guy Debord's canonical articulation of spectacle is compromised in the late twentieth century by diffuse operations of flow, connection, and immanence. He explains,

> For Debord, writing in 1967, at the last high tide of the "Pax Americana," the auratic presence of the commodity was bound up with the illusion of its utter tangibility. But since that time, we have witnessed the gradual displacement of aura from images of possessible objects to digitized flows of data, to the glow of the V D T and the promise of access embodied there. It is a reversal of the process indicated by Debord, in which the seeming self-sufficiency of the commodity was a "congealment" of forces that were essentially mobile and dynamic. Now, however, with pure flux itself a commodity, a spectacular and "contemplative" relation to objects is undermined and supplanted by new kinds of investments. There is no opposition between the abstraction of money and the apparent materiality of commodities; money and what it can buy are now fundamentally of the same substance. And it is the potential dissolution of any language of the market or of desire into binarized pulses of light or electricity that unhinges the fictive unity of spectacular representation. Figurative images lose their transparence and are consumed as simply one more code.[17]

This "undoing of the spectacular consumption of commodity" that Crary describes means that images "never surpass their functioning as abstract code" and operate instead as strings of representations whose content is the very flow of their own presentation.[18] This condition was in many ways prefigured by the shift in media sequencing from programming toward "flow," an experience which eschews discrete units of consumption in favor of a more generalized experience of immersion. As television networks attempted to capture the attention of their audience for an entire evening, intervals or breaks within programming were gradually smoothed over with commercials. Accordingly, the semi-autonomous units of prior modes of content distribution such as newspapers or theatrical performances broke down as the spectator's experience became an uninterrupted continuity, a field of becoming which was populated by asignifying and prerepresentational intensities as much as or more than content. As the goal in this arrangement is precisely *not* to watch closely so as to preserve and affirm "the promise of exciting things to come," the audience "watches television" more than a particular program, performance, or image.[19]

At first glance, recent transformations in media consumption appear to contradict this diagnosis. Platforms such as YouTube, TiVo, and Netflix would seem to reintroduce the very interval that network television sought to efface. These technologies offer the viewer the ability to pause, rewind, or repeat programs according to their own desires and schedules. In conjunction with the mobile device, they even give the user the ability to segment the viewing experience within the context of daily life (we begin the latest episode of *Mad Men* while in the waiting room of the doctor's office, then restart it while in a meeting, and finally catch the end when we return home after work). However, situating this transformation within a larger logic of spatial montage suggests that while these new modes of content delivery may shift the parameters of media consumption from a temporal to a spatial register, they nonetheless preserve, if not perfect, the relations described above.[20] The evolution of the Windows operating system over the past thirty years embodies this familiar narrative. During this time, the platform moved from the layering of multiple windows introduced in version 3.0 to a full-on simultaneity with the recently released Windows 8, which effectively absorbs once-cascading windows into a single graphical user interface (GUI). While Renaissance and baroque painters once utilized the image to showcase the exotic items available for consumption for a newly empowered viewer/consumer, contemporary technologies transform the screen itself into a commodity. Now the pictorial plane itself functions as a kind of virtual "real estate," the term mobile device designers use to refer to the precious screen space of their medium, reminding us that "every small area of the screen [is] a potentially lucrative ad."[21] A similar shift is visible in the post-continuity aesthetics of contemporary film, which juxtaposes and layers spatially and temporally discordant images with little interest in the kind of totality of the twentieth-century filmic diegesis, as well as its pervasive reliance upon compositing and CGI.[22] Like the bitmapped computer display or object-based programming, these latter artifacts simply internalize the logic of flow within the boundaries of the frame itself. The result is a densely layered image whose extraordinary use of onscreen real estate enacts a kind of digital *horror vacui,* which only confirms Foucault's declaration that the new era be an "epoch of juxtaposition . . . of the side-by-side."[23]

Throughout this evolution from temporal to spatial articulations of flow, the spectator's investment takes place "not into images of actors, but onto the formal management of images."[24] The net effect is that, as Leslie Kan observes, "the televised spectacle ceases to have content."[25] Obviously, media still traffic in actual products, personalities, and events, but this presentation of content is, at times, overwhelmed by the allure of the flux of becoming. In this context, absence, that motif which from the Holocaust to Hiroshima has become something of an official visual language of disaster, loses its negativity. Like McLuhan's light bulb, which contains no content but produces a situation, in the context of 9/11 these relations bestow a unique agency to the image of absence and the absence of images, both of which would structure the experience of the disaster in equally formative fashion relative to the image proper.

In this new role, absence testifies to a larger self-effacing tendency of the spectacle which McKenzie Wark refers to as the "disintegrating spectacle." As the successor to Debord's "integrated spectacle," the disintegrating model is based in, and in fact co-opts, its own capacity for deformation and thereby offers a less Manichean base from which to approach these absences. Its power is, paradoxically, rooted in the ability of dominant image to collapse and de-compose without necessarily losing its hold on the relations which fuel the ascendancy of the visible.[26] In this dynamic model, the equation of the dominant image with excessive presence gives way to a fluid exchange in which the spectacle embraces its own death and rebirth and in so doing dovetails at a structural level with disaster. Following this dynamic through the visual culture of 9/11 and its aftermath expands the discourse of the event beyond what Debord called the spectacle's "affirmation of appearance" into a more formative drama surrounding the image and its entanglement with absence.[27]

ICONOCRACY AND THE INVISIBLE

As the dominance of spectacle theory served to establish an illusory opposition between the frenzy of the visible and the primacy of absence, the discourse of 9/11 appeared suspended in a dizzying set of contradictions. At the same time Orbán was claiming the event to be driven by "maximum exposure rather than concealment," Nicholas Mirzoeff was proclaiming the end of the "pictorial turn" as the visible, that locus of global power, seemed to take on a new "opacity" that fundamentally "resist[ed] the viewer." Likewise, just as Žižek stressed the spectral, visual nature of the terrorist threat, Marita Sturken described a general "aesthetics of absence" at work within the visual culture of 9/11. Despite the apparent opposition posed by these positions, taken as a whole they nonetheless reveal a crucial structural relation of the disaster. Indeed, read through the work of Mondzain, the interrelation or "economy" between these seemingly incompatible drives form the conditions of possibility for the vivid visual presence and global dominance of the image in the twenty-first century.

Mondzain's genealogy of contemporary media goes back to the iconoclastic controversies of the eighth and ninth centuries when the church was forced to formulate a new doctrine of the image which would both safeguard it from the charge of idolatry and at the same time preserve its proselytizing function. In order to grant the image the power to make manifest an essentially invisible God, mimesis was recast in terms of the Christian concept of incarnation. Summarizing this distinction, Mondzain explains,

> To incarnate is not to imitate, nor is it to reproduce or to simulate. The Christian Messiah is not God's clone.... The image is fundamentally unreal; its force resides in its rebellion against becoming substance with its content. To incarnate is to give flesh and not to give body. It is to act in the absence of things. The image gives flesh, that is, carnal visibility to an absence in an irreducible distance from its model.[28]

This "irreducible distance" provides the interval of difference through which the image grants flesh to the invisible while withholding full embodiment. The intertwining of the visible and invisible that the icon enacts presents a model of the image in which the latter appears as the active, primary force behind the visible. This interpenetration is made possible by a duality of the invisible through which the absence of the image takes shape as presence. In contrast to the image's sensual presence, which tends to present a singular noncontradictory aspect, this invisible presence "addresses itself to the question of being at the very moment where it allows a glimpse of its nonbeing in the luminous flesh of an object."[29] This luminosity of the object is the result of the performativity of the image which animates the stasis of representation in such a way that renders the process of becoming-image synonymous with "shar[ing] space" with God.[30] By way of overseeing this relation, a process that occurs through both discourse and artistic practice, the church's power was galvanized in the icon. As this logic bled into imperial authority, it made possible the kind of globalization of which we are today the inheritors.[31] With the media now assuming this task of managing the interrelation of the visible and the invisible, Mondzain poses the question: is there really a significant difference in "submitting to a church council or to CNN?"[32] Summarizing this affinity, Susan Buck-Morss claims, "Live news is the living body of today's iconocracy. Satellite-video is the world-become-flesh."[33]

While the model of "iconocracy" formulated by the early history of the church provides a crucial prehistory to the contemporary image, Mondzain acknowledges that the relation it manages has shifted. At the core of this distinction is a move from the metaphysically driven model outlined above to what is often portrayed in terms of a "flattening out" of the image. On account of a variety of interrelated forces which include the advent of digital representation, a general move away from "documentary culture," and a skepticism regarding master narratives, images in the contemporary sphere are no longer engaged in re-presenting signifieds in the world, let alone the Absolute. Instead, the image is enmeshed in a horizontal structure of self-referentiality whose relation to the real does not precede or transcend the parameters of representation itself. This seemingly self-sustaining network of images is the basis for global formations of power which, according to Mondzain, employ the logic of the incarnation not necessarily to summon the Divine but to reinforce the hold that these formations have on the visual economy itself. These relations are made legible in the twenty-first-century disaster where the kind of metaphysically charged invisibility discussed above manifests as traumatic "breaks" in representation. It is on these grounds that Baudrillard christens 9/11 as "the first historical spectacle of the death of the image in the image of death," a symbiotic exchange which he refers to as the "spirit of terrorism."[34]

Meaghan Morris's anecdote regarding the loss of signal during an Australian broadcast illustrates the way in which the death of an image and the image of death become interchangeable, resonating with one another in a self-sustaining circuit of exchange. While watching television with her family one Christmas Eve, Morris found the show suddenly cut short by the familiar words, "We interrupt this regularly scheduled program . . ." An anxious news anchor soon appeared and began: "Er . . . um . . . something's happened in Darwin," the capital of Australia's Northern Territory. Viewers anxiously awaited additional information only to find that there was none, at least not until the next morning, when they learned that the city had been hit by a hurricane. In that window of time when the event remained unknown, a panic gripped the viewing audience. Morris describes the onset of her own anxiety in terms of "the mechanization of bodily habituation to crisis [taking] over to see me through."[35]

The instrument of panic was not the cyclone (the signified), but the absence of information, an absence that, in effect, made the entire city of Darwin disappear for a span of twenty-four hours. As the spectacle sustains itself through a proliferation of images, crisis, emergency, and disaster now define themselves as a state without pictures, without reports, without information, a state of silence. This anxiety is reinforced by a history in which nonrepresentation is continually equated with catastrophic violence. In this, the static of the smart bomb camera seems almost a pastiche of the collapsing images from the San Francisco earthquake of 1989 or the Tiananmen Square protests of the same year, where only after media coverage stopped did the killing begin.[36] These precedents reinforce the anxiety of the non-image so that eventually the public comes to conflate real-life tragedies with the loss of the signal – so much so that any image, even one depicting a horrific scene, is preferable to the absence of the image. As Mimi White states, "In a context in which loss of TV signal carries greatest cause for alarm, even images of destruction have the capacity to reassure the viewer that everything is ok."[37] As these scenarios suggest, the negativity of absence is activated in the context of disaster, achieving a presence within the image which, while taking place in a secular context, mimics the structural duality of the invisible that Mondzain ascribes to the icon.

0.4. Still from the World Series Broadcast during the earthquake of 1989.

These images without content confound conventional analysis as they convey a highly contingent and historically specific epistemology rather than re-present per se. However, as the primary role of the image in Mondzain's theory is "the incarnation of a duality," it is the very coming into being or the making-contact-with of an image that takes precedence over its narrative or symbolic elements. This means that what is typically read in terms of propaganda, i.e., the indoctrination of a people by a given set of beliefs typically assumed to be embedded in the message of the image, is for Mondzain secondary to a more foundational aspect of visual presence, the very process of becoming-image itself.[38] As a result, the critical project must center on the management of the duality of the visible and its other, a strategy particularly apropos to the context of disaster which is often denoted by a sudden precariousness of the image.

This relation is succinctly illustrated by Art Spiegelman's iconic cover for the September 24, 2001, issue of the *New Yorker*, one of the first commemorative images to find its way into the public sphere after 9/11. The design presents what at first glance seems to be a black, monochromatic cover without detail. Only with a subtle shift of light does the faint impression of the now-missing towers appear within the emptiness. In this, the processes of memory are made manifest in the subtle interplay between presence and absence, allowing the image's coming into being to be placed on view. The image "takes shape" in a dual sense, becoming both the instantiation of an outside which summons the terror of the event and the reaffirmation of presence through which the symbolic order is reinstated. In this ghostly image, the interplay between visible and invisible dramatizes both the crisis of representation spawned by the event and the reconstitution of the image that would take place after.

Commenting on Spiegelman's subsequent graphic novel, *In the Shadow of No Towers*, Marianne Hirsch points out the way in which so many of the motifs of the work "architecturally mirror the structure of the towers and thereby allow . . . us to keep them in view even as they collapse in front of our eyes, again and again."[39] Some months later, a similar logic would manifest within the New York skyline itself. On March 11, 2002, eighty-eight search lights filled the night sky with an immaterial presence that commemorated if not resurrected the suddenly sacred structure.[40] This relatively short-lived performance in turn prefigured the permanent memorial that would eventually be constructed at Ground Zero. Michael Arad's *Reflecting Absence* presents the "footprint" of the towers as empty plots which the visitor interacts with from the intimacy of an underground corridor. According to Arad, the intent of the memorial is to "to make visible what is absent. The primary responsibility we have is to those we lost that day."[41] Throughout the visual culture of 9/11, the towers seem to dramatize a making visible with each appearance, an action that engages with and springs from an enduring absence.

TOWARD A VISUAL STUDIES OF THE INVISIBLE

This project attempts to stake out a middle ground in reference to a series of polarities which comprise the discourse of 9/11. In the aftermath of the disaster, the European response, represented primarily by the 9/11 Verso series of works by Baudrillard, Žižek, and Virilio, deployed a familiar theoretical discourse of spectacle and the Lacanian real in order to diagnose the event as a wound to the symbolic order.[42] On the heels of these works, American scholarship sought to eschew abstractions in favor of personal experience, foregrounding the familiar critical lenses of trauma studies (E. Ann Kaplan's *Trauma Culture: The Politics of Terror and Loss in Media and Literature,* or the early anthology *Trauma at Home: After 9/11,* edited by Judith Greenberg) and cultural studies (Marita Sturken's *Tourists of History: Memory, Kitsch, and Consumerism from Oklahoma City to Ground Zero*). In step with larger pedagogical divisions between these groups, this latter body of work was formulated as a conscious rebuttal to what Kaplan referred to as the "very abstract and theoretical approach" of scholars on the other side of the Atlantic.[43] Through these early exchanges, a division was established in the aftermath of the event that to a large extent continues to persist in the scholarship on 9/11 to this day. Because of this opposition, the productive relation of theory to *specific* images, motifs, and visual experiences, as well as the necessity of historicizing the iconographic and theoretical assemblages within the visual culture of 9/11, have often been left out of the discussion.

Using visual studies as an arbiter between these two camps, this project attempts to open the discourse of 9/11 and, more generally, the visual culture of disaster to these blind spots. While integrating the theories of Kittler, Flusser, Barthes, Deleuze, Freud, and others, the work heeds the warnings of Kaplan, who cautions against "overstat[ing] the political/psychic symbolism" and in turn viewing the event from "a distant intellectual perspective."[44] Accordingly, the investigations of this project are focused on precise objects of inquiry and are historicized via iconology and discourse analysis. For example, the motif of the empty city which figured prominently in film and photography after 9/11 is situated in relation to Cold War disaster films; the image of falling bodies is contextualized within the pervasive myth of suicide leapers after the stock market crash of 1929; and the post-9/11 monument is read in terms of a codified visual trope of absence that originates in post–World War II Germany. While attempting to add specificity to the early deployments of theory, this project also implicitly calls attention to the shortcomings of the American perspectives, pointing out, for example, the lack of engagement with digital photography in trauma studies and the problems of the humanist base of cultural studies, both of which I suggest benefit from an encounter with poststructuralism, theories of autopoiesis, and the "inhuman turn."

This balancing act is made possible by conceiving of the visual experience broadly, approaching photography, film, graphic novels, monuments, and new media not simply in terms of the purely symbolic, but as constructions of vision. While this approach is a by-now-familiar one, several caveats should be made with regard to the kind of visual studies that this project aligns itself with. The first of these is evident in the sheer irony of a project which utilizes *visual* studies as means to engage and analyze the *in*visible. As W. J. T. Mitchell points out, the field has a penchant for being easily seduced by grand pronouncements of a "visual turn." This affirmation of a "hegemony of the visible" is problematic as it overlooks the role of extravisual sensorial experiences such as the haptic or aural, the enduring presence of text within contemporary culture, and the historical resonance of such pronouncements with a recurring anxiety regarding the image which goes back at least to the classical world. In this spirit of questioning the absolutism of such grand statements, this project posits the visual as at least partially the product of an encounter with its other. Indeed, the following chapters will suggest that, in the case of 9/11, it is this encounter which to a large extent makes possible the disaster as a legible, historical event.

The second stipulation concerns the place of materiality in the experience and, indeed, the construction of vision. Despite early anxieties regarding the "disappearance of the object" at the hands of an eye-centric model, visual studies has proven more than amenable to the close study of images and their formal properties. Whitney Davis succinctly summarizes the circular relation that recent revisions to the field have come to articulate between objects and visuality. In *A General Theory of Visual Culture,* he both portrays the material surface of visual culture as the creative product of "the period eye" which apprehends them, and at the same time acknowledges these surfaces as themselves accumulations of layers of acculturation which oversee what becomes visible. The interrelation of these two dynamics occurs via a "feedback loop . . . [a] complex relay or recursion of vision into visuality and vice versa."[45] Placing the eye within such "feedback loops" necessarily involves shedding, whenever possible, the idea of a singular model of vision, and with it the notion of the "privileged spectator" that often populated early forays into visual studies.[46] Instead, this dynamic interaction suggests a model of what Nicholas Mirzoeff calls intervisuality, the simultaneous display and interaction of a variety of modes of visuality."[47] As these modes of seeing coexist in fragile formations rather than seamless or totalizing constructs in the context of 9/11, these instances of absence and erasure come to mark a site of conflict in which images, modes of seeing, embedded histories, and hybrid media circulate. It is this formative drama that occupies this project.

Chapter 1, "From Latent to Live: Disaster Photography after the Digital Turn," considers the unique position of the photographer as of 2001, the first year that digital cameras outsold their analog counterparts. While trauma studies has established an enduring connection between the delayed temporality of the camera and the psychic processes of deferral, these relations were thrown into contention by the instantaneity of the digital format. At the same time, the actual experience of photographers "on the ground" suggests that this familiar narrative of digitization was incomplete or partial, as the "most photographed disaster in history" was just as often captured in celluloid as in binary code. This chapter considers the ways in which this hybrid medium of photography produced new modes of non-seeing in the context of the disaster, especially in relation to the analog film camera.[48]

Perhaps the most memorable image of 9/11, aside from that of the collision of the passenger jets with the towers, is the *Falling Man* photograph by Richard Drew. Chapter 2, "Origins of Affect: The Falling Body and Other Symptoms of Cinema," attempts to position this image in the context of a history of the representation of falling bodies so as to grapple with an enduring paradox. Despite its disproportionate representation in popular culture, jumping from tall buildings has never been a statistically significant form of suicide.[49] Why is it, then, that the image of the suicide leap figures so prominently in film, photography, and other visual media of the last century when its actual occurrence is such a rare event? From where does the kind of grand cinematic leap originate if not from reality? In order to pursue the origin of this charge, this chapter extracts a structural affinity between the representation of falling in psychoanalysis (primarily Freud and Winnicott) and the cinema, so as to better understand the unique articulation of the fall that surfaces in the visual culture of 9/11.

In the aftermath of 9/11, the motif of the empty city in film and photography operated as a means to indirectly engage with an event that seemed otherwise off limits. Chapter 3, "Remembering-Images: Empty Cities, Machinic Vision, and the Post-9/11 Imaginary," engages with this phenomenon by contextualizing these images within a larger historical narrative. Whereas in Cold War cinema the paradox of witnessing a world without humans is utilized to issue a powerful clarion call to its viewers regarding the endgame of nuclear war, in the context of 9/11 these same relations are inscribed within more timely debates regarding the autonomy of media. Drawing from this iconography of emptiness, these images infuse the destructive violence of the disaster with anxieties regarding the "obsolescence" of the human in the face of increasingly self-sustaining audiovisual systems. Exemplary of this dynamic are the photographs of empty cities by Thomas Struth and Michael Wesely in which the prospect of a world without people is presented not as a prophecy or a threat but rather as the underlying condition of contemporary "mediality" and its undercurrents of surveillance and military force.

Almost immediately, the targeting of the World Trade Center was attributed to its status as a "monument" to capitalism. While the association of the towers with excessive commercialism has been with the site since its inception, the rhetorical connection to the monument in the aftermath pinpoints something precise about the conditions of 9/11. Chapter 4, "Lights, Camera, Iconoclasm: How Do Monuments Die and Live to Tell about It?," attempts to draw out this relationship by reading this metaphor in literal terms. Approaching the everyday operation of the towers and their destruction through the unique status of the contemporary monument sheds light on the ways in which these two trajectories of the structure are intertwined via a formative relation to media. However, in the course of pursuing this reading of the destruction of the towers, these insights reflect back upon the status of the monument, introducing a theme which will be taken up in the concluding chapter. Whereas this initial analysis of the monument will seek to establish the form as a kind of latent presence, an absence whose virtuality makes possible an interconnection to the image, the final chapter will look at the ways in which this potentiality is systematically contained and delimited via the larger power operations which inscribe it. Ironically, this reversal will transpire in the context of a visual motif which has historically signified the openness of nonhierarchical, participatory modes of articulating history.

Born out of what Thierry Groensteen describes an "art without memory," the mnemonic function of the graphic novel could not contrast more starkly with the permanency and timelessness of the more officially sanctioned cultural form of the memorial.[50] However, it is this opposition which allowed these two disparate media to form the virtual bookends to the period of iconoclasm that followed 9/11. The concluding chapter, "The Failure of the Failure of Images: The Crisis of the Unrepresentable from the Graphic Novel to the 9/11 Memorial," considers the way in which the progression instantiated by Art Spiegelman's *In the Shadow of No Towers* (2002) and Michael Arad's *Reflecting Absence* monument (2011) reflects a broader trajectory within the visual culture of the disaster which effectively bridges the gap between an unthinkable image and a permanent installation. Animating this narrative are questions regarding the representation of personal experience and the viability of the "unrepresentable" in the face of a ubiquitous and increasingly homogenized image of disaster.

Throughout these inquiries, the image of absence visualizes what Mondzain describes as the crossing of a threshold through which power is expressed. In light of the instability that such images seem to mark in the context of disaster, the intent of this book is less to give a totalizing theory of the invisible than to trace the ebb and flow of a complex interaction which undergirds the visual culture of the event. It pursues momentary linkages between images, modes of seeing, intellectual histories, and often hybrid media forms. In this it reiterates the kind of concatenation of detail that Irit Rogoff connects to the field:

> In the area of visual culture the scrap of an image connects with the sequence
> of a film and with the corner of a billboard or the window display of a shop we
> have passed by. . . . Images do not stay within discrete disciplinary fields.[51]

And yet in pursuing these chains of visual phenomena in the context
of 9/11, this model comes to articulate a more radical proposition of looking at the spaces both between and within images, not just their interrelation or collective contributions to a visual field but their articulation
of a realm of possibilities through which one witnesses the emergence
of 9/11 as a legible event. It is this dialogue which is on display in the
exchange between the visible and its other in the wake of the disaster.

Every time I press the shutter, the viewfinder closes. And
it happens so fast that what I'm mostly seeing is black. . . .
I didn't know what was occurring in front of my lens.

DAVE BRONDOLO,
New Yorker, on photographing 9/11

Armed with a lens to inject between myself and the world . . .

GEOFFREY WOLF,
The Sightseer

ONE

From Latent to Live

As the first year that digital cameras outsold their analog counterparts, 2001 marked a tipping point in the digital turn, one that would forge a new relation between the medium and the spectacle of disaster.[1] With its dematerialization into code and capacity for instant transmission, the digital format allowed photography, perhaps for the first time in its history, to satiate the desire for "live" images. As a result of this sudden acceleration of the still image, the cultural position and function of film photography would endure an equally profound redefinition. In an attempt to retain legitimacy in the face of what John Roberts calls the "intrusion" of digital technologies and a "defeated documentary culture," film photography in the twenty-first century appeared to relinquish its hold on the now in favor of more reflective and distanced role.[2] As David Campany explains, in ceding "the representation of events in progress . . . to other media," the postdigital identity of the medium became bound to the role of the "undertaker," that shadowy figure who "turns up late, wanders through the places where things have happened" in order to document "the aftermath of the event" rather than the event itself.[3]

However, the experience of photographers "on the ground" on 9/11 suggests that this familiar narrative of digitization was momentarily compromised by the disaster. Within minutes of the collision, gift shops that surrounded the World Trade Center reported selling out of disposable film cameras. The manager of a Duane Reade drugstore in the vicinity of the towers even claimed to have sold between sixty and one hundred film cameras in the first hour of the attacks.[4] These accounts, along with the numerous exhibitions of amateur photography from that day, confirm that the most photographed disaster in history was just as often captured on celluloid as in binary code. While one is tempted to diagnosis this phenomenon as a nostalgic return to a more familiar mode of seeing in the face of uncertainty, framing the issue in these oppositional terms tends to overlook the unique circumstances of this resurgence. As the rivalry between these formats was momentarily eclipsed by a larger desire for visibility, photography in the context of the disaster was no longer simply in a transitional state as of 9/11, but was rather a hybrid medium.[5]

As analog and digital platforms coalesced at the level of practice, new modes of vision were momentarily made possible which would challenge reigning assumptions regarding disaster photography. Under the influence of trauma studies, the camera's presence at the scene of the catastrophic events is typically read in terms of a defense mechanism which safely removes the subject from a scene that is too great. Manifesting as a kind of blindness within the operator's field of vision, this phenomenon is understood in terms of a failure to fully comprehend let alone experience the reality before the lens. However, as a result of the convergence of a series of conflicting forces which center on the delayed temporality of the analog medium and the disaster's demand for instant images, the non-seeing of analog practice was taken to such an extreme that it pushed what is under normal circumstances a deferral of vision into an indefinite suspension. As a result, the model of "looking away" which has characterized the relation of trauma to the camera came to disclose the possibility of what I will call non-seeing, a blindness in which the traumatic experience does not return in a newly encoded symbolic image, but rather remains within this absence as an unfathomable event. This overwhelming of the capacities of the film camera recalibrates familiar models of the sublime according to a new techno-imaginary where enduring metaphysical or transcendental associations are jettisoned in favor of a more immediate redistribution of the senses.

Given the evocative power of the photographs that came out of that day, it is on some level understandable that the operator's experience would take a back seat to the image in the scholarship on 9/11. However, subordinating the act of taking pictures to the lure of images not only threatens to naturalize the interventions of both operator and apparatus, but also reinforces certain elisions within photographic theory more broadly. (It is telling in this respect that the two dominant figures of the field in the last half-century, Roland Barthes and Susan Sontag, both attest to a dislike for taking pictures.) For these reasons, this inquiry will begin before the image, or rather at a moment when the image exists in latent form, clouding the vision of the operator as a virtual presence. This broadened configuration of practice, which I will call the "photographic situation," understands the immediate phenomenological experience of the camera as a simultaneously futural event in which the present is roped to an impending image. Approaching the act of photography as the creation of an interval within experience serves to draw out the critical relationship between practice and image and in turn bring into view the larger transformations of the medium that were under way at the time of the disaster.

DISASTER PHOTOGRAPHY AND
THE ABSENT OPERATOR

While the motivations behind the impulse to take pictures in the face of the 9/11 disaster are admittedly as varied as the images they produced, it is telling to find a recurring thread running through the accounts of those who either found themselves reaching for the camera or witnessed this response from afar. For example, E. Ann Kaplan describes her own urge to photograph in terms of "a desire to make real what I could barely comprehend."[6] David Friend similarly attributes this pervasive response to the realization that "only rendering this act visually would confirm its reality."[7] Citing the photograph's ability to forge order in the place of chaos, Barbie Zelizer describes its role in 9/11 as "a powerful and effective way of visually encountering the horrific event."[8] Reflecting a larger position within the critical study of 9/11, these comments attribute the resurgence of the still image to a collective need for clarity in the face of an unfathomable event, a desire to slow down and make sense of an event that happened "too fast" and that was because of its sheer scale and unprecedented nature incomprehensible at the time of its occurrence.

While photographs certainly allow for the kind of careful contemplation that the disaster itself does not, this possibility is more often than not contingent upon an impoverishment or at least displacement of the now at the level of the operator. The most well-known articulation of this relationship is found in Susan Sontag's *On Photography,* which famously argues that the act of taking a photograph functions first and foremost as a way of avoiding experience in the present. As an instrument of "non-intervention," the camera, according to Sontag, effectively removes its operator intellectually and even emotionally from the reality before the lens, a dynamic that becomes especially disconcerting in the face of human suffering. Sontag states,

> Photographing is essentially an act of non-intervention. Part of the horror of such memorable coups of photojournalism . . . comes from the awareness of how plausible it has become, in situations where the photographer has the choice between a photograph and a life, to choose the photograph. The person who intervenes cannot record; the person who is recording cannot intervene.[9]

The binary between immersed participation and detached observation is admittedly less restrictive in the context of everyday photography, as the operator seamlessly moves between positions in order to coax his or her model or simply arrange the scene before the lens. However, this scenario is often condensed into an either/or proposition in the disaster, where issues of life and death are often decided in a single, fleeting moment.[10] Even if a given photograph does not itself embody the "pregnant" or "decisive" moment, the potential for such images structures the scene of photography, fueling a prolonged production of images which sustains the disengagement of the operator. The interconnectedness between this pursuit of the image and the violence of the disaster is embodied in Carolee Schneemann's *Terminal Velocity* (2001), in which the artist arranges thirty images of the falling bodies of 9/11 in serial format. Emphasizing the downward motion of these bodies, the grid of images not only renders the compulsive nature of disaster photography visible, but also, in Warholian fashion, portrays this activity as somehow inseparable from the impending death of the camera's subjects.

However, when read in the context of her larger project it is clear that Sontag is, like so many of her contemporaries, interested more in diagnosing the alienation of the "image world" that the apparatus al-

1.1. Carolee Schneemann, *Terminal Velocity,* 2001. Black and white computer scans of falling bodies from 9/11. Enlarged sequences of seven columns by six rows—forty-two units, each 16 × 12 inches. Image courtesy of the artist. © 2013 Carolee Schneemann/Artists Rights Society (ARS), New York.

legedly produces than in the specific operations which determine the moment of photography. By working backward from this recurring diagnosis of spectacle, a misleading conception of the noninterventionist quality of photography emerges. Specifically, what is considered an active denial on the part of the operator in these formulations is in reality a symptom of a larger sacrifice of vision that takes place via the photographic operation. From this standpoint, the operator does not so

1.2. Thomas Hoepker, *A Group of Young People Watch the Events of 9/11 from a Brooklyn Rooftop*, 2001. By permission of Magnum Photos.

much choose the camera over reality, but rather suspends the possibility of such a choice within the interval between blindness and sight that the processes of chemical photography introduce. Once incorporated within the photographic environment, the disaster no longer appears as a space of intervention; in fact, it no longer appears. This capacity of the photographic operation to produce non-seeing is illustrated by two controversial images produced during 9/11, both of which depict a disavowal of the camera at the moment of disaster.

In his 2006 *New York Times* article entitled "Whatever Happened to the America of 9/12?," Frank Rich wrestles with the larger implications of a photograph taken by Thomas Hoepker on September 11. The image shows a group of lounging New Yorkers, "taking what seems to be a lunch or bike-riding break, enjoying the radiant late-summer sun and chatting away as cascades of smoke engulf Lower Manhattan in the background."[11] Published on the fifth anniversary of 9/11, Rich's editorial portrays the image as representative of the growing nonchalance of the American public following the disaster: "Traumatic as the attack on America was, 9/11 would recede quickly for many. This is a country that likes to move on, and fast."[12] Though the piece does not blame the medium per se for the troubling disconnect the image seems to visualize, Hoepker's photograph is nonetheless prompted to engage with its role in producing this disconnect by virtue of the photographer's implied participation in this practice of passive looking.

Ironically, Chris Schiavo, the second woman from the right in the photograph, is herself a photographer and would later confess to wrestling with these same issues of disaster photography on that day. However, unlike Hoepker, she decided to

> not touch a camera that day. Why? For many reasons including a now-obvious one: This somewhat cynical expression of an assumed reality printed in the *New York Times* proves a good reason. . . . But most of all to keep both hands free, just in case there was actually something I could do to alter this day or affect a life, to experience every nanosecond in every molecule of my body, rather than place a lens between myself and the moment.[13]

Hoepker's photo suggests that Schiavo's refusal of the camera is motivated not only by a desire to fully experience the event and thereby save it from reification, but more immediately to *see* the disaster. Its internal spectators – whether dismissive or seeking communal support in the face of uncertainty – compose themselves around the act of looking and thereby distinguish their experience from that of the camera and its operator. The stopped bicycle, the two chairs pulled up as if to allow those sitting in them to get a better look, and even the faces of those figures who momentarily turn away from the burning towers, suggest a verbal communication of what has just been seen. As such, the photograph presents two forms of looking: one based in direct apprehension and social engagement, and the other a remove, a virtual blindness that permeates the photographer's own vision of the disaster and perhaps even the "coverage" of the event more broadly.

Fellow Brooklyn photographer Tim Soter responded to the disaster in a similarly anti-photographic manner. Rather than capturing the event itself, the photographer chose to nonchalantly pose for the camera with the burning towers as his backdrop. While some have objected to the image and its seemingly opportunistic memorialization of human suffering (the work landed on the "wall of shame" in the *Here Is New York*

1.3. Tim Soter, *Self-Portrait*, 2001. By permission of the photographer.

exhibit), it nonetheless reveals something critical about the operation of the camera in the moment of disaster. According to the photographer, the image was born out of a simple desire to include himself in the narrative of a truly historic event and to perhaps even provide a document for his grandchildren who would one day "read about the event in a textbook."[14] In the process of fulfilling this witnessing function, the image necessarily presents the photographer's attempt to evade the camera and its eradication of the event. Accordingly, what might first appear to be a callous mode of apprehending the trauma of that day suggests the exact opposite. Rather, in posing for his own camera, Soter's reflexive gesture equates freedom from the apparatus with the possibility of communion with the disaster. Paradoxically, in order to make good on what John Berger describes as the most basic promise of the photograph, the assertion that "this particular event or this particular object has been seen," both Soter and Hoepker actively present a negation of the photographic process. They testify to "having seen" by foregrounding the act of not photographing and in the process ascribe a kind of blindness to the apparatus that is willfully avoided.

The anxiety that these images visualize regarding the capacity of disaster photography to suspend vision would be validated by a roundtable discussion among the photographers of 9/11 in the weeks after the attacks. In this exchange, David Handschuh, who captured the collision of the jet with the towers in a now-iconic image, confessed to never seeing an airplane enter his frame. The next morning when a neighbor brought over a copy of the *Daily News* to his door he was stunned to find his byline underneath the image. Similarly, it was only after receiving a call from a lab technician that Richard Drew realized that his photograph of the exploding tower had also captured a person holding on to a piece of the crumbling building.[15] Like so many other New Yorkers, Will Nuñez raced to the local newsstand to buy a disposable camera after seeing the smoking crater in the North Tower. While shooting his colleague standing in front of the window of the thirty-second floor of One State Street Plaza, he inadvertently captured the second plane streaking through the frame, a detail that only became apparent after he got the film developed weeks later.[16]

Such instances dramatize the euphoric blindness which, as Vilém Flusser describes, shadows instances of "photo-mania." In these cases, photographers "are not 'in charge of' taking photographs, they are consumed by the greed of their camera, they have become an extension to the button of their camera. . . . A permanent flow of unconsciously created images is the result."[17] It is the very alterity of this flow of inanimate and mechanically produced images for which Walter Benjamin praised the medium. Transcending the limitations of vision, the camera's eye excavated that which was invisible to the everyday sensorium, the end result of which was a "salutary estrangement between man and his surroundings."[18] As the disaster confirms, the overcoming that Benjamin and other modernists celebrated is, however, the product of a negative relation to sight that is made possible by the camera's implicit promise to return experience as image. As the expectation of an ensuing image promises to fill in the blanks, the operator is relieved of the burden of fully experiencing the now and perhaps even subsequent reflection upon it. Consequently, the photographer's experience of the moment itself is one of inexperience and non-seeing. Sylviane Agacinski explains,

> In counting on a retrospective vision, in entrusting my memory to the material trace, I can save myself the effort of a subjective recollection, indeed even an attentive look at the present. This is how the amateur photographer risks depriving himself of any present.[19]

This guarantee of the return of the experience as image grants the photographer a bye so to speak, as it ensconces him or her in between the "not yet" and the "already no more" of the visible. Such is the unique position of the photographic interval, which effectively defers vision until a later date, leaving the photographer in what artist Ariel Goldberg calls "a place of delay and darkness."[20]

Through the relinquishing of vision that occurs in the practice of film photography, the impending image is able to establish the sight of the operator retroactively. However, at the time of its occurrence, the act of photographing leaves only a promise of return in its place. Barthes captures the future tense that this exchange ascribes to the photographer's vision (or lack thereof) in the following terms: "The photographer's 'second sight' does not consist in 'seeing' but in being there. And above all, imitating Orpheus, he must not turn back to look at what he is leading – what he is giving to me [the viewer]!"[21] By disentangling seeing from bearing witness, the camera offers a kind of godlike oversight of the world by which the very origins of reality are placed at the disposal of the operator, not so much in terms of content of the image or the deployment of technique, but rather in the simple and dramatic act of bringing vision into being once again. The euphoria of this possibility is dramatized in the opening of Italo Calvino's short story "The Adventures of a Photographer":

> [The weekend photographers] come back as happy as hunters with bulging game bags; they spend days waiting, with sweet anxiety, to see the developed pictures. . . . It is only when they have the photos before their eyes that they seem to take tangible possession of the day they spent, only then that the mountain stream, the movement of the child with his pail, the glint of the sun on the wife's legs take on the irrevocability of what has been and can no longer be doubted. Everything else can drown in the unreliable shadow of memory.[22]

As Calvino explains, the camera's suspension of experience/vision leaves a vague but "sweet anxiety" regarding its return as image while all that escapes the confines of representation is left to "drown in the shadow of memory," if it ever achieves entry into conscious life at all.[23]

Drawing upon the psychoanalytic understanding of trauma, scholars have tended to regard this disassociation of the photographic operation as a form of "looking away" that recalls the traumatic moment when the child perceives "the lack." In reaction to an unassimilable signifier which threatens to unravel the symbolic order, the subject in this model directs the gaze elsewhere, usually onto a fetish object whose presence momentarily restores the stability of self and world. The act of photographing, like the inner workings of trauma itself, allows us to evade experience in the moment so as to postpone our encounter with the event. The processes of chemical photography require that we wait for the image to be developed, whereupon we can engage with it in a more contemplative and controlled fashion. Commenting on this affinity, Ulrich Baer states, "Because trauma blocks routine mental processes from converting an experience into memory or forgetting, it parallels the defining structure of photography, which also traps an event during its occurrence while blocking its transformation into memory."[24] In the moment of taking the image, this deferral manifests within the visual register as a kind of blindness that is, under normal circumstances, eradicated or at least smoothed over with the return of the experience in the form of an image.

From this perspective, the persistent blindness among 9/11 photographers would seem to confirm the camera's role in providing what Bob Rogers calls "a substitute for assimilating the psychological and sociological implications of what has been witnessed."[25] Yet there are numerous complications with this association. Despite working through a similar logic of belatedness, the temporal delay of trauma cannot so easily be collapsed with the processes of chemical photography. Such a position overlooks the fact that, in the case of photography, the reappearance of the image is under the explicit control of the subject, whereas Freud's understanding of "deferred action" is one in which the traumatic resurfacing of the event is traumatic in part because of its sudden and unpredictable appearance. As Jean Laplanche points out, it is for this reason that sexual development proves so fertile a ground for the experience of *après coup*, as it proceeds according to an "unevenness" that has a tendency to abruptly introduce the subject to a body of knowledge which drastically revises his or her understanding of past events. From Dora to the Wolf Man, Freud's case studies repeatedly illustrate the way in which this process often occurs against the will of the subject or at least without conscious consent. The reactivation of this previously elided event more often occurs by chance than intentionally, the result of an encounter with situations or ideas that bear some superficial similarity to the "psychic representatives" of the unassimilated event. Perhaps the most problematic element of this association of the camera with the psychoanalytic understanding of trauma is the assumption that the image is somehow synonymous with the event itself, as if the former operates as a transparent window upon the latter. Though certainly capable of triggering memories, an encounter with a two-dimensional representation must be distinguished from the resurfacing of a psychic event itself. Putting aside these not-unimportant issues, 9/11 exposed a more immediate clash between photography and the conceptual rubric of trauma which demands further scrutiny.

As one of the first large-scale disasters to be captured by amateur and professional photographers in digital form, 9/11 would require a reconsideration of many of the basic assumptions of disaster photography.[26] In the process of engaging this important yet still unresolved question of the role and significance of digital technology as a medium for recording disaster, I would like to shift the emphasis backward, so to speak, and look at the ways this new medium transformed the above relations of the analog film camera. From this perspective, the incongruence between the temporality of the analog still and the disaster's thirst for live images meant that the model of "looking away" which has characterized the relation of trauma to the film camera came to disclose a new mode of vision, one that was intimately connected to the historically specific conditions of the image as of 9/11.

THE VIEWFINDER IN THE SHADOW OF THE SCREEN

Beginning with William J. Mitchell's canonical text *The Reconfigured Eye*, scholars have painstakingly cataloged the ramifications of the digi-

tal turn in terms of the image, noting a greater instability that has resulted from the fluidity of transmission, a non-indexical relation to the
real, and an overall dematerialization. However, the advent of digital
photography has also had important ramifications at the level of practice,
perhaps the most immediate of which concern issues of temporality.
As taking and viewing the photograph occur in what for all intents and
purposes are the same, indivisible moment, the accelerated temporality of digital photography reduces the interval of its analog counterpart
to near nonexistence. Nicholas Mirzoeff presents this condensed temporality of the digital image in terms of an "expanded present" which
"intrudes briefly into the past but is experienced as a continuum."[27] Accordingly, the act of taking pictures is no longer structured around the
expectation of return but rather is experienced as what Pavel Büchler describes as an encounter with a "found object," something that we "come
across without knowing what we are looking for."[28]

The recoding of the still image as live flows in large measure from the
digital process of (pre)view which presents the scene before the lens as
moving image rather than supplement or prosthetic to "natural" vision.
As an extension of systems of perspective, the optical, embodied experience of the analog SLR tends to incorporate vision in its entirety. From
the black curtain to the matte finish of the camera body, the obscuring
of direct visual apprehension of the outside world allows for a near-perfect conversion of binocular to monocular vision. This prosthetic character of the analog camera is, however, largely absent from digital practice
as the camera is disconnected from the body, is held at arm's length, and
consequently produces an image that is in visual dialogue with the object
or event it purports to record. This shift in photographic practice from
prosthetic or "natural" vision to autonomous view is reflective of a larger
dynamic of premediation which undergirds the digital experience. By
substituting an already coded image for what film theorists once called
"the pro-filmic event," the operator's task is recast in terms of enacting
screen captures within an enclosed flow of data, a conjuring of the image
through an intermedia exchange between movement and stillness. As
such, the practice of photography produces an image which remediates
rather than represents, recurs rather than returns. This relation is both
the basis for the virtual simultaneity that the still image achieves with

the present and the motor by which the practice of photography loses its future orientation.[29]

Artist Scott Kildall illustrates the way in which this new temporality of the still image collides with existing expectations to create a heterochronic experience of the camera. In his *Video Portraits* series (2006–2008), Kildall approaches strangers with his digital camera and asks if he can take their picture. While the subject assumes and then struggles to hold a pose for the impending photograph, Kildall records them with the camera's video function. The sitters are then left to wait for the click of the camera, which never comes. In the context of this indefinite suspension, both the subject and the viewer of Kildall's work eventually become aware of the futility of waiting for the image. Not only does the seemingly interminable length of these pieces eventually give up the ruse, but so does the unabridged access to the now that the camera presents in its place actively displace the expectation of such an image. Eventually, one comes to realize that the portrait they await is right before them, a suspicion that is confirmed by the work's title, which is not *Photos in Waiting* or something of the sort, but *Video Portraits*. As the "portrait" and the moment of transcription come to exist in the same singular moment, the deferral that we expect from the camera is eradicated as the still "photograph" is rendered not only animate, but live.

In the following passage, Johanna Drucker describes the larger implications of the painfully awkward performances that ensue in Kildall's work:

> Their expressions change and flickers of mood – anxiety, annoyance, frustration, question, flirtation – show dramatically that they have internalized the idea of "the photograph" as a final event, a flash, a quick slice through ongoing life, a record, an instant. They dodge toward and lunge away from the camera, waiting for the moment, the snap, the action of the shutter. Their movements are always anticipating immobility, and as Kildall stretches out the clock in an unspecified stretch of time, they begin to exhibit a restless uncertainty about exactly how to define what it is that the photograph is. Have they missed it? Is it coming? What is the *it*, the phenomenon, the photograph? A limited frame, a time frame, cut, held, fixed, defines the photograph. And Kildall refuses to fix the frame, take the picture.[30]

By disclosing those intimate moments of preparation which betray the kind of affectation that the "good" photograph successfully conceals, the

1.4. Still from Scott Kildall's *Video Portraits* series, 2006–2008. By permission of the artist.

work compromises the medium's enduring connection to memory and death.[31] As Barthes points out, the static postures and artificial expressions that comprise this "making of oneself into image" form a ritual which has from the medium's inception been regarded as a prefiguration of death. However, while the practice of analog photography obliterates the now as a precondition for its future resurrection, the image in digital practice provides an anterior future, confirming what one has already seen, delivering immediately what was once irrevocably lost to the moment. In this way, the "givenness" of the image, its precession in the form of a live preview, acts as a guard against the very loss that motivates the analog experience.

Kildall's work thus dramatizes not only the enduring artificiality of the photographic portrait, but more importantly for the purposes of this chapter, the way in which the experience of deferral that is built into the analog process is suddenly rendered palpable in the shadow of the digital image. Now the image appears missing, more distant and less connected to the time of its taking than it once was. An ad campaign launched four months before 9/11 for the Sony Cybershot camera capitalizes on this relative lag. The commercial features a group of young women whose lunch is suddenly interrupted as Aerosmith lead singer Steven Tyler walks across the room. As they frantically reach for their cameras, the table is upended, wine splashes against a white tank top, and the once-tranquil scene begins to resemble an Aerosmith video. Within this chaos, one woman effortlessly removes her digital camera, tracks her prey on screen, and then captures the perfect image while a film camera falls from her girlfriend's purse and pops open upon hitting the floor. In the meantime, the women are crowding around the playback screen of the digital camera, which has not only sidestepped the dangers of exposing film but delivered the image for inspection before Tyler even leaves the room. The tagline which follows reinforces the camera's newfound capacity for instant review: "The great little camera with a great big screen."[32] Reversing the hierarchy between the screen (viewing) and the image (taking) that traditionally accompanies photographic practice, the slogan distills a larger dynamic which will culminate in the disaster, one which allows the apparatus to function as an instrument for seeing rather than representation.

As these examples suggest, not only does the digital format allow for a virtual simultaneity between taking and viewing images, but so does it in turn bring the interval of the film camera to light in almost irritating vividness. As such, the unconscious processes of deferral that were implicit in film photography now move to the level of conscious experience. While prompted by the arrival of the digital format, this consciousness of deferral is only exacerbated by the disaster, where the urgent need for images pushed photography even further toward instantaneity and away from the model of deferral discussed above. As the analog image collided with the digitized media sphere of 9/11, the film camera was subject to a relative "loosening" or deceleration of the interval between the click of the shutter and the return of the experience as image. Indeed, these relations momentarily made possible a disconnect between the terms of the interval, a collapse between taking and viewing images. This possibility is illustrated by stories such as that of Gulnara Samoilova, who, after photographing the events of 9/11, hurried home to develop the film in her kitchen. While waiting for the chemicals to process the film, she turned to her TV to see the second building collapse.[33] Suddenly, the urgency was gone as the instantaneity of one medium trumped the belatedness of another, sending its image into a state of extended deferral.

While such anecdotes literalize the notion of an imageless experience of the camera discussed above, the larger claim is not simply that the immediacy of the image in the coverage of 9/11 made developing the filmic image a moot point, although this seems to be a not-uncommon response. [34] Rather, as a result of the unique position of the medium as of 9/11, analog practice offered the possibility of an indefinite deferral of vision, a non-seeing which in opening the interval of photographic practice would undermine the very distinction between seeing and its other. Far from impoverishing or eradicating experience, this absence within vision, like the "negative presentation" of the sublime experience, allowed for an encounter with the unfathomability of the event that the image itself seems bound to delimit and contain. At the same time, these historically contingent and fleeting assemblages of vision would disconnect the sublime from its intimations of the absolute, disclosing the film camera as not only an instrument of the imagination but also a means of de-imaging a disaster which from the beginning appeared to take place within and for the image.

DOES THE DISASTER WANT TO BE PHOTOGRAPHED? NEGATIVE PRESENTATION AND THE ANALOG SUBLIME

Of the varied reactions to 9/11, two seemed to take center stage, forming a sort of mantra of the witness in the aftermath. Over and over, firsthand accounts described the event as both "like a movie" and "unreal." The seeming paradox of this simultaneity, which posits both unrepresentability and an image-like quality, reflects the central paradox of the sublime. While the sheer intensity of the sublime experience would seem to ally it with those events perceived as vividly real, somehow more fully present than the banal occurrences of everyday life, philosophy has consistently pointed to cognitive failure as its founding characteristic. As an overwhelming of the faculties, such experiences have generally been understood as the tendency of larger-than-life events or objects to exceed, interrupt, and thereby expose the inadequacy of our ability to fully apprehend, let alone make sense of, an extraordinary reality.

In the *Critique of Judgment*, Kant refers to the perception of such phenomena in terms of a "negative presentation" in that they prompt a failure of the imagination which manifests as an image of the absence or, at least, incompleteness of the object or event in question. According to Kant, this short-circuiting of perception occurs in two modes: the mathematically sublime and the dynamically sublime. In the case of the former, we are presented with something that "is large beyond all comparison" such as a mountain as seen when standing at its base, or the pyramids in Egypt when taken in from a similarly overwhelming vantage point. However, as this sublime is rooted in the incompatibility of perception and those *a priori* conceptual categories used to process such a perception, it is not the size of the object in itself that overwhelms. Rather it is only through a particular vantage point or mode of seeing that such experiences exceed human scale and thereby come to refuse the gestalt that our preexisting frames of reference seek to bestow upon them. The consequences of this "failure" of the imagination to adequately present the object to the mind are twofold: first, we are presented with the limits of our normative ability to process and perceive reality, and, second, the discrete forms on which these processes rely unravel into a state of "formlessness," thereby allowing the mind to "progress without hindrance to infinity." In order to understand how this violence to the imagination is the condition of possibility for the photographer's engagement with the disaster, a peculiar paradox of Kant's text must come to light, one that is perhaps best illustrated by his discussion of the dynamically sublime and its relation to reason.

In the case of the dynamically sublime, size is replaced with power, as in, for example, the unbridled strength of a stormy sea (actual) or the abyss beneath a cliff (imagined). Kant departs from his predecessor Edmund Burke by distinguishing the dynamically sublime from the experience of fear, claiming that, despite the initial danger, these phenomena must be witnessed from a relative position of safety in order to occasion the sublime. This caveat reflects a larger interest in claiming the sublime as "purposive," i.e., as reaffirming reason, despite its initial overwhelming of this faculty. Kant insists that while the initial experience of the sublime is one of confusion and excess, the very ability to ponder something that exceeds the senses and the imagination (mathematically sublime) or to contemplate and cope with a potentially life-threatening experience without giving in to it (the dynamically sublime) reaffirms the supersensible faculty of reason. With this position Kant runs into an obvious problem, as this compensatory gesture seems wholly incompatible with the kinds of experiences the sublime would seem to describe. One does not immediately associate the experience of, for example, being at sea in the midst of a roaring hurricane or leaning against the glass of the observatory deck of the Sears Tower with this kind of intellectual satisfaction. Clearly, an account must be made for the lingering shock of the sublime alongside this affirmation of reason. For this, he introduces the notion of "negative pleasure," which presents the movement between these two phases not in terms of an irreversible, causal relation but as a "vibration" or "oscillation."[35] In light of this "rapid alternation" reason's superiority is momentary and partial, subject to the same inability to fully manifest as the very sublime event itself.

This relation is perhaps most clear in the context of the mathematically sublime, where the unboundness of the initial experience is accompanied by an idea, if not a direct apprehension, of its totality. The classic example here is the night sky. While processing the size and distance of such an object proves impossible, an idea of the universe persists which to a certain degree contains this "unbounded" object. In turn, the non-seeing of the sky, our inability to create and process an image in its totality, gives way to a particularly vivid mode of seeing. This occurs through a simultaneity between, on the one hand, a failure of perception, and, on the other, a persisting mental image of that which exceeds perception. In this way, the subject of the sublime successfully contemplates the scale and power of the event while at the same time tasting its incomprehensibility, simultaneously mastering it and letting him- or herself be mastered by it.[36]

In the context of the disaster, this duality of the sublime experience finds its correlative in the film camera and its transformation of vision. As the apparatus bifurcates the operator's gaze it similarly presents visual experience in terms of a reconciliation between two conflicting images – one which manifests within the viewfinder as an incomplete image, the other the product of an imaginative act through which the impending photograph comes to shadow the present as latent presence. Alejandro González Iñárritu's contribution to the anthology film *September 11* integrates this unique mode of vision into its mode of address and in so doing illustrates the formative relationship that the camera maintains to the sublime experience in the context of this event.

The work begins with a slowly building soundtrack of panicked voices and ambient sound which plays against an entirely black screen. After almost a full two minutes of darkness, an image flashes and then disappears. As similar images begin to appear more rapidly and eventually remain onscreen long enough to be deciphered, they come to reveal bodies falling from the World Trade Center at almost incomprehensible speeds. Immersed in darkness for the majority of the film, the viewer struggles to situate him- or herself within this filmic space as desperate voices and occasional screams seem to come from all directions. With the viewer's eyes adjusted to the darkness, the flash of images is intrusive, literally difficult to watch. Its afterimage lingers in the absent spaces from which it emerges, merging the work's claims to visibility with its outright refusal to do so. While the film's scenes of falling bodies are composed of video footage, their momentarily flash mimics the photographic act and as such asks the viewer to extrapolate the logic of the film to the experience of the camera. Indeed, the spectator position of the film is in many ways that of the disaster photographer whose precarious oscillation between survival and image, seeing and non-seeing, appears written into its very form.

It is telling that the film conjures such an intense affective charge by mimicking the experience of the camera, integrating its structure of delay and return, opening its intervals to interminable durations before finally delivering the tortured image. Clearly, in a world where disaster is signified by a swarm of cameras, the photographer's experience appears as both psychic code and visual shorthand for the experience of trauma. However, in merging the camera's transformation of vision with the psychic experience of disaster, the film suggests a larger interpenetration, one which is at the center of Flusser's theory of the photographer and the arrival of a "techno-imagination."

1.5. A body falls from the World Trade Center in Alejandro González Iñárritu's segment of the anthology film *September 11* (2002).

As a postindustrial form of labor which displaces work onto the apparatus, the "photographic gesture" in its normative instance is one of play, an incessant recombination of possibilities within a given "program." The givenness of these space-time manipulations is central to what Flusser describes as the Kantian base of the photographic operation:

> One time and space for extreme close-up; one for close-up, another for middle distance, another for long distance; one spatial area for a bird's-eye view, another for a frog's-eye view; another for a toddler's perspective; another for a direct gaze with eyes wide open as in olden days; another for a sidelong glance. Or: one area of time (shutter speed) for a lightning-fast view, another for a quick glance, another for a leisurely gaze, another for a meditative inspection. . . . The result is a mass culture of cameras adjusted to the norm; in the West, in Japan, in underdeveloped countries – all over the world, everything is photographed through the same categories. Kant and his categories become impossible to avoid.[37]

The apparatus's articulation of these universal categories not only provides the condition of possibility for translating experience into a codified and legible image, but also decenters the processes of cognition through a dynamic exchange between camera and operator. In applying these categories to their subjects, photographers ("functionaries") manifest the apparatus's preprogrammed possibilities at the same time that they subject this process to their own desires ("The camera does the will of the photographer but the photographer has to will what the camera can do").[38] While imagination ("the specific ability to abstract surfaces out of space and time and project them back into space") serves as "the precondition for the production and coding of images," the camera itself supplies what Kant refers to as the "ontological predicate" of perception, those categories through which thought takes place and in turn the world comes into being.

This externalization of Kant's representationalist philosophy is in many ways prefigured by Max Horkheimer and Theodor Adorno, who understand the selective function of the culture industry as a displacement of once-internal processes of cognition. They explain,

> Kant's formalism still expected a contribution from the individual, who was thought to relate the varied experiences of the senses to fundamental concepts; but industry robs the individual of his function. Its prime service to the customer is to do his schematizing for him. Kant said that there was a secret mechanism in the soul which prepared direct intuitions in such a way that they could be fitted into the system of pure reason. But today that secret has been deciphered.[39]

For Horkheimer and Adorno, the self-realizing demographics of marketing combined with the predictability of genre and the sheer ubiquity of mass culture allow the culture industry to effectively supplant the individual so as to reproduce the material conditions of exploitation.[40] Flusser's revisions to Kant, on the other hand, suggest a less deterministic relation which proceeds according to reciprocity rather than repression. For Flusser, photographing operates as a means of "post-ideological manipulation" in that it relies upon the seeming autonomy of choice at the same time that it delimits and contains the possibilities in which this "freedom" can take place. This departure from the top-down deployment of power complicates the relation of the camera to vision, as the enigmatic "black box" is in this exchange neither a prosthetic extension of its operator nor an autonomous agent which covertly reprograms the sensorium. Rather, echoing Foucault's abandonment of the "repressive hypothesis," Flusser's camera oversees a reciprocity or "unity" in which the subject's seemingly autonomous operation of the device serves to reproduce (at the level of form rather than content) the authority of those underlying parameters of experience which the apparatus articulates. This circle establishes a "symmetry between the function of the photographer and that of the camera, [so that the] apparatus functions as a function of the photographer's intention [and] this intention itself functions as a function of the camera's program."[41]

For Flusser, the static quality of these givens ("Photographers can only photograph what they can photograph") is at the root of the medium's connection to totalitarianism, as it provides the universal language through which large-scale processes of homogenization can take place. In the context of 9/11, the same immutability of these analog "camera-categories" prompts a confrontation between the camera's mode of seeing and the accelerated urgency of disaster in the face of the digital turn. As these latter forces resist the film camera's attempts to process the scene, they come to fuel an overwhelming of these mechanized categories, thereby prompting this "techno-imagination" to reproduce the Kantian experience of formlessness. Paul Crowther explains the latter in the following terms:

> If we view a mountain in the distance it has a characteristic shape which enables us to describe it as a "mountain." But suppose that we are standing at its base with, perhaps, its higher reaches shrouded in mist. Under these conditions . . . the mountain seems . . . to be a limitless phenomenal mass or aggregate, without any defining shape or form.[42]

While on the one hand the negativity and formlessness of the sublime event testifies to a violence performed upon the imagination, on the other, it is precisely this inability to "see," or at least to see fully, that grants us access to a beyond representation for Kant. As Derrida points out, "In this violent renunciation . . . the imagination gains by what it loses. . . . It gains in extension and in power. . . . [The] potency is greater than what is sacrificed." Understanding the productive nature of this breakdown in the context of 9/11 involves recognizing the ways in which this concept is literalized for the film photographer. As the apparatus comes to function more as means of looking than imaging, it aids the exchange between operator and "black box" described above at the same time that it makes possible the increasingly inconceivable prospect of an experience without an image. In holding off rather than producing images, the disaster thus offers what Flusser calls "meta-programming," a *detournement* of the camera by which this "anti-apparatus" comes to work against the camera's most essential functions.[43]

The unfathomability that the analog camera produces is in this relation clearly not the transcendental outside to representation, nor does it offer the thinly veiled intimations of an absolute which has historically accompanied the concept of the sublime. As the camera furnishes the categories through which sensation can be translated into experience, what were once *a priori* categories of the soul materialize in Flusser's theory as mechanical conventions. As such, these "camera-categories" form not only the ground from which the photographic act emerges, but also the conditions for their own overwhelming. In this regard, one can read the sublime's "negative presentation" of the disaster in a dual sense – not only as the Kantian overwhelming of categories of reason, but also as the return of the unique and specific cultural conditions which are necessarily elided by the universal image.[44] As the image "ensnare[s] the cultural conditions like a net with a limited view through its mesh," the photographer must endure a kind of blindness in order to see the contents of this web. The unique position of the camera as of 9/11 momentarily made such an experience possible.

PREMEDIATION AND SUBLIME SPECTATORSHIP

Nearly half a century ago, Guy Debord famously declared that "all that was once directly lived has now become mere representation."[45] While intended to diagnose a larger cultural condition of postwar consumerism, this statement succinctly describes the transformation of vision that occurs as the photographer raises the camera to his or her eye. By collapsing vision with a virtual image to come, the gaze of the photographer presents what Heidegger explained in a different context as "[not] a picture of the world, but the world conceived and grasped as picture."[46] The dual temporality of this "world picture" enacts a bifurcation within vision whereby the now of the viewfinder is intertwined with the futural dimension of a latent image. While the above discussion has focused on the way in which this interval can emulate the sublime's "radical openness," it is important to point out that, in its everyday instantiation, this interstice or in-between is also the site where photographic practice is co-opted by the spectacle.[47] The ramifications of this interpenetration are illustrated by the following scene from Don DeLillo's novel *White Noise.*

> Several days later Murray asked me about a tourist attraction known as the most photographed barn in America. We drove 22 miles into the country around Farmington. There were meadows and apple orchards. White fences trailed through the rolling fields. Soon the signs started appearing. THE MOST PHOTOGRAPHED BARN IN AMERICA. We counted five signs before we reached the site. There were 40 cars and a tour bus in the makeshift lot. We walked along a cowpath to the slightly elevated spot set aside for viewing and photographing. All the people had cameras; some had tripods, telephoto lenses, filter kits. A man in a booth sold postcards and slides – pictures of the barn taken from the elevated spot. We stood near a grove of trees and watched the photographers. Murray maintained a prolonged silence, occasionally scrawling some notes in a little book.
> "No one sees the barn," he said finally.
> A long silence followed.
> "Once you've seen the signs about the barn, it becomes impossible to see the barn."
> He fell silent once more. People with cameras left the elevated site, replaced by others.
> "We're not here to capture an image, we're here to maintain one. Every photograph reinforces the aura. Can you feel it, Jack? An accumulation of nameless energies."
> There was an extended silence. The man in the booth sold postcards and slides.
> "Being here is a kind of spiritual surrender. We see only what the others see. The thousands who were here in the past, those who will come in the future. We've agreed to be part of a collective perception. It literally colors our vision. A religious experience in a way, like all tourism."
> Another silence ensued.
> "They are taking pictures of taking pictures," he said.
> He did not speak for a while. We listened to the incessant clicking of shutter release buttons, the rustling crank of levers that advanced the film.
> "What was the barn like before it was photographed?" he said. "What did it look like, how was it different from the other barns, how was it similar to other barns?"[48]

The scene illustrates how ubiquitous and excessive mediation undercuts the future orientation of the photographic practice and in the process introduces a nonproductive conception of blindness into vision of the operator/spectator. Photography in these instances functions as a reaffirmation of the status quo, a "taking pictures of pictures" which only reproduces the dominant image of reality. As such, the photographer's gaze is simultaneous to a destruction of vision as it delimits and destroys experience outside of this pervasive image ("No one sees the barn"; "It becomes impossible to see the barn"). Contrary to the negative presentation of the sublime, this blindness is nonactive; it is simply the placeholder for a no-longer-accessible real. These relations are made possible through a vast collectivization, what Flusser describes as "an embodiment of the social apparatus of representation" whereby users reaffirm the authority of this dominant image through individual practice.[49] In this way, the network of "nameless energies" that the narrator of *White Noise* senses in the swarm of clicking shutters before him dramatizes a "mass culture of cameras adjusted to the norm."[50]

The capacity of photography to reproduce the spectacle is particularly pronounced in the context of the disaster, where the virtual image manifests in accordance with what Christine Battersby refers to as "our over-familiarity with framed images of apocalypse and tragedy."[51] As these images "distance us from the force of uncontained power," the operator can and often does close the interval discussed above, thereby evoking DeLillo's circular narrative.[52] However, it is the sheer unavailability of analog photography's program to the user, its refusal of easy reconfiguration, which both granted the medium its dominance and universality and opened the photographer's vision to the kind of overwhelming of these categories in the context of 9/11. As a result of the convergence of multiple dynamics, which include the near-perfect distribution of analog and digital media at the time of the disaster and the relative deceleration of the film camera at the hands of a pervasive desire for live images, the photographer's gaze became entangled in a web of conflicting temporalities and expectations. In these instances, the logic of deferral which characterizes the analog image clashed with the larger desire for instant visibility, leaving an activated absence in the place of the virtual image. As a result of this absence, the apparatus came to work against itself, holding the balance between image and non-image in an indefinite suspension so as to present the shattered landscape before its assimilation into an image. However, this apparent escape from representation must be qualified, as its articulation of the outside is dependent upon and at least partially the product of the techno-imagination of the camera which presents this deferral of vision not as negation or erasure but as an active production of invisibility. While the structure of disavowal and delay has long been the basis for an enduring connection between the psychoanalytic understanding of trauma and the seemingly universal phenomenon of disaster photography, such assemblages problematize this enduring approach. Rather than a "motivated" gesture of disconnect by which an autonomous unconscious intervenes, this unique mode of vision recognizes the formative role of media in the sensorium's processing of time and space and, in turn, removes the negative connotations of the disaster photographer for whom looking away no longer functions as a means of circumventing contact.

An excess of speed turns into repose.

ROLAND BARTHES

In 1900, the soul suddenly stopped being a memory in the form
of wax slates or books, as Plato describes it; rather, it was
technically advanced and transformed into a motion picture.

FRIEDRICH KITTLER

TWO

Origins of Affect

THE FALLING BODY AND OTHER SYMPTOMS OF CINEMA

During the stock market crash of 1929, it was widely circulated that disheartened financiers began jumping from the windows of their Wall Street offices in record numbers. A London newspaper described Manhattan pedestrians' having to wade through bodies of jumpers that "littered the sidewalks."[1] Mexican painter José Clemente Orozco, who was in New York working on a mural for the New School, explained, "Many speculators had already leaped from their office windows, and their bodies gathered up by the police. Office boys no longer bet on whether the boss would commit suicide but whether he would do it before or after lunch."[2] Comedian Will Rogers claimed that "you had to stand in line to get a window to jump out of," while Eddie Cantor joked that hotel clerks were asking guests if they wanted rooms "for sleeping or jumping."[3] One imagines the scene on that day as a kind of perverse realization of René Magritte's *Golconda* (1953), in which bankers in bowler hats and black suits fall *en masse* from the urban sky.[4]

Almost as remarkable as the horrific scenes these tales describe is their utter lack of truth. As John Kenneth Galbraith pointed out in *The Great Crash,* suicide rates remained unchanged in the wake of the crash. Of the few that did take place and could be traced back to the events of Black Thursday, very few occurred via jumping from a skyscraper. In fact, as Nina Shen Rastogi reports, between Black Thursday and the end of 1929, one hundred suicides took place in New York, of which only four were related to the stock market crash, and only two of those were performed by jumping.[5] Karen Blumenthal's book on the crash goes even further in debunking the myth by claiming that there were in fact no suicides on Wall Street that day.[6] Despite this absence of leapers, virtually the only one immune to the hysteria of falling bodies seemed to be Winston Churchill, who describes in his book *The Great Republic: A History of America* his having witnessed a man "being dashed to pieces" after leaping from the room beneath his at the Savoy Plaza Hotel. After observing the panic that a workman perched on a steel girder created for a crowd below who figured him for a "ruined capitalist," Churchill, for one, was able to brush off the death he had witnessed as sheer coincidence.[7] However, for the rest of the public, the image of the falling body remained not simply bound to the historical "reality" of the event, but in some essential way representative of the trauma itself.[8]

Despite its disproportionate representation in popular culture, jumping from tall buildings has never been a statistically significant form of suicide.[9] The Empire State Building, the most popular architectural site for leapers in the United States and for many years the tallest building in New York, has had just over thirty suicides since its completion in 1931. As these leaps tend to follow a pattern of "temporal clustering," around half took place between the years 1931 and 1946, which means that in the sixty years since, the site has averaged around one suicide every four years. Not only is this mode of suicide generally uncommon, but, in relation to other countries, it is especially rare in the United States, where the cinematic leap ironically originates. Despite the United States' maintaining a fairly average overall suicide rate, less than 4 percent of all American suicides occur by jumping from buildings. Compared to Singapore where this method comprises 60 percent of all suicides, or Hong Kong where the same figure is 44 percent, this percentage is exceptionally low.[10]

Not only does the sheer prominence of the falling body in popular culture contradict its actual infrequence, but so do the conventions of representation more often than not betray the actual experience of leaping from a skyscraper. As George H. Douglas explains, the shift in the 1970s from open observation decks to glassed-in or fenced viewing platforms in buildings such as the Sears Tower and the Empire State Building significantly reduced the kind of grand suicide leap that figures prominently in movies and television. Even before the enclosure of observation decks, the nature of modernist architecture so prevalent in American cities such as Chicago and New York made the kind of free fall that we tend to associate with such leaps nearly impossible. As city regulations in the early twentieth century began requiring skyscrapers to maintain a "setback" structure in order to allow more sunlight to reach the street below and to prevent the spread of fire between buildings, the path to the ground was no longer a straight shot. This is especially prominent in New York, where, beginning in 1916, zoning ordinances set aggressive restrictions on a building's "sky exposure plane," an imaginary, inclined plane that the building's exterior was not allowed to come in contact with.[11] However, because of an optical illusion that makes these setbacks appear pencil-thin from a great height, the jumper believes that he or she can easily clear the obstacle and make it to the street below. In reality, most suicides from prominent American skyscrapers are interrupted by the structure itself.[12]

All of this begs a series of questions: Why is it that the image of the suicide leap figures so prominently in film, photography, and other visual media of the last century when its actual occurrence is such a rare event? From where does the kind of grand cinematic leap originate if not from reality? Why is it that the image of the falling body seems to assume such a unique cultural position in the wake of disaster? These questions have become particularly poignant in the wake of 9/11, when the image of the falling body, which existed only within the imaginary in 1929, was actualized in a series of stunning yet immensely disturbing photographs. As many of the trapped occupants of the World Trade Center chose to leap from their upper-story windows rather than be burned alive, photographers on the ground snapped their descent in rapid succession, producing Muybridge-like contact sheets that charted an eerily stunted progression. Despite the intoxicating quality of these horrific images, the photographs of leapers were soon pulled by the major news outlets, which deemed the photographs "too disturbing" for a general audience. After the initial publication of these images, the closest the mainstream audience would get to the horror of these bodies was the sound of ominous thuds that issued from outside the Trade Center lobby in CBS's documentary *9/11*.[13]

2.1. Richard Drew, *Falling Man,* 2001. AP Photo/Richard Drew.

In order to pursue the origin of the intense, unruly affective charge that such images carry with them, this chapter will first consider the motif of falling in the context of psychoanalysis. Tracing this image through the work of Freud, Winnicott, and others reveals several plausible answers to the aforementioned questions regarding the source and cathartic power of the fall. However, more important than the truth value of any one of these theories over another is their underlying similarities, which collectively reveal a structural affinity between psychoanalytic discourse of the fall and its representation in commercial cinema. Pursuing this dual articulation of a "fall without impact" compromises the directionality of the psychoanalytic position, suggesting a circular trajectory whereby the memory of the event is retroactively produced as much as it is resuscitated by images. As a result of this dynamic, these images came to mark a conflict in the visual culture of 9/11 whereby the photographs of "leapers" would position the falling body as a primary nodal point around which the memory and experience of the disaster would materialize. At the same time, these "falling-images" threatened to interrupt the causal relations of narrative upon which the ensuing discourse of national identity and military intervention depended.[14]

ORIGINS OF THE FALL

It is only fitting that this inquiry begin in the theater of dreams, where the fall is experienced with an intensity and regularity that rivals the cinema. In this regard, however, it is disappointing that in *The Interpretation of Dreams,* a book of nearly seven hundred pages, Freud deals only tangentially with what is certainly one of the most common experiences of sleep.[15] There are two possible reasons behind the relative absence: first, his claim to have never had the dream of falling himself, and, second, and more probable, his inability to track down the source of the anxiety that tends to accompany the dream. Analysis has convinced Freud that dreams of falling reference the childhood game of being repeatedly tossed in the air and caught by an adult family member. However, whereas the initial occurrence gives rise to sexual pleasure (as with wrestling and other forms of "romping about," Freud claims the repetitive motion and physical nature of the game provides sexual gratification for the infant or toddler), its subsequent resurfacing in the dreams of the adult carries with it an anxiety that he admits to not fully understanding.[16]

Seven years after the publication of Freud's book, Jack London's interrogation of the same dream in his novel *Before Adam* would in-

advertently attempt an answer to this lingering question. Being something of an armchair psychoanalyst, London approaches the dream
state as one in which the subject is granted direct access to an otherwise
opaque unconscious.[17] However, whereas Freud tended to locate the origin of the fall and much of the material upon which dreams themselves
are based in childhood, London sees a more distant past resurfacing in
this familiar narrative.[18] For London, the universality of the "falling-
through-space dream" suggests the presence of a shared, intersubjective
archaic past whose residues continue to haunt the "civilized" individual.
The protagonist of Before Adam finds evidence of this relationship in his
own recurring childhood dreams of landscapes and natural life which
have no basis in the lived experience of this self-proclaimed "city boy."
From this perspective, the image of the fall would be a particularly affective vehicle for bringing these residues to the surface of the psyche, due
to its significance to the daily life of our predecessors. Seeing as though
our ancestors lived high up in the canopy, such an experience would have
posed a traumatic and real danger and it is therefore no accident that it
would be singed with such vividness in our "racial memory."

Despite its speculative, even fantastic nature, London's proposition nonetheless introduces an important point for the psychoanalytic
understanding of the fall, namely, that the affective charge of the experience is one that is based in memory. The resurfacing of this event,
whether traceable to the conscious experience of the individual or not,
is spurred by a certain coincidence of form between the present experience and some prior originary memory of the fall. London inadvertently
stumbles upon this idea when turning to the question of why it is that we
never hit the ground in these dreams of falling. Pigeonholed by the larger
framework of "racial memory," his answer to this question is, despite its
cleverness, virtually unprovable. Only the memories of the survivors
of the fall are written into our collective memory, says London, since
those who were not able to catch hold of a branch or stop themselves
by other means would most likely not live to pass on the recollection
of that experience.[19] While Freud never directly concerns himself with
this question, the very nature of the childhood game that he cites as the
source for dreams of falling suggests a similar formal structure. In the
act of being repeatedly tossed in the air and caught before striking the

ground, the child is spared impact over and over again. As Freud tells us, subsequent dreams of falling simply "leave out the hands" so that the dreamer "float[s] or fall[s] unsupported."[20] It is here that the question of affect becomes all the more mysterious, as one would think that this form of the fall, which omits the moment of impact and therefore the true violence of the experience, would eradicate or at least diminish the intense anxiety that it carries with it. However, in the work of D. W. Winnicott it becomes clear that quite the opposite is true.

In his concept of "falling forever," Winnicott explains the form, universal character, and affective intensity of the image of falling without recourse to an ancestral past or what is assumed by Freud to be shared childhood experiences (surely there are cases of children who were not tossed in the air in this fashion and still experienced dreams of falling as an adult?).[21] Instead, he attributes the power of this image to the early drama of establishing selfhood. According to the analyst, in the course of the formation of the ego, the infant is subject to a traumatic oscillation between "subjective omnipotence," wherein he or she experiences the world as undifferentiated from the self, and "objective reality," in which a separation is achieved through which it becomes possible to delineate self and other. Attempting to negotiate the "me" from the "not me" brings about an overwhelming anxiety in the infant, one that trumps what are typically considered the primary concerns of early childhood (fears of abandonment and neglect of basic needs).[22] By focusing on the adequacy of a stabilizing environment through which to weather this more primary process of ego formation, Winnicott's object relations externalize Freud's ego-driven model which places the oral drives and their management at the center of development. In order to safely transition the infant from a world in which "subjective objects [those items which the child regards an extension of him or herself] dominate," to objective reality, "the mother" is paramount.[23] At the core of Winnicott's portrayal of the infant's anxiety, and in turn the ramifications of the mother's success or failure in establishing adequate support for this drama, lies the motif of falling.

Prior to the experience of "deprivation," the separation and establishment of independence from the mother, the infant is plagued by what Winnicott refers to as "unthinkable anxieties."[24] These anxieties are

comprised of four interrelated varieties: going to pieces, having no relation to the body, losing all orientation, and falling forever. This "trauma
of annihilation" is part and parcel of a spatial disorientation, a separation of the mind and the body, and a loss of control and organization
between the self and the physical world, all of which are encapsulated by
the figure of "falling forever."[25] The mother-infant relationship is central
in warding off the "impingement" of these anxieties through the establishing of a "holding environment," which refers most immediately to
the ability to cradle the child in her arms and thereby provide a position of security and safety from falling, but more generally to the ability
to provide a stable, nurturing environment. While children who have
been "let down," both literally and figuratively, carry this anxiety more
closely to the surface, it is present to varying degrees within even the
fully integrated adult.[26] The prospect of falling forever in this latter context is essentially a repetition of the initial experience of preintegration
and as such maintains the capacity for ego regression. As Mary Jacobus
points out, the adult's fear of falling forever is essentially "the fear of a
breakdown that has already taken place – an unthinkable collapse of the
defenses and a return to an unintegrated state."[27] Insisting that anxiety
is not a strong-enough word for such dread, Winnicott referred to these
psychic events as "primitive agonies."

Running through each of these psychoanalytic theories of the fall
is the idea that representations (oneiric or otherwise) achieve a certain
affective intensity as a result of their ability to conjure a memory of an
"originary fall." This mnemonic relation is contingent upon a specific
form of the representation, one which articulates a fall without impact, or, as Winnicott puts it, a "falling forever." This suggests a certain
paradox in that what would appear to be the removal of harm, i.e., the
withholding of impact, might in fact be precisely the condition through
which the image achieves its affective intensity. In this way, the "primal
fall" encases a duality in that it is both a fall without impact and therefore
a sparing of the subject from physical harm and even death, and a "falling forever," a literally unthinkable unraveling of identity which proves
anything but a reaffirmation of safety. In this distillation, the very real
prospect arises that the common thread holding together these theories may not be psychoanalysis at all. It is, after all, undeniable that the

psychoanalytic formula of the fall that has just been articulated (going to pieces, falling forever, having no relation to the body, and having no orientation) reads more like a Hollywood staging of the fall than a clinical diagnosis.

FALLING-IMAGES AND THE CELLULOID UNCONSCIOUS

Looking back upon the history of film, it is clear that falling from a skyscraper is, along with the self-inflicted gunshot wound, the method of choice for Hollywood suicides. Cinematic conventions of representing this event almost uniformly dictate an absence of impact. Typically, this is accomplished by interjecting an ellipsis between the descent and the presentation of the lifeless body below. Exemplary of this tendency is the 1932 film *Skyscraper Souls,* which clearly references the stock market collapse three years earlier. At the conclusion of the narrative, the secretary and lover of a bankrupt mogul climbs to the top of the hundred-story building that is the source of both her financial and her romantic woes. Upon leaping from the edge, a dizzying superimposition fills the screen as the descent layers over a bird's-eye view of the street below. Just as the figure approaches the ground, the film cuts abruptly to a montage of close-ups showing the faces of screaming pedestrians against the soundtrack of police sirens. More well-known is the opening sequence of *Vertigo* (1958), in which James Stewart slips after chasing a criminal and finds himself hanging from the ledge of a roof, high up in the San Francisco skyline. In the course of attempting to save him, a fellow police officer loses his footing and plummets to the ground. The ensuing sequence begins with the falling body of the officer and then cuts to a close-up of Stewart's panic-stricken face before returning to the aerial view which reveals the motionless body on the sidewalk below.

The affinity between the cinema's articulation of the fall and the psychic image which pervades the discourse of psychoanalysis prompts a reconsideration of the basic parameters of the questions that began this chapter. This structural homology necessitates that the investigation be recast from one that attempts to answer the circular question of the origin of affect to a more reflexive hermeneutic which centers on the conditions of possibility for the question itself. From Icarus's

2.2. James Stewart loses his footing in the opening sequence of *Vertigo* (1958).

famed descent to the biblical account of the "fall of man" to Dante's descent into a "deep place where the sun is silent," the figure of the fall has certainly been a recurring motif throughout history. However, by considering why it is that the interrogation of this *bottomless* fall appears in psychoanalysis virtually simultaneously with the birth of cinema, a more sensible but no less provocative answer to London's inquiry into the uniformity and universality of this motif emerges. Clearly, the medium of moving pictures allowed for both a visualization and a level of "experience" of this event that were virtually unimaginable prior to its arrival. More fundamentally, however, the formulation of a fall without impact is the product of the medium's most basic operation of dissecting and reassembling a given action into a larger whole, a dynamic which from Taylorism to surrealism runs throughout modernism. This ability to present reality in terms of what Walter Benjamin refers to as the "multiple fragments . . . assembled under a new law" is the precondition for the reconfigured image of the fall which psychoanalysis finds embedded in the modern psyche.[28]

At the same time, the commercial cinema's articulation of a fall without impact is also the product of the industry's observance of certain social taboos against excessive violence. Indeed, prior to the implementation of the Production Code in the early 1930s, which established a self-censoring body of the industry in order to avoid governmental regulation, one finds several exceptions to this convention. For example, D. W. Griffith's *The Birth of a Nation* (1915) contains the now-rare occurrence of a suicide leap captured in a single uncut sequence. In a famously problematic scene, Flora Cameron, a young white girl and darling of the South, is pursued through the forest by a crazed African slave. Rather than giving herself to Gus the "Renegade Negro," and thereby sullying the purity of the white race, a theme that recurs throughout the film in the dreaded figure of the mulatto, she heroically jumps off a cliff. We see her body, or rather a fairly unconvincing rag doll that plays her stunt double, in long shot as she/it falls from the cliff ledge and strikes the ground below. Prior to Griffith's film, one finds multiple representations of the unbroken fall. For example, as a Selenite grabs hold of the departing spaceship in Georges Méliès's *A Trip to the Moon* (1902), the descending spacecraft and its unofficial passenger crash into the sea through the use of dazzling superimposition. Likewise, in Edison's *Dream of a Rarebit Fiend* (1906), a dreamer floats above the city in nocturnal bliss. However, after being caught on a weathervane by his pajamas, the man soon falls through the ceiling of his bedroom and into his bed with back-breaking force.[29]

While the code did not explicitly stipulate that the crashing of falling bodies be removed from the screen, one can't help but think that such an event would fall under the "brutality and possible gruesomeness" that the "don'ts and be carefuls" actively discouraged. The revisions to Frank Capra's *Meet John Doe* (1941) confirms such a suspicion. The script's initial call for Doe to commit suicide by leaping from the Golden Gate Bridge was quickly nixed by studio executives. While the official explanation was that test audiences considered the ending too dark, Gary Morris can't help but notice that this avoidance of Doe's suicide establishes a "striking parallel to the human propensity for side-stepping this phenomenon, and specifically, in the film's context, the Golden Gate

Bridge's board of directors' inability to confront the dark side of what happens on one of San Francisco's landmarks."[30]

The film's deferral to a familiar narrative device in its earlier conclusion inadvertently captures the larger significance of this overlap between the cinematic articulation of the fall and the psychic image which pervades the discourse of psychoanalysis. Originally, Doe was to be dissuaded from leaping by an angel who would, in typical Capra fashion, show him a "film" of his life in order to convey the devastating consequences his suicide would have for those around him. As Friedrich Kittler explains, such sequences visualize the interpenetration between memory, interiority, and media that is catalyzed by this new figure of the falling body:

> Around 1900, immediately after the development of film, it appears that there was an increase in the number of cases of mountain climbers, alpinists, and possibly also chimney-sweeps who, against the odds, survived almost fatal falls from mountains or rooftops. . . . A theory immediately began to circulate among physicians like Dr. Moriz Benedict and mystical anthroposophists like Dr. Rudolph Steiner that the experience . . . of falling was allegedly not terrible or frightening at all. Instead, at the moment of imminent death a rapid time-lapse film of an entire former life is projected in the mind's eye. . . . In 1900, the soul suddenly stopped being a memory in the form of wax slates or books, as Plato describes it; rather, it was technically advanced and transformed into a motion picture.[31]

Kittler's joke regarding the survival of victims of the fall at the turn of the century positions a cinematic core at the center of experiential knowledge. As such, this brush with death reveals not the unconscious's storehouse of the past, as psychoanalysis would have it, but rather an externalization of memory and selfhood. The primacy of the image in this mnemonic function of the fall is the subject of Steve Cutt's recent short film entitled "In the Fall" (2011), in which a man slips while watering his rooftop urban garden and embarks on an action-packed descent to the ground below. Seconds into his descent, a projector, boom box, and pull-down screen arrive thanks to the help of some well-meaning pigeons. This media assemblage then begins to recount "the best bits" of the anonymous man's life in fragmented but familiar fashion. At the conclusion of this presentation, the man's anxiety-ridden face goes calm as he leans back, lights up a cigarette, and awaits his collision with the ground. The film concludes with a dramatic iris-in, which leaves the collision itself to the imagination.

The biopic flashback which often accompanies the fall only magnifies a larger capacity of the cinema's image of falling forever to be internalized as subjective memory. This is precisely the predicament of London's hominid alter ego in *Before Adam,* who on the first page of the novel inadvertently reveals the formative role that visual representation plays in his pursuit of the supposedly pure and primal state:

> Pictures! Pictures! Often, before I learned, did I wonder whence came the multitudes of pictures that thronged my dreams; for they were pictures I had never seen in real wake-a-day life. They tormented my childhood; making my dreams a procession of nightmares. . . . Only in my days only did I attain any measure of happiness.[32]

Just as dreams function for London's protagonist as a kind of passive possession by the image, so does the discourse of psychoanalysis, with its internalization of this cinematic fall as unconscious memory, bear witness to this unraveling of interiority at the hands of the filmstrip. The vehicle for this movement is in many ways the elision of impact, which recasts what is primarily a physical threat in psychological terms. As a result of the cinema's gradual eradication of impact, the straw dummy was replaced with an ellipsis or absence that left the body to fall endlessly. The ensuing limitlessness of the fall has meant that its trajectory has continued within the psyche where, as the work of London, Freud, and Winnicott attest, it gains momentum, becoming stuck in a web of the imaginary which confuses directionality and undermines origins. It is precisely this scenario which is played out in the visual culture of 9/11.

PHOTOGRAPHY AND 9/11: FALLING-IMAGES / FALLING MAN

While photographing the smoking towers on the morning of September 11, Richard Drew overheard disbelieving onlookers reacting to a series of dark specks falling from the structures. After his zoom lens revealed that these shapes were indeed bodies, the photographer followed over a dozen of them in his viewfinder as they plummeted to the ground. Equipped with a motor drive, the camera extracted a stop-motion sequence of the descent, from which a single image would emerge that would become a mainstay of post-9/11 visual culture. Entitled *Falling Man,* the image depicts an anonymous man whose descent from the World Trade Center would be replayed across a variety of media. Alejandro González Iñárritu's contribution to the anthology film *September 11* (2002) utilizes flashing images of the falling bodies from that day; Carolee Schneeman appropriates still images of these descents in her photocollage "eulogy" entitled *Terminal Velocity* (2001); Don DeLillo's 2007 post-9/11 novel *Falling Man* takes its name from the phenomenon; the final pages of Jonathan Safran Foer's 9/11 novel, *Extremely Loud and Incredibly Close* (2005), concludes with a graphic representation of a body as it descends into space; and Tom Junod's influential piece on the falling man in *Esquire* magazine was turned into a feature-length documentary in 2006. Through the endless appropriation of this image in the aftermath of the event, a metonymic relationship would emerge whereby the falling man would come to serve as visual shorthand for the event itself.

This relationship was confirmed by the reception of artist Sharon Paz's *Falling,* a work which positioned eleven nondescript white silhouettes of falling bodies in the windows of the Jamaica Arts Center in Queens on September 10, 2002. Like Eric Fischl's anonymous *Tumbling Woman,* which was removed from Rockefeller Center just weeks before, or the ad campaign for the fifth season of the T V series *Mad Men,* in which an anonymous silhouette seemed to be frozen mid-descent, Paz's piece drew almost instantaneous ire from the public, who regarded the work as an insensitive and premature memorial to the victims of 9/11 despite its lack of overt reference to the event.[33] Putting aside the complicated issue of when and how a culture should appropriately grieve tragedy, these incidents confirm a larger collapse of the attacks with the image of the falling body in the collective imaginary. Interestingly, running through these remediations is a familiar formula, one which emanates from the formal relations of Drew's initial photograph at the same time that it conjures the psychocinematic fall discussed above.

In "The Imaginary Fall," Gaston Bachelard repeatedly employs photographic metaphors to represent the kind of objectivity that is in opposition to the imaginary of the "pure fall," a bottomless plunge that unravels the coordinates of "solid" space. As this latter phenomenon is

2.3. Eric Fischl, *Tumbling Woman*, 2002. By permission of the artist.

distinguished from a "cinematographic description of exterior phenomena," the writer who seeks to conjure its transformative power must "find the means of inducing this imaginary fall in the soul of the reader before unrolling the film of objective images."[34] Tied as it is to "circumstances that are completely external," the photographic base of moving pictures is, for Bachelard, at odds with the kind of qualitative transformation that he associates with the pure fall.[35] Despite Bachelard's misgivings, Drew's photograph and the images that it seems to spawn present a possibility of transcending these limitations.

This process is set in motion by the spatial compression and aggressive cropping of the photograph, both of which initiate a destabilizing play between surfaces. The perfect symmetry of the striations of the exterior of the building, the meeting of this surface with that of the adjacent tower, which creates a play of depth within an otherwise two-dimensional picture plane, and the stark contrast of light and dark created by the interplay of light and the recesses of the surface cannot help but bring to mind classic minimalist works. As problematic as this blurring of high art and tragedy might be, it nonetheless helps to illuminate the peculiar visual experience of the photograph. Similar to standing before a work of Frank Stella or Sol LeWitt, to stare at the photograph for an extended amount of time is to lose perspective, to unravel the solidity of space. The uniform lines of the towers appear to vibrate in stroboscopic-like fashion in the background (a motion that is invited by the interchangeability of these structures' design) as the viewer focuses on the anonymous body in the foreground. In the process, what were once the instantly recognizable, iconic buildings of the New York skyline are suddenly rendered foreign, even illegible.

At the same time, the aggressive zoom of *Falling Man* eliminates any contextual information such as the New York skyline or, for that matter, the proximity of the falling body to the ground. We are left only with the vertical striations of the Trade Center facades, which as Ada Louise Huxtable noted in a *New York Times* piece from 1973, "are curiously without scale."[36] The cutting of space performed by the zoom, in combination with the disorienting effect of the undifferentiated surface of the towers' facades, grants the out-of-frame an ambiguity or undecidability. As the movement of the figure is no longer foreseeable beyond the instant in which it is frozen, the fall is characterized less by objectivity than indeterminacy. Perhaps the ground is just out of frame and this figure is moments from death, or perhaps he has just begun his descent from one of the top floors and has one hundred and ten stories of empty sky beneath him. This indecipherability grants the body a sense of weightlessness that undercuts what we know intellectually to be the inevitable result of the fall. As Tom Junod observes, "If he [the falling man] were not falling, he might very well be flying." In this, the work is exemplary of what I will call "falling-images." These photographic presentations of the falling body conjure the psychocinematic constellation in the wake of 9/11 by presenting an image which is as much about a falling apart or melting away of the mode of representation and reference itself as about the subject it represents.

Animating this disruptive ambiguity is an almost uncanny sense of movement which corrupts the photograph's temporal and spatial immobility and thereby liberates the image from the material base of the medium that Bachelard references. The still image's capacity for motion is at the center of Henri Cartier-Bresson's notion of the "decisive moment," a fleeting arrangement in which the "instantaneous lines made by the movements of the subject" converge into an image of balance.[37] Cartier-Bresson defined the concept primarily in terms of practice, i.e., as "a formal flash of time when all the right elements were in place before the scene fell back into its quotidian disorder." However, as Liz Wells suggests, the result of such an arrangement was also the articulation of a specific kind of "movement" which would be legible within and, indeed, constitutive of a narrative trajectory on the side of the image.[38] As Cartier-Bresson put it, the content of such an image should "radiate out from it [so that] this single picture is a whole story in itself," a prescription that is succinctly embodied in the photographer's seminal image of an outstretched foot hovering inches above the ground.[39] In "hold[ing] this equilibrium immobile," the photograph weaves the past and future reverberations of the represented action into an extended event and in the process transforms an otherwise mute reality into what Cartier-Bresson called "the organic rhythm of forms."[40]

As David Bate points out, Cartier-Bresson's conceptualization of the moment is best situated within a long discursive tradition regarding the most effective means by which still images (most notably history paintings, but also sculpture and theatrical staging) can best articulate extended narratives.[41] Of crucial importance in this discourse is Gotthold Ephraim Lessing's influential concept of the "pregnant moment," which posits the preferred moment for representation as one that would engage the imagination in such a way so as to expand the depicted scene beyond itself. This moment was not to be the climax itself, but a preclimactic moment whose proximity to the former was to be close enough so as to be thoroughly colored by it, while at the same time far enough from it so as to both garner suspense for its arrival. This configuration would then prompt the imagination to push the image beyond its material presentation. David Wellbery summarizes the effect of such an arrangement as follows: "From the sensuous presence of the single painted moment the imagination moves backward and forward, unfolding as it does so an unwritten narrative."[42] In this way, Lessing's "free reign of the imagination" occurs simultaneously with a liberation from the plasticity of the work as the temporal dimension and overall experience of the piece transcend the limitations of its sensible form. In Roy H. Quan's description of Cartier-Bresson's "decisive moment," one hears the reverberations of this position: "The viewer [of such images] is asked to ponder the consequences, to infer purpose, to hypothesize a possible outcome, to go beyond the photographic information in order to complete the meaning of the image."[43] Indeed, as the "presentiment of the way in which life itself unfolds," the photograph prompts a similar extension which transcends both the given content of the image and the inherent stillness of the medium. [44]

While this imaginative extrapolation can open the image beyond the given, the ensuing narrative often takes place within strictly delimited parameters, as for example in photojournalism, where the reconstruction of an event and the telling of a story are paramount. Peter Wollen delineates art photography from its photojournalistic counterpart precisely on this basis, claiming that whereas the former presents states or conditions, the latter utilizes an implied sense of process so as to present the represented action as a completed event.[45] As Cartier-Bresson puts it, the photographer "craves to seize the whole essence, in the confines of one single photograph."[46] The resulting image summons this totality by eliciting and then answering questions of causality. The central question that the news photograph grapples with, according to Wollen, is, "What was it like just before and what's the result going to be?"[47] The falling body is in fact particularly well suited to such a formula. Utilizing the stillness of the photograph as a means to make sense of an incomprehensible event, the internal organization of the image presents the suspended body within a continuum through which the viewer is prompted to expand the depicted moment and in turn reproduce a predefined chronology. In these instances, the image comes to illustrate Barthes's description of "the pregnant moment" as the "presence of all the absences . . . to whose rhythm History becomes . . . intelligible."[48]

A photograph of the famous Triangle Shirtwaist Factory fire of 1911 presents the fall as an entirely offscreen event. Attempting to register the scale of the catastrophe, the camera focuses on the accumulation of bodies on the ground. In the process, the image constructs a restraining before and after which act as the symbolic bookends which contain

2.4. Triangle Shirtwaist Factory fire, 1911.

the missing event. Lying lifelessly in the foreground, the bodies of three female factory workers are sprawled out before us. However, as if to suggest an event even more horrible than the one we gaze at, the living subjects of the photograph are almost uniformly looking ominously toward the sky, perhaps waiting for the next leaper or actively following a body in its descent to the ground. The exception is the well-dressed man in the background whose gaze penetrates through the composition to meet our own. This figure adds a reflexive layer to the image, as he models a certain form of spectatorship for the viewer. The blankness of his expression reflects our own inability to process or make sense of the event before us. It is precisely this bewildered wonderment, perhaps the face of trauma itself, that is dissipated by the solidity of the photograph's narrative. In comparing this image to William G. Shepherd's famous reporting of that day, it becomes clear that the overdetermined quality of this narrative serves to safely contain an inscrutable event which exceeds representation. In his article, language breaks down and the reporter resorts to pure sound in order to convey the inability of words to capture a horror beyond recognition: "I learned a new sound – *a more horrible sound than description can picture*. It was the thud of a speeding, living body on a stone sidewalk. . . . Thud-dead, thud-dead, thud-dead, thud-dead" (emphasis mine).[49] While the reporter cannot find words, the camera can nonetheless find an image through which this otherwise incomprehensible event is made legible.

Whereas the Triangle Factory fire photograph presents these components of the image as an interconnected continuum, I. Russell Sorgi's *Suicide, Buffalo* (1942) achieves its pathos by presenting the same temporal markers as tragically disconnected. The photograph shows a woman falling to her death from the window of the Genesee Hotel in Buffalo, New York. The painful irony of the image springs from the lack of coincidence between the police officer who, oblivious to the falling woman, enters the hotel presumably to "talk her off the ledge," and the presence of the woman's body on the right-hand side of the photograph that tells us he is too late. By rendering this disconnect visible, the camera's ability to freeze an instant lends the image its tragic character, as it means that the two events are forever separated by the singular click of the camera. Confirming this disconnect is the coffee shop manager who peers out the window, most likely at the crowd that has no doubt gathered outside, but also at the viewer, who is, as a result of this almost accusatory stare, asked to intervene. However, being privy to the body that the officer and the coffee shop manager are not, we are all too aware of the irreversibility of her death. The woman's body is suspended precariously only several feet above the ground. It is a moment that does not allow ambiguity, let alone salvation. Yet, as the practice of the photographer acknowledges, all of these narrative threads emanate from the suspension of the body. In his notes, Sorgi describes waiting until the body "passed the second or third story" before opening the shutter.[50] Clearly the intent was to capture the inevitability of impact, to come as close to death as possible without actually touching it. In short, Sorgi waited for the pose that would rewrite the event as a story.

More recently, Jon Bushell's 2006 photograph of Katherine Ward, a successful corporate lawyer living in London, depicts a woman as she leaps to her death from a fourth-floor Kensington Hotel room window.

2.5. I. Russell Sorgi, *Suicide, Buffalo*, 1942.

The *Times* story presented the image along with another photograph that shows Ward standing on the edge of the parapet, peering down below as if contemplating whether or not to jump. In this latter image, her arms seem to both push off against the wall behind her and grab for its safety. It is as if in the split second before she leaves the ledge she realizes the horror that awaits her. The next image shows the body in mid-descent, crouched in a near-seated position, mere seconds before impact. The aggressive cropping of the image has removed all contextual information save for the building itself, a few tree branches, and a streetlight. The slender proportions grant the photograph an extreme verticality that stresses the downward motion of the fall. At the same time, the uncannily suspended body, with its sharp focus and awkward position, presents a stasis that both resists that movement and in turn allows the two bodies to be connected in causal fashion.

The transformative nature of this intervention becomes clear when contrasting such images with the firsthand accounts of witnesses who observed such suicide leaps.[51] Relaying the report of an eyewitness, a 1904 *New York Times* article about a suicide leap explains, "So fast did it [the body] descend that the boys did not at first realize that it was a man."[52] In fact, the sheer speed and sound of the event, which was described as being "like the report of a large calibre pistol," was so disorienting that the boys actually reported it as a shooting.[53] James Logozzo, an employee who worked for Morgan Stanley on the seventy-second floor of the World Trade Center's South Tower, describes the experience of witnessing the jumpers of 9/11 in like terms: "It took three or four [bodies] to realize: They were people." As another witness from that day recalled, "dark spots fell from the sides of the building, at first it wasn't clear what they were."[54] Interestingly, the day after running the controversial photographs of Ward's suicide, the *Times* ran an article by Tim Lott that acknowledged both the image's active imposition of a storyline upon its passive subject and the broader historical relevance of this phenomenon:

> The image of Katherine Ward leaping to her death from a hotel window in Kensington on Tuesday was profoundly shocking, not simply because it was an act of self-destruction frozen in time, but because it was a rarely captured moment of preserved and exhibited despair. But the shock of the image went further. We have all been marked by images of the "flyers" from the World Trade Centre who chose to leap to their deaths rather than face being incinerated, but these were people who were, in a way, making a rational choice in a crazed, unbearable situation.[55]

Despite Lott's insistence, the temporality and accompanying sense of "movement" or narrative of Richard Drew's image contrasts starkly to the above images of the fall. Instead of articulating a causal relation upon which narrative threads could be woven, the work presents a radically different conception of "extension," one which eschews the spatial and indexical base of the photograph. Exemplary of this phenomenon is Richard Misrach's *On the Beach* series (2007), which interrupts spatial continuity, confusing direction and eradicating depth so that the descent of the body turns upon itself. As a result, the falling body takes on an impossible simultaneity of ascension and descension, death and transcendence.

FALLING IN MISRACH'S *ON THE BEACH*

Despite their being cited as the inspiration for the work, at first glance it is difficult to see how the falling bodies of 9/11 work in relation to the leisurely scenes of *On the Beach* (2007).[56] The images of sunbathers and swimmers scattered across placid expanses of sand or water seem about as far away from Ground Zero as one could imagine. At the same time, it is nonetheless readily apparent that within these seemingly innocent scenes something is off kilter. The photographs are littered with bodies, which lie in near-fetal positions or with arms outstretched, appearing as lifeless detritus washed up on the shore after some catastrophic event downstream. Floating strangely on top of the water as if pieces of wreckage or positioned in the hollows of the sand, they are often half-buried, perhaps by the fallout from a recent explosion or simply the passage of time. Throughout the possible scenarios that these images elicit, the out-of-frame looms large and yet remains indistinct and inaccessible. With no definitive connection to be made between the structuring absence of a recent disaster and the image proper, the contents of the latter are left disturbingly open.[57]

Despite refusing overt reference to the falling bodies of 9/11 at the level of content, Misrach's photographs nonetheless conjure the event through a formal interruption of diegetic space which mimics the trauma conveyed by the images of "leapers" from that day. Because of the extreme elevated viewpoint (the photographs were taken from Misrach's hotel window in Hawaii), the often-isolated figures of *On the Beach* are enveloped by the limitless, undifferentiated, and depthless space that

2.6. Untitled #893-03, 2003. © Richard Misrach, courtesy Fraenkel Gallery, San Francisco, Marc Selwyn Fine Art, Los Angeles and Pace/MacGill Gallery, New York.

surrounds them.[58] In this, the works reference the spatial character of the news photograph, which Barbara Rosenblum describes as "linear planar, that is, the lines are parallel to the picture plane. . . . In other words, news pictures are flat."[59] While these attributes signify the "news mood," as Paul Zucker phrases it, the disorienting and impenetrable quality of Misrach's photographs could not be more incompatible with the function of photojournalism. The enormous book of the series published by Aperture exacerbates this contrast by placing a blown-up detail of the figure on the adjacent page of the corresponding image, an arrangement that prompts the viewer to search for the hidden figure in the original image and to lose him- or herself in the expanse of the image in the process.[60] However, it is not simply the scale that disorients the viewer and transforms the scene before him or her. Like the whiteout sequences of George Lucas's futuristic *THX 1138* (1971), the exceptionally flat, uniform space in which these bodies are placed frustrates the viewer's spatial perception and overall orientation. There is no horizon to orient oneself by, no presence of the sky at all for that matter, nor are there significant shadows that would help us to position ourselves in relation to the sun. There is only a seemingly endless swath of sand or water that offers no indication of which end is up or down.

2.7. Untitled #857-02, 2002. © Richard Misrach, courtesy Fraenkel Gallery, San Francisco, Marc Selwyn Fine Art, Los Angeles and Pace/MacGill Gallery, New York.

Within this largely dimensionless diegesis, Misrach's photographs introduce a curious form of movement. While the elevated position of the camera and the lifeless bodies at the bottom together imply a fall of sorts, it is the works' play of depth which puts these falling bodies in motion. This phenomenon is especially apparent in those images in which the body floats on top of perfectly transparent water. As the water all but disappears in these images, the viewer perceives the ocean floor as the ground itself, so that the bodies seem to be suspended in air moments before impact. At the same time, the utter stillness of the image, let alone the beach scene in which he or she is enmeshed, confirms that this would-be leaper is clearly floating upon the surface of the water. The indefinable spatial position of these bodies, their strange simultaneity within multiple planes of the image, introduces a movement which defies the coordinates of Cartesian space and in so doing articulates a descent that embodies contradictory trajectories.

At a recent talk in New York, Misrach described the elevated viewpoint used throughout the series as identical to that of Drew's *Falling Man*, only reversed. Instead of staring up from the ground at a figure falling from the sky, we now look down at a body whose descent is measured against the ground itself. This elevated, disembodied point of view undercuts the conventional mode of identification whereby the camera's position on the ground assures us of the presence of the photographer, through whom the viewer reexperiences the event. It also serves to complicate the directionality of the fall. In light of the image's nonspecific articulation of space, the viewer simultaneously reads the fall in terms of this convention, which presents the descent as seen from the ground below. As this vantage point exists in virtual simultaneity with its mirror image, these bodies appear to be lifted up into the sky at the same time that they retract into the sand and/or water.

In this spatial ambiguity, the series establishes an ironic relationship to the Cold War sci-fi movie that it takes its title from. In the film, *On the Beach* (1959), which is based on Nevil Shute's novel of the same name, all of the inhabitants of the United States have perished or fled after nuclear fallout and as a result the major cities have been left entirely vacated. As a cloud of radiation blows south toward Australia, the last inhabitable place on the globe, the American servicemen are overwhelmed by nostalgia for their homes in the States and decide to sail one last time to the West Coast. Yet, in the final minutes of the film, which depict the final minutes of the world itself, the only images the film can produce seem to prevent access as much as they grant it. Because of the threat of nuclear contamination we see the empty streets of San Francisco from the safety of a periscope, or a vacated power station in San Diego from within a special radioactive suit. The title of the film is, then, something of a dramatic tease, in that the narrative builds the desire to place us "on the beach" once again (the beach functioning as a sort of Edenic space before the fall). It even builds the expectation that it can deliver that experience to the viewer. Yet the larger point of the film is that it is precisely this experience that the nuclear situation has made impossible, and as such the images of cities it presents necessarily substitute a strained and heavily mediated presence for the traditional immersive cinematic experience.

The title takes on a similar irony in relation to Misrach's series. At first glance, these images carry out exactly what this very matter-of-fact phrase suggests: they grant us access to the carefree life of vacationers and beach bums and, in a larger sense, place us "on the beach." Yet, at the same time, the extreme bird's-eye view which distances us from the

2.8. Untitled #394-03, 2003. © Richard Misrach, courtesy Fraenkel Gallery, San Francisco, Marc Selwyn Fine Art, Los Angeles and Pace/MacGill Gallery, New York.

action, the haunting presence of a catastrophic event that seems to loom in the offscreen, and the spatial disintegration of the undifferentiated surfaces against which the bodies are presented all undercut the image's presentation of that space, leaving the bodies to fall through a seemingly dimensionless space.

The larger implications of this duality manifest in the gruesome contortions of the falling bodies of 9/11. Their balletic writhing speaks to a process of decorporealization whereby the body is freed from its physicality (Lyle Owerko's series is exemplary in this respect) at the same time that the impending collision reaffirms its corporeal nature. In discussing a similar tendency in Francis Bacon's figures, Gilles Deleuze describes a process through which the body "escapes from itself" so as to represent a movement between states of being rather than the movement of a discrete object through space. As all possibilities are present as virtuality within such a movement, seemingly opposed terms coexist, their tension serving to preserve possibility as such.[61] In this formulation, the fall is simultaneous to a reversal of the fall; it rescues the anonymous figure at the same time that it documents his death. This process is made literal in the concluding pages of Jonathan Safran Foer's 9/11 novel, *Extremely Loud and Incredibly Close*, where the reader is confronted with a succession of still images of a falling man that bears an uncanny similarity to Drew's image. Individually, each page chronicles his descent toward death. Yet, if the reader flips the pages fast enough, these still images come to life, creating a movement which serves to lift the body upward and away from impact. The downward trajectory becomes simultaneous to an upward ascension. The figure is both dead and saved from dying. The story is both told and yet to be told. As these contradictory positions are embodied in a single figure, the once-discrete "instant" gives way to a nonchronological, "thickened" temporality that complicates, even undermines, the stories these images tell.

ANONYMITY AND WAR

While psychoanalysis diagnosed the affective charge of the image of the fall in terms of its ability to engage a preexisting memory, the above analysis has suggested a formative role of media in the recall and structure of this "prior" experience. Rather than engaging a previous event, the image of the fall maintains the capacity to actively constitute an "origin" or locus around which memory is both conjured and recast. Exemplary of this trajectory is Richard Drew's *Falling Man*, which in the wake of 9/11 gave rise to an iconography of the descending body that continues to populate the collective imaginary. As nodal points within a broader mnemonic network, these images are not only multiple, but interconnected around the motif of absence in such a way that amplifies memory's power of immanence (Drew himself seems to acknowledge this dynamic in his description of the image as "the most famous picture nobody's ever seen"). The political valence of this scenario becomes apparent when this absence, which has thus far been construed in terms of an absence of impact made possible by the disintegration of the spatiotemporal continuum of the image, is extrapolated to the parameters of identity and selfhood.

The anonymity of these descending bodies not only functions as a cenotaph or placeholder for the thousands of unrepresented deaths that day, but also inadvertently engages the problematic position these images occupy within the visual record. Without ethnicity, nationality, class, or gender, these anonymous figures present something akin to what Giorgio Agamben refers to as "bare life," that category of the living (*zoe*) which exists outside of what the body politic construes as human (*bios*) but which nonetheless makes possible the polis as such.[62] The repression of the falling body, though always partial and incomplete, similarly allowed for the construction of national identity as means to mobilize the country for war. Henry A. Giroux describes a shift in the wake of 9/11 whereby the spectacle no longer utilized visual symbols to build consensus (fascism) or embolden collective rituals (consumerism), but rather actively dictated "who is safe and who is not, who is worthy of citizenship and who is a threat, who can occupy the space of safety and who cannot, and ultimately who may live and who must die."[63] As this operation was directed at reconstituting the body politic after the attack, one can quickly see why it is that bare life must be excluded. It is not that it is on the other side of these binaries per se, but rather that it exists outside of and indeed undermines the entire operation of subject formation, which as Giroux points out almost immediately became entangled with militarization in the wake of 9/11.

This relationship between the impending invasion of Iraq/Afghanistan and the formation of national identity in the wake of the disaster was made visible in the controversy surrounding another iconic image of that day.[64] Recalling Joe Rosenthal's famous World War II image on the shores of Iwo Jima, Thomas E. Franklin's *Raising the Flag at Ground Zero* (2001) depicts three firefighters sending the Stars and Stripes up a makeshift pole amidst the wreckage of Lower Manhattan. When this now-iconic image came to be translated into a work of sculpture to be displayed at the New York City Fire Department's Brooklyn headquarters, a significant revision was made. In an effort to be more "inclusive" with regard to those who had perished that day, the subjects in the sculpture were portrayed with rather transparent political correctness – the three Caucasian men of the photograph were replaced with one African American, one Hispanic, and one Caucasian male.[65] As Susan Willis points out, the "sliding signifier" of a racially heterogeneous image served to displace the significance of the event from the confines of New York to the national stage, a shift necessary to mobilize a *nation* for war (as Willis puts it, the piece "facilitates a shift from the local to the international, from the work of recovery to war").[66] As the work insinuates that it was the United States rather than New York City that was attacked, it addresses (and forms) a collectivity in the hopes of moving our attention from Lower Manhattan to Afghanistan and ultimately Iraq.[67]

In turning to the work of Maurice Blanchot, it becomes clear that this operation of subject formation is mirrored by the psychoanalytic diagnosis of the fall. In *The Writing of the Disaster,* he bemoans Winnicott's concept of "falling forever" for its assumption of a continuous and discrete self. However, the consequences of this "fictive application designed to individualize that which cannot be individualized" go beyond that of a simple misunderstanding.[68] The very ego whose formation and entry into objective reality the concept claims to passively narrate is, according to Blanchot, the product of the discourse itself. As such, the concept of "falling forever" does not simply describe the maturation of the subject, but rather actively participates in its formation. The circularity of this process is made possible by the position of what psychoanalysis posits as an early memory within the adult psyche. As an experience that predates the formation of the self, it is an event that is never experienced in the fullest sense of the word and as such is not accessible to conscious memory. Winnicott explains this paradox in the following terms: "It is not possible to remember something that has not yet happened, and this thing of the past has not happened yet because the patient was not there for it to happen to."[69] Consequently, he goes on, "there are moments when the patient needs to be told that the breakdown, a fear which destroys his or her life, has already been."[70] As the liminal state of this memory opens the individual to this productive nature of discourse, the psychoanalyst's request that the patient remember is perhaps not as innocent as Winnicott would have us believe. Indeed, the authorial tone of the analyst as he or she essentially describes informing the subject of a memory he or she never had lays bare the active intervention of the discourse of the diagnosis.

However, *Falling Man* complicates this retroactivity by undercutting both the parameters of identity and the spatial/geographic boundaries through which the ensuing military campaign would be articulated. Instead, its formal structure conjures a whole host of affective intensities that would refuse incorporation, haunting the visual record as a remainder of a larger transformation of an incomprehensible event into a narrative of history. In this regard, the repression of the image reproduces the tendency of psychoanalytic discourse of the fall to reinstantiate the subject at the cost of a state of pure potentiality or outside. Without this most basic division between self and other, a division which globalized subjectivity tends to couch within a dialectic exchange rather than render obsolete, the rhetoric of war unravels and the falling man is left to fall forever. In this, the image speaks to the way in which the curtain of censorship, which sought to restore the spatial and temporal coordinates of sovereignty through which warfare would be made possible, remains porous, often revealing glimpses of a whole host of deterritorializing potentialities embedded within the visual record of that day.[71]

The thing seen doesn't need [the operator/viewer] to be there to be seen. The photograph is precisely . . . [a] "world seen without a self."

ANN BANFIELD

THREE

Remembering-Images

From the early perspectival diagrams of the Renaissance to the modern models of city planners, the image of the empty city has historically operated as what Barthes calls "a pure signifier," an empty sign "into which men put meaning."[1] In this capacity, such images provide the "degree zero" of the built environment, that substrate of underlying possibilities from which the city is reimagined from a seemingly omniscient viewpoint. Despite the interventions of theory in the postwar era, it was the popular culture of the nuclear age that compromised the apparent neutrality of the image of the empty city.[2] Cold War sci-fi films such as *The World, the Flesh and the Devil* (1959), *Five* (1951), *On the Beach* (1959), *Target Earth* (1954), and *The Day the Earth Caught Fire* (1961) recast the emptiness of such images as the aftereffect of a horrific event rather than the condition of possibility for a perfect legibility of space, and in the process intertwined the narrative of progress with an unimaginable violence. While "the bomb" has since moved to the back burner of collective anxieties, the motif of the empty city has persisted, accommodating more timely forms of disaster such as climate change (*The Day after Tomorrow*), biological warfare (*I Am Legend*), global infertility (*Children of Men*), drug-resistant viruses (*The Andromeda Strain*), and, most recently, terrorist attack. Throughout this varied history, the image of the vacant city has forged what Vivian Sobchack refers to as an enduring "iconography of emptiness . . . [which] marks the American cinematic imagination of the post-holocaust city."[3]

In negotiating the unofficial taboo against representing scenes of terrorism in the wake of 9/11, films such as *The Day after Tomorrow* (2004),

28 Days Later (2003), and *I Am Legend* (2007) called upon the image of the empty city to indirectly reference what was considered too sensitive for public consumption. While the affective intensity, if not the sheer readability, of these images is partially contingent upon historical resonances with the above iconography, in the post-9/11 context the motif also came to speak to new modes of power and correlative ways of seeing which exceeded the existing visual language of disaster. Attempting to extract these relations from what appear to be empty, even neutral images may seem counterintuitive. Yet, as these images often oversee the existence of the world within the narrative or media imaginary in which they exist, they inadvertently take as their subject the conditions of visibility which inform the disaster and its aftermath. The internal processes by which these images produce (or fail to produce) a world (filmic or otherwise) are made legible in a series of formal "problems" that the empty city necessarily introduces.

This reflexive dialogue originates in Cold War cinema, where the contradictions introduced by the prospect of viewing a world without humans surface as an ellipsis in the filmic diegesis. This break or interval in the cinematic illusion prompts the spectator to intervene in order to reanimate the stalled narrative and, more broadly, reinstate the possibility of a world in the face of nuclear annihilation. As the task of reversing the course of destruction is entrusted to the viewer, the empty city becomes the site of an extracinematic agency through which the film experience extends beyond the theater. In post-9/11 cinema, this existential drama is displaced onto the onscreen protagonist, as the spectator is circumscribed within conventional codes of cinematic identification. Not only is the question regarding the destruction of the human race definitively answered by these films, but the very drama itself is safely enclosed within the confines of the frame. In the process, the drive to repopulate the city, to in effect save the world, is co-opted and internalized by familiar post-9/11 narratives of perseverance, individualism, and American exceptionalism.

The metatextual capacities of the empty city are, however, reactivated after 9/11 in the realm of photography, where the contradictory relations that have historically accompanied such images are inscribed within more timely debates regarding the increasing autonomy of media.

Through the paradoxes of spectatorship that these images inherit from their Cold War predecessors, a reflexive image emerges which takes the prospect of a world without people as not simply a prophecy or threat but rather the condition of contemporary mediality in the aftermath of the disaster. In visualizing the disappearance of the subject/operator at the hands of a catastrophic event, these works intertwine the iconography of disaster with the basic operations of the contemporary martial image, collapsing literal death with a symbolic eradication of the human in the face of an apparently self-sustaining audiovisual system. Less a conflict than a state of being, this condition is intimately connected to the peculiar suspension of the empty city between what Susan Sontag describes as the twin prospects of sci-fi disaster, "unremitting banality and inconceivable terror."[4] Through this simultaneity, the image discloses the processes by which the incomprehensibility of disaster is already narrativized, premediated by a militarized gaze which renders the spatial and temporal boundaries of war fluid, if not obsolete. It announces a mode of conflict which lacks the formal declarations and goals of war and as such eschews the conventional signs of combat. Rather, within these multilayered cognitive maps of post-9/11 lines of force, the visual signifiers and operation of military incursion overlap with those of contemporary mediality, laying the groundwork for the "everywhere war" of which we are all subjects.

AGENCY WITHOUT IMAGE: THE EMPTY
CITY IN COLD WAR CINEMA

This "iconography of emptiness" discussed above has been built upon the negotiation of a series of formal problems which coalesce around the motif of the empty city in the cinema. Despite often dramatic leaps in time and space, narratives of commercial film tend to be governed by an essentially behaviorist, stimulus-response logic that Gilles Deleuze represents with the equation of SAS' (Situation→Action→New Situation).[5] Such an interval is said to be "rational," in that it acts in accordance with a chain of like intervals that together form an organic totality in which each shot presupposes that which it precedes and follows. This means that the SAS' configuration of the interval in any given scene functions as

3.1. Still from Kiju Yoshida's "Hiroshima," 1995.

a means of extending this logic globally within the narrative as a whole.[6] The disaster film is no exception. Indeed, as Carl Abbott explains, the genre is intimately "structured by the arrow of time – the contrasts of before and after, cataclysm and rebirth."[7] Dominated by "the negative and nihilistic value of emptiness," the image of the empty urban center, however, threatens this narrative coherence by marking the death of the city as a functional space.[8] Without a governing subjectivity or onscreen body to organize the experience of this space (what Deleuze calls the sensory motor schema), the empty city and its intimation of disaster pose "a basic problem [to] the narrative structure."[9] This image cannot make formative connections within and between plot points, much the same way as the "foreign body" of the traumatic event foregoes the associative structures through which memory typically takes place.

Such images threaten to undermine not only the conventions of storytelling, but, more broadly, the larger frame through which we might read and understand the world (filmic and otherwise). Through a series of mirroring effects, the codes of commercial cinema elicit a primary identification with the camera so that, in effect, the viewer relates to the image as a pure act of seeing.[10] In the context of the disaster film this means that seeing reaffirms the transcendental subject that the apocalypse necessarily eliminates. While the conventional cinematic form is built upon the persistence and survival of the viewing subject, the truly successful disaster film would, in other words, leave no witnesses. Acknowledging this tension between the vision of a world without people and the necessary persistence of the viewer, the editors of *Life* magazine felt obliged to remind their readers of their continued existence after the publication of their impressive visual catalog of the H-bomb's devastating power. While the note was obviously intended to introduce some levity into an otherwise tense situation, such reminders prove detrimental to the suspension of disbelief that the cinema requires. It is this tension that forms the basis of Kiju Yoshida's short film entitled "Hiroshima."

The piece begins with a video image of the filmmaker making the following declaration: "Now people tend to believe the cinema can describe all the events in the world, even the cosmic universe, as in science fiction. On the contrary, I believe that the cinema cannot show any image. This is what I will try to show you." The film then cuts to a grainy black-and-white film image that shows Yoshida and his cameraman staring back at us while filming the scene before them. We hear only the slow ticking of the camera which Yoshida's assistant methodically cranks. Through a slow wipe, an image of the ravaged Hiroshima Prefecture building is revealed, whereupon we hear the sound of a distant explosion.[11] The film then cuts back to the image of the director and his cameraman through a wipe in the opposite direction, as the sound of the camera once again returns. Suddenly, the filmstrip unravels, returning us to the video image that introduced the film, only this time we see a group of elderly Japanese staring into the camera. Over this scene, the director explains,

> Can the cinema describe that instant 50 years ago? It is totally impossible. If we had been shooting then, me and the cameraman would have been destroyed by the atomic bomb. We mustn't be presumptuous. The cinema can't describe everything. Bearing this reality in mind, we have to think about the part cinema can play from now on.

Acknowledging this "impossible" spectator position of the disaster film, Robert C. Cumbow describes Cold War films such as *Testament* (1983) and *On the Beach* as both antisurvival films and anti–*survival films*, as the untenable position of the witness in these films threatens to undermine the cinematic form itself.[12] The contradictory position of the spectator in combination with the breakdown of the narrative's "behaviorist logic" initiates a kind of collective trauma at the level of both form and content, conveying the literally unimaginable image of life without humans while emulating the unassimilable psychic position of this trauma at a structural level.

How is it that the image of the empty city became so deeply entrenched in popular culture, given that its presence threatens to undercut the basic tenets of the cinematic illusion? The answer can be found in the early years of the Cold War, when this diegetic breakdown is effectively recuperated by film as a powerful clarion call for action on the part of the viewer, enacting a kind of extracinematic suturing in which subjectivity is (re)constituted through the introduction of an indeterminate future. Exemplary of this process is the final sequence of *On the Beach*, which features a morose montage of empty San Francisco where newspapers and debris blow across the streets like tumbleweeds in a classic Western. Suddenly, the sorrowful dirge heard on the soundtrack is interrupted by an urgent crescendo as the film cuts to a close-up of a banner which reads, "THERE IS STILL TIME.. BROTHER." As the appearance of the empty city has paralyzed the narrative, agency is necessarily transferred to the viewer, who is asked to intervene, in essence, to repopulate this city. Similarly, at the conclusion of *The Day the Earth Caught Fire,* the world waits as atomic bombs are about to be detonated in order to push the earth's orbit away from its impending collision with the sun. The newspaper that employs the film's protagonist has printed two versions of the next day's front page. One reads "WORLD SAVED," the other, "WORLD DOOMED." The image of the protagonist running through an otherwise empty city, which begins the film, returns and then abruptly disappears. As the credits roll without resolution, the viewer is asked to write the concluding scene, to reanimate the stasis of the film.

3.2. Edward Judd walks through a deserted London in
The Day the Earth Caught Fire (1961).

This formula is perhaps most overt in the concluding scene of the
1983 made-for-TV movie *The Day After,* where the camera pulls back from
a single pair of survivors to reveal the wreckage left by the bomb. As the
image fades to black, a disembodied voice is heard speaking over a telephone: "Hello? Is anybody there? Anybody at all?" To the more than one
hundred million viewers that tuned in, the target of this address would
be driven home by the scrolling text that followed: "It is hoped that the
images of this film will inspire the nations of this earth, their peoples
and leaders, to find the means to avert the fateful day."[13] As these examples illustrate, the contradictory status of the camera/spectator that
the empty city introduces is utilized in the Cold War in order to issue a
direct form of address, one which in effect reinstates the spectator that
the film itself would seem to abolish.

Interestingly, a similar strategy was articulated via still image in
Edward Steichen's famous *Family of Man* photography exhibition at the
Museum of Modern Art in 1955. After journeying through an immense
catalog of images which visualized the interconnectedness of human-
kind, the viewer was confronted with a final ominous image which featured a six-by-eight-foot mushroom cloud. This concluding photograph
was not only the sole color image in the show, but was also transparent
and positioned in such a way that allowed the viewer to look back upon

the images of the show through this apocalyptic frame. As these incompatible images overlapped with one another, the prospect of a peaceful planet was literally put in peril by the threat of the atomic bomb, and yet by simply stepping to one side or another, the viewer could effectively rearrange the images according to an alternate future in which the human race would be reborn. Borrowing from the cinematic convention of the empty city, this arrangement forged an empowered spectator who upon leaving the museum was charged with preserving not simply the imaginary world of the image, but reality itself.

BAYARD AND THE UNDEAD IMAGE:

THE EMPTY CITY AFTER 9/11

While in the Cold War disaster film the empty city functioned as a call to action for the American public, in post-9/11 cinema this same dynamic came to reinforce passive spectatorship. Rather than transferring agency to the viewer, such films repopulate the city by their own accord, typically by way of the heroic struggle of a lone survivor (*I Am Legend*) or the last family or clan (*The Day after Tomorrow, 28 Days Later*). Shifting this task of resurrecting the city to the onscreen agent allows these films to utilize familiar conventions of the "just war" and the "warrior spirit" to reaffirm Western individualism and American exceptionalism. In this, the role of the empty city dramatizes what David L. Altheide describes as the immediate expansion of the events of that day into an "interpretative schema that connected the attacks with renewal, revenge and deference to leaders" who would in turn articulate a collective political and military response adequate to the devastation.[14]

More immediately, however, this shift served to restore the integrity of the filmic illusion and with it the conventional relations of spectatorship. As Laura Mulvey famously observes in her essay "Narrative Cinema and Visual Pleasure," "the subordination of the gaze of both the onscreen actors and the audience to that of the camera itself [serves to] eliminate intrusive camera presence and prevent a distancing awareness in the audience."[15] By containing the powers of the image of the empty city within the frame, so to speak, the paradox of instantiating a witness in a world that is without humans is safely absorbed by the

3.3. The Twin Towers in *City by the Sea* (2002).

narcissistic powers of the filmic illusion. The resulting inaccessibility of this underlying tension extends beyond the realm of cinema in post-9/11 visual culture, resurfacing in the television series *Life after People* (2008–2010), in which computer-generated sequences of decaying cities and landmarks seem to emanate from an operatorless camera, and in Alan Weisman's lyrical work of post-apocalyptic nonfiction entitled *The World without Us* (2007). Like their cinematic counterparts, these seamless images seem to never reveal the underlying paradox of chronicling a world without humans in an image that is made for and by a supposedly extinct race.

This redefinition of the cinematic codes of the empty city can be understood as supplanting an ethical spectator with a neoliberal subject. As David Harvey points out, when all other justifications failed for a preemptive invasion of Iraq, it was the "triumph of freedom" which took center stage in American political rhetoric and eventually materialized in the Bush administration's rationale for military action. According to this logic, it was not enough to save the Iraqi people from the tyranny of Saddam Hussein. To ensure lasting freedom, a government must be set up wherein "individual freedoms are guaranteed by freedom of the market and of trade."[16] The neoliberal agenda behind the war on terror conflicted with the kind of agency that Cold War cinema attempted to bestow upon its viewer. That agency exemplifies ethical spectatorship, a mode of subjectivity defined not so much in terms of the capacity to

decide right and wrong within the narrative of the film, but more foun-
dationally as an awareness of one's own relation to the systems of representation. This position is made possible by ruptures in the imaginary
coherence of the film whereby the viewer's interactions with the screen
transcend identification and in turn sidestep subject/object distinctions
and their concomitant hierarchies. The sacrifice of this safe interpel-
lated subject position initiates a metatextual relation which prompts
the viewer to scrutinize his or her relation to the image. Following Em-
manuel Levinas and his discussion of the face-to-face interaction, this
gaze also carries with it a responsibility, even an obligation, to others. By
returning rather than absorbing the gaze it issues a request which rever-
berates within the social sphere. On the other hand, the reconstituted
subject position of post-9/11 cinema prompts the viewer to lead humanity out of the apocalypse via an onscreen idealized self. In the context
of the disaster film, this relation furnishes the subject with an imaginary
mastery without actually granting the subject the ability to change or
even acknowledge the conditions of "military and neoimperial violence"
through which he or she is empowered. Mimicking the neoliberal valo-
rization of the individual, the subject's immersion within the onscreen
image articulates a desocialized, deculturalized agency, which appears
to transcend even the end of humanity itself.

Whereas the narcissism of the disembodied spectator of post-9/11
commercial cinema allows the viewer to negotiate the paradox of the
empty city without necessarily introducing the conundrum to conscious
thought, the photograph cannot so easily circumvent such an impasse.
What Barthes describes as the image's most basic assertion, the "that-
has-been," is partially contingent upon the ability of the viewer to work
backward from the image, to acknowledge that someone witnessed and
decided to photograph this event.[17] As John Berger explains, photographs, unlike cinema, "bear witness to a human choice being exercised
in a given situation. A photograph is the result of the photographer's decision that it is worth recording that this particular event or this particular object *has been seen*" (emphasis mine).[18] As a result, the photograph
is always partially coded as past and as such inevitably brings with it an
awareness of the conditions in which it was produced. This vestigial presence of the past opens the image to the possibility of a conflict with the

viewing present, an exchange that was recognized in 1840 by Hippolyte Bayard as an integral component of the medium's creative force.

At the urging of an associate of Daguerre, Bayard postponed the announcement of his discovery of the direct positive printing process to the French Academy of Sciences, a decision that would cost him the notoriety and payout he deserved. To communicate his anguish at this turn of events, Bayard staged the end of his life for the medium that had in some sense already taken it. The resulting image shows Bayard as corpse, a seemingly lifeless body that is laid out for the viewer in such a way that suggests a funeral viewing. By negating the presence of the operator, Bayard's *Self-Portrait as a Drowned Man* appears to be an image without an author, an autopoiesis whose legitimacy is reinforced by a suicide note written on the back of the image. Yet, at the same time, the very existence of the photograph testifies to the persistence of the operator/subject through whom it was brought into being. This play between conflicting temporalities smashed the positivist realism which the nineteenth century ascribed to the medium. Instead, as Michael Sapir points out, Bayard presented the photographic image as "a crossroads at which issues of recognition, authorship, display, visibility, invisibility, truth and illusion meet and play off of one another."[19]

In like fashion, the photographs of empty cities by Thomas Struth and Michael Wesely actively problematize the witnessing function of the still image by mobilizing the anxiety of automation which has accompanied the medium since its inception. Pushing the camera beyond its anthropocentric base, these images accumulate data rather than see; organize and retrieve information rather than remember; and perceive the geometry of the city as an empty vector space rather than a window of desire. At the center of this articulation of what Paul Virilio calls "sightless vision" is an attempt to visualize an alterity of memory which appears to exclude the viewing subject not simply from the event itself but also from its recollection. In this, the image intertwines the possibility of a cataclysmic disaster with a new vulnerability regarding the category of the human. In the wake of 9/11, this dynamic resonates with the increasingly automated networks of image/weapon systems which would define both the impending military incursion and post-disaster subjectivity more broadly.

3.4. Hippolyte Bayard, *Self-Portrait as a Drowned Man,* 1840.

TIME IMMEMORIAL: THE NEVER-ENDING
NOW OF THOMAS STRUTH

According to Maria Morris Hambourg and Douglas Eklund, Thomas
Struth's first hint of artistic proclivity came when his father brought
home a book of photographs of New York City by Don Hunstein. What
impressed the young Struth was the energy and movement of the pe-
destrian-filled streets, a vitality and freedom that he contrasted with the
"angst, enervation, and decimation of postwar Germany."[20] Years later,
after Struth had himself become a practicing photographer, he returned

to shoot these same city streets while attending PS1 in New York. In the process, a strange displacement would take place. In works such as *Dey Street, New York* (1982) and *6th Avenue at 50th Street* (1978), the American city appears dark, dank, and eerily empty, as if taking the shape of the photographer's impressions of 1960s Germany. The collapse of these two historically disparate referents reflects what Carole Naggar refers to as the "variable-time effect" of Struth's empty cities, a dynamic that she maps in the following terms:

> 1978 in both Manhattan and Naples looks somehow like the 1930s. Shanghai, photographed in color in 2002, looks like the 1970s. Tokyo in 1991 looks like William Klein's "Hollywood by Light," shot in the 1960s, except for the *London Sunday Times* magazine-like colors, both vivid and faded. Venice's Calle Tintoretto will always look like the seventeenth century, while Duittenburg in 1991 looks exactly like the late 1940s.[21]

From this web of interrelations, Naggar extracts a larger statement in Struth's work regarding the subjectivity of time, its reliance upon place, and its tendency to "pass ... at different speeds in different parts of the world, and even sometimes in the same spot."[22] But the dizzying narrative that she weaves exceeds not only the firsthand experiences of most viewers but perhaps even the capacity of human experience itself. While Struth's empty cities certainly maintain an antagonist relationship to the idea of a discrete, autonomous unit of time, the uniformity of the lighting and the lack of an inherent center of interest, let alone an explicit time of day, also appears to problematize if not refuse the presence of a subject through which time might be processed and organized. Accordingly, rather than a relational or subjective aspect of time, these images seem instead to articulate a simultaneity within time itself.[23]

This condensation of time in Struth's empty cities is bolstered by a strategic deployment of absence. Discussing the way in which the disparate historical references of the skyline fail to congeal into a singular present in *Dallas Parking Lot* (2001), Charles Wylie notes the image's tendency to prompt contradictory associations of the "computer punch cards of the 1960s, the laptop and the wireless device."[24] This sense of temporal nonspecificity is reinforced by *Sommerstrasse, Dusseldorf* (1980), where the overhanging cable car wires dramatize the deep space of the empty city. The rigidity of the lines formed by these cables, their perfect symmetry and convergence at the central vanishing point of the picture plane, also recalls the strict orthogonals of perspectival diagrams, and yet the instantiation of a spectator that one associates with this arrangement is rejected by the absolute lack of human activity and/or presence within the frame. As Charles W. Haxthausen observes, "the centrality of the perspective signifies a positioned subject encountering public spaces that themselves shape private subjectivity."[25] However, rather than offer a seamless operation of interpellation, the image seems to ask the viewer to bear witness to the formation of subjectivity from a distance.

Describing the peculiar "exclusion of the viewer" that occurs in Thomas Struth's empty cities, Michael Fried notes a sense of "heightened meaningfulness" and a "subliminal influence" which comes about as a result of the image's *lack* of a singular subjectivity that organizes them.[26] Through an exploitation of the indexical basis of medium, Fried explains,

> the places in Struth's photographs typically represent the collaging together of traces of multiple intentions, traces laid down at different, even widely disparate moments, thereby modifying, covering, or effacing the traces of previous intentions, so that the scene as a whole presents itself as everywhere stamped by intention albeit (with a few exceptions) not by a single or collective intention to produce the scene, the place, the milieu as it appears to the viewer.[27]

As the ambiguity of the operator in the post-apocalyptic image combines with Struth's "objective" and analytical style, the image comes to testify not only to a disappearance of its "author" but to a denial of the human in general. Writing on the vacant landscape of Chernobyl, Slavoj Žižek compares the experience of the empty city to "witnessing the act of one's own conception ... [or] burial" in that such scenes present the possibility of "a gaze which observes the world in the condition of the subject's non-existence."[28] As if dramatizing this possibility, *Crosby Street, New York* (1978) offers a single legible sign, a one-way street arrow which directs the viewer out of the frame.

It is telling in this respect that Ann Goldstein locates the origin of these photographs of empty cities in Struth's participation in the psychoanalyst Ingo Hartmann's *Familie Leben* project. Recalling August Sander's photographic series *Das Antlitz der Zeit (The Physiognomy*

of Our Time) (1929), Hartmann and Struth organized snapshots brought
in by Hartmann's patients into a series of categories which included siblings, parents, weddings, and so on. As each of the fifty patients brought
in three to four images, the result was an extensive collection which,
while shown publicly on two occasions, has never been published, in order to respect the privacy of those depicted.[29] Interestingly, however, the
project specified that the patients must either be absent from the images
or at least unrecognizable in them. Accordingly, Hartmann and Struth
requested photographs of the patients' families before the patients were
born or photographs which showed them as very young children. Struth
describes the affinity between the *Familie Leben* project and his earlier
photographs of the city in terms of a shared emphasis on "unconscious
places."[30] In this he reinforces the idea that the absence of subjectivity,
in terms of both a built-in position from which to view the scene and the
representation of the human in the frame, is the condition of possibility
for a flattening-out and, indeed, disappearance of time.

Freud famously pursues such an image of the city in *Civilization
and Its Discontents*. However, despite an undeniable similarity between
the way in which cities retain their past alongside their present and the
nonchronological character of the unconscious, he concludes that the
urban landscape cannot serve as an adequate visual representation of
this relationship. In order for the metaphor to work, says Freud, this
simultaneity would have to be taken literally, so that, for example, the
Palazzo Caffarelli would stand at the same time as the Temple of Jupiter
that took its place. In fact, each discrete structure would have to contain
all previous versions within itself. As if implicitly engaging Freud on
this point, Mulvey points out that "because the photograph captures
the presence of life stilled, the instantaneous nature of human movement and the fragility of human life, it confuses time more thoroughly
than, for instance, the presence of a ruin or landscape in which traces
of the past are preserved."[31] Struth's images of the empty city reinforce
this point, successfully materializing Freud's failed metaphor within the
confines of the image.

As stone walls are reflected in glass and steel facades in works such
as *Water Street / Maiden Lane, New York* (1978), the previous presents
which each structure represents layer on top of one another, compris-

ing a dizzying cognitive map of history. A similar condition is visible in *Ferdinand-von-Schill-Strasse, Dessau* (1991), where the interchangeability of housing tenements pushes the modernist pursuit of universality into sheer atemporality. In denarrativizing the skyline of these cities, the camera articulates a world in which there is no past that can be separated out from the present moment of viewing. There is only a now in which all of history has arranged itself without distinction and without the markers of decay. In this, the image visualizes an exchange between the material city and the imaginary which from Proust to Calvino has long been the muse of writers.[32] What is unique in these images, however, is that the image itself seems to have internalized these interior processes of the subject, picturing the world in semi-autonomous fashion. This dual nature of Struth's "depopulation" of the image, its capacity to not only empty the frame of humans in a literal sense but preclude their presence at some deeper, structural level, also informs the empty cities of Michael Wesely. Citing a desire to shake off the influence of Cartier-Bresson's "decisive moment," the photographer describes his work in terms of a deceleration of the time of modernity. Yet, as his exceptionally long exposures accumulate "all" of the moments of a given place and present them without discrimination, slowness becomes indistinguishable from stillness, and time in its normative sense slows to a crawl and dies.

THE BEFORE, AFTER: MICHAEL WESELY
AND THE LONG EXPOSURE

One month before the attacks of September 11, Michael Wesely trained four cameras on Manhattan in order to chronicle Yoshio Taniguchi's renovation of the Museum of Modern Art. In the photographs that resulted from these two-to-three-year exposures, the streets of New York are bisected by the persisting lines of headlights, buildings appear in various forms of construction and deconstruction, and, in general, the city disappears under the weight of an exhaustive visual catalog of human activity. In light of this immense layering of time, the viewer is prompted to work backward, asking what absent event might have caused those repeated arcs of light to be strewn across the sky. Why is it that this

9.8.2001 - 2.5.2003 The Museum of Modern Art, New York

3.5. Michael Wesely, *Open Shutter* series, August 9, 2001–May 2, 2003.
© 2013 Artists Rights Society (ARS), New York / VG Bild-Kunst, Bonn.

particular bus appears in recognizable form while the rest of the traffic is reduced to a single contiguous blur? Indeed, part of the initial pleasure of these photographs is derived from tracing narrative threads through this vast network of time.

However, it doesn't take long before the viewer quickly finds herself in a vicious circle, as the more she is immersed in this pursuit of the past, the more the directionality of time is compromised: Is the scaffolding which appears buried within this structure the sign of its construction or of a slow disintegration which has left only this skeleton? Is the provisional plywood sign on the right-hand side of the frame a holdover from a bygone era or an announcement of rebirth? The image provides no consistent answer to these questions at the same time that the voluminous impressions that cover its surface, as if forming some perfect index of time itself, call out to be deciphered and read.

As Vilém Flusser explains, the components of a photograph typically relate to one another via a "mutual significance" whereby the time of "scanning" the image, the experience of having seen *this* detail before another, is absorbed by some larger overdetermined narrative. In order for this latter process to occur, a single element must be elevated to the status of "carrier of meaning" so that "the before [of scanning] can become after [and vice versa]."[33] However, without this "carrier" the time of scanning, simply the narrative of visual apprehension, circles around itself and cannot form a cohesive, deterministic trajectory. Flusser associates this level of experience with the Nietzschean concept of eternal recurrence, as the same elements return to consciousness without distinction, without, in effect, having passed. In like terms, as Wesely's images jettison the notion of a singular present, the aura of pastness which typically informs the medium no longer holds. Perhaps the bus, the one which is inexplicably legible relative to the rest of the traffic, was stopped for an extended time. Maybe it broke down and spent several hours on the side of the road, or maybe the light of a bright sun simply flared off the roof during an otherwise routine stop. Without the selection of a present against which the past can arrange itself in legible form, the photograph appears unable to support linear time, let alone the very concept of narrative.

The photographer first encountered this alternate logic of time in his first successful one-year exposure, which was taken in the office of Helmut Friedel, the director of the Städtische Galerie in Munich. The enigmatic presences which missing events achieve in the resulting image belie the thousands of occurrences which took place before the lens and disappeared into the image. For example, while the man who occupied this space on an almost daily basis is ominously absent from the frame, an event which lasted only a few of the nine thousand hours the camera recorded would leave an imprint. During a television interview that took place in the office, the rectangular light box which refracted the lights, though present only briefly relative to the total exposure time, nonetheless left a subtle impression due to its sheer intensity.[34] In like fashion, Wesely notes that much to his surprise the workers at the museum renovation site do not appear in his *Open Shutter* series despite having eaten lunch in almost the exact same spot each day. Meister sug-

3.6. Michael Wesely, *Open Shutter* series, July 8, 2001–July 6, 2004.
© 2013 Artists Rights Society (ARS), New York / VG Bild-Kunst, Bonn.

gests one possible explanation for such disappearances with his claim
that in the course of these extended exposures the negative can develop
dead spots where light has burned away its surface. After such events
the camera, like the human psyche stunned into shock, cannot record
the events that follow, despite their importance or intensity. As a result
of this dynamic, these images confound expectation; for example, it is
the older architectural elements that achieve a definitive presence while

the newly constructed facades which cover these interior frames appear with only a ghostly presence. The past is, in other words, just as accessible and at times even more present than the present itself. In the end, what is initially experienced as the image's resistance to memory gives way to the recognition of an alternate mode of memory, one that has, in seemingly autonomous fashion, documented the past according to a wholly foreign set of drives and economy.

While contemporary technology no longer dictates such lengthy wait times, the work of Michael Wesely nonetheless calls upon the long exposure in the wake of 9/11 to actively depopulate the city. Struth's early morning photographs utilize a similar absence to confound time and the expectation of an organizing subjectivity. As such, these images intertwine the violent destruction of the human race via disaster with a growing anxiety regarding the obsolescence of the human in the face of our media-infused reality. However, in considering other contemporary images of the empty city it is clear that these relations are not necessarily inherent to the motif of the empty city, but are dependent upon a certain mode of presentation.

One year after Wesely's camera closed its shutter, the Korean artist Atta Kim began his ON-AIR series, in which he photographed popular tourist destinations in Midtown Manhattan with shutter speeds of eight hours or more. Drawing upon his *Deconstruction* series in which bodies are "violently tossed around" desolate fields so as to suggest "the aftermath of a horrific catastrophe," these eerily suggestive images of Times Square, Fifth Avenue, and Grand Central Terminal also maintain an unsettling quality despite their lack of bodies.[35] The missing subjects appear to have been sacrificed to the disaster which crowds the offscreen, reminding the viewer of Walter Benjamin's characterization of Eugène Atget's empty streets as the scene of a crime.[36] Not only is the event legible as a structuring absence in these photographs but so is a viewing position affirmed. The inhabitants, like the missing revelers of a Dutch still life, speak through their absence, as the motion of the city is preserved underneath the image's stillness in a series of streaks and blurs. The past in these images is less placed in contention (Wesely, Struth) than actively eradicated by way of what Siegfried Kracauer calls the camera's ability to "annihilate" that which it records. In this regard, the work resonates

3.7. Atta Kim, ON-AIR *Project 110-7,* from the series "New York," eight hours, 188 × 248 cm, chromogenic print, 2005. By permission of the artist.

with the artist's interest in chronicling various "modes of disappearance," from melting ice sculptures of the Parthenon to the erasure of the population of some of the world's largest cities. These images of disappearance reaffirm a separation between past and present, a longing for some unrecoverable past that, as Barthes and others have continually affirmed, lies at the root of photography's power.

In Kim's empty cities, photography's affinity with death is fully on display, allegorized as blurs, disintegrations, and other detritus from some now-extinct existence. However, in the photographs of Michael Wesely and Thomas Struth the medium's association with death and, in turn, its normative relation to memory move from the literal to the symbolic by way of the image's unwillingness to organize the indices of time it has captured. Through the long exposure and the interruption of the image's implicit viewer, these images visualize a remembering that seems to take place without and even at the expense of the rememberer.

This dynamic is exacerbated by the post-9/11 context, in which the clash between the desire to find some indirect impression, perhaps even truth, of the disaster amongst this dense web of indices and the apparatus's seemingly arbitrary organization of the past only further magnifies the otherness of these memory-images.[37]

ALLEGORIES OF AUTOMATION:

THE EMPTY CITY AS AUTOPOIESIS

An 1840 cartoon by Gerard Fontallard depicts a daguerreotypist who has propped himself against a rooftop chimney and fallen asleep while waiting for the camera behind him to record the scene. Scattered around the photographer are signs of the accumulation of time: an empty wine bottle, a well-smoked pipe, a pocket watch, and even the huddled body of the operator himself, who appears to have weathered the cold for longer than he would like. The mise-en-scène suggests that the extended exposure times of the apparatus are not simply a time-consuming nuisance but a palpable reminder of the irrelevance of the operator in the face of the automatic quality of the mechanism. That this "automatic" quality occurs at the expense of the operator (and more broadly the human in general) is confirmed by the scale of the photographer, who, like Durer's personification of melancholy, appears overgrown, bumbling, and unable to act in the world.[38]

While in the nineteenth century the "automatic" quality of the photograph often served as the basis for its dismissal as a noncreative, inferior medium relative to the "organic arts," in the early twentieth century this same feature would be embraced by theorists and photographers for its ability to open new possibilities of perception.[39] Summarizing the newfound freedom that the advent of photography made possible, André Bazin famously declared, "For the first time an image of the world is formed automatically, without the creative intervention of man.... All the arts are based on the presence of man, only photography derives an advantage from his absence."[40] Decades later, Stanley Cavell staked out a similar position in *The World Viewed* with his claim that "by removing the human agent from the task of reproduction ... photography satisfied ... the human wish to escape subjectivity and metaphysical isolation, a

3.8. Gerard Fontallard, *The Daguerreotypist,* 1840.

wish for the power to reach this world, having so long tried, at last hope-lessly, to manifest fidelity to another."[41] At the core of these "automatist" positions is the recognition that the mechanical processes of the camera provide a replacement or at least an alternative to what was once a human action, and do so, as Gary Snyder summarizes, "by means or steps that are roughly parallel to those the device is supposed to replace."[42] Recent work by Vilém Flusser, Diarmuid Costello and Dawn M. Phillips, and others have qualified the technodeterminism of these positions with more nuanced readings of the photographic operation which emphasize a give and take between automation and agency. Rather than get embroiled in this complex and important debate, I wish to extrapolate from photography's historical expectation of automation toward a more contemporary media environment so as to disclose the ways in which the above images of the empty city engage with a broader context of media violence, surveillance, and subjectivity after 9/11.[43]

The discourse of automation which surrounded early photography may appear trite in the face of contemporary imaging systems which utilize heat signatures, facial recognition, and behavioral patterns to read and classify subjects via database query. However, the process of recording light by mechanical means is, in many ways, the origin of an enduring anxiety which follows media of the last century. In recent years, this anxiety has taken on an additional layer of meaning as the automation of seeing has been rendered inseparable from the operation and semiotic currency of both military aggression and post-9/11 surveillance, forming a joint constellation which Nicholas Mirzoeff refers to as the "post-panoptic visuality of global counterinsurgency."[44] At the center of this phenomenon is a shift from a prosthetic construction of vision to what John Johnston calls "machinic vision," which takes place within "an environment of interacting machines and human-machine systems [and produces a correlative] field of decoded perceptions that, whether or not produced by or issuing from these machines, assume their full intelligibility only in relation to them."[45] In this formation, the collapse of symbolic and literal death that was visualized in the photography of empty cities dovetails with a machinic gaze which in construing seeing as targeting produces the conditions for the "everywhere war."

After a decade of pilotless airstrikes, it is clear that the camera eye no longer serves as a simple tool of reconnaissance. Rather, within the increasingly autonomous kill chains of contemporary weapons systems, sighting reproduces the Bergsonian model of perception as virtual action. We see, says Bergson, in order to act and in so doing configure a world around this impending action. As a result, vision is always already

a projection of an impending event. This scenario is reproduced algo-
rithmically in, for example, the U.S. Navy's phalanx gun system, which
detects and automatically engages incoming threats; the Israeli Harpy
"fire-and-forget" unmanned aerial vehicle (UAV), which seeks out and
destroys radar installations without direct operator control; or South
Korea's army of sentry robots, which are equipped with machine guns,
thermal imaging cameras, and laser range finders capable of detecting
and eradicating enemies several miles away. The parity that Snyder's
description of photographic automation establishes between the operation of the eye and its mechanical stand-in functions structurally
within these formations of vision. Rather than simply extend the eye
in prosthetic fashion, they internalize and perform a kind of automatic
perception, which, though open to reprogramming and human influence, regularly demonstrates an uncanny ability to act in the world. As a
result of this machinic gaze, the subject/target appears, to use Bergson's
term, as an "extended object"; his or her very presence within the system
is conflated with an implicit course of action.

The conflation of seeing and attacking that occurs at the site of these
automated weapons systems produces a unique temporality which is
represented in popular discourse by the phrase "target of opportunity."
This phrase was used in the media to describe the alleged hiding place
of Saddam Hussein and, as Samuel Weber points out, quickly became
representative of a larger logic of the war on terror. As Weber explains,
while the enemy had to be "identified and localized, named and depicted" in familiar fashion, what is new in the post-9/11 context is the
"mobility, indeterminate structure, and unpredictability of the spatiotemporal medium in which targets had to be sited."[46] In this kinetic
and unstable environment of networked intelligence, targets/subjects
became opportunities, a moment which had to be made use of. The very
singularity of such phenomena became intertwined with what Weber
describes as "the generality of an established order, scheme, organization or plan, in respect to which the event defines itself as exceptional
or extraordinary."[47]

This scenario is illustrated in Jamal Penjweny's series of photographs
Saddam Is Here (2010). The work depicts everyday Iraqis holding photographs of Saddam Hussein in front of their faces while driving to the

3.9. Jamal Penjweny, *Saddam Is Here,* 2010. By permission of the artist.

market, sitting in the dentist's chair, or simply getting ready for bed. As viewers, we are made aware of a kind of absurd displacement of the operation of targeting from tyrannical leaders to a collectivity or country. The post-9/11 fluidity of what Carl Schmitt called the "friend or foe distinction" is made palpable in these works, as not only is the target anonymous and thereby anticlimactic relative to the spectacle of "shock and awe" or 9/11 itself, but so too is it, in the end, simply an image. It is telling in this regard that the gesture of the figures reads as both a revelatory act of display for the camera and a shielding from the consequences of this performative gesture. As culturally specific as Penjweny's images may be, they also speak also to a mode of representation that is pervasive in everyday life after 9/11. As the visual cues from these technologies are themselves increasingly embedded within popular culture, it is apparent that the notion of seeing as automated targeting is not isolated to the electronic battlefield, the virtual cockpits of the UAV or the remote locations of netwar. Rather, it is vastly becoming part of not only everyday discourse, but also the visual language through which our cultural understanding of conflict takes place.

In the absence of the kind of immersed photojournalism that characterized Vietnam, automated image systems often supply the images of contemporary war. As a result, the unforgettable images of war from the last century, such as Nick Ut's *Napalm Girl,* Eddie Adams's *Saigon Execution,* or Joe Rosenthal's *Raising the Flag on Iwo Jima,* are increasingly supplanted by the new visual icons of war, the self-destructing smart bomb camera or the leaked footage from the drone's-eye view. In fact, John Broughton points out that after several decades of this automated visual culture of war the very construct of "seeing without an eye" has come to serve as a "mnemonic for previous U.S. military action."[48] The result of this overlap between the media presentation and actual experience of war is that a series of categories have come to coincide in the automated image – these include operator/viewer, experience/reproduction, trauma/entertainment, and so on. James Der Derian describes this phenomenon in terms of the arrival of a "military-industrial-media-entertainment network" (MIME-NET), which escalates the intrusion of Vietnam's "war waged in the living-rooms of America" to one waged within the global networks that constitute daily life.[49] The advent of "spectator warfare" is made possible not so much because of the intensity of these media presentations and their ability to convey the "reality" of war, but rather the exact opposite. It is the product of a shared level of mediation, through which even "combat" itself now flows.

This dynamic is a recurring theme in the budding genre of "drone art," which utilizes the visual codes of the UAV camera eye to destabilize the spectator's relationship to the onscreen image, unsettling the once-secure boundary between a passive spectator of a distant war and the firsthand experience of military personnel. For example, in his short film *5,000 Feet Is the Best,* Omer Fast stages a fictitious encounter between a drone and an American family in the Nevada desert near Creech Air Force Base. The film overlays the audio of firsthand accounts of drone operators with aerial shots of the barren American landscape, before eventually moving to the Las Vegas Strip. These images are enframed with the metadata and scale markers which comprise the drone's-eye view, forcing the viewer to see as the drone/drone operator. Similarly, Trevor Paglen's *Drone Vision* presents extended loops of drone camera footage which have been secured by an amateur satellite hacker. As the presentation of these images mirrors the visual language of leaked footage such as the "Collateral Murder" video, which shows the killing of around a dozen Iraqi civilians and two journalists by an air-to-ground strike of U.S. Apache helicopters, its seemingly banal content is overpowered by the sense of a breach of security. Through these formal interventions, the viewer is asked to engage with the shared interface of war, which incorporates even those empty, disconnected spaces which Deleuze termed "any-space-whatevers."

The presence of these visual codes in the empty cities of Struth and Wesely similarly recast the city as a martial space. While this no doubt stems in part from the sense of a recent attack that the image of the empty city carries with it, these images also speak to a less palpable mode of subject formation which extends beyond immediate sites of conflict. For example, as the automated eye of engagement overlaps with new modes of surveillance, these empty cities illustrate the way in which a shared experience of mediated war becomes entangled with larger forces of post-9/11 subjectivity. They are, in other words, reflexive constructions of the "war image" in the sense that Mirzoeff describes, a performative image which in a self-fulfilling prophecy stages an American victory that is then realized in circular fashion.[50] In this regard, it is telling that Wesely's layered images are not only produced by an invisible camera mounted several stories above the ground, but also read more like data accumulation than photography. His camera is archival; it charts flows of information, perfect indexical exchanges of unknowing subjects. In its lack of a central organizing agent from which to view or decode the image, its spatialization of time and emphasis on the vectors of exchange and movement, the work exemplifies recent reevaluations of Foucault's panopticism.

Greg Elmer describes the advent of a diagrammatic version of the panopticon which works through a multiplicity of processes whereby the subject is "continuously integrated into the act of collecting, storing, and cross referencing . . . data."[51] McKenzie Wark terms this new apparatus the transopticon, "a distributed monitoring and commodified feedback, with no central node, necessarily, but autonomous and automated feedback loops, . . . where it is no longer even a goal for the 'subject' to internalize the perspective of visibility."[52] The familiar model of "automatic power," whereby the subject lives as if he or she is being seen regardless of whether or not this is the case, is replaced by less invasive, more seamless mode of cataloging via algorithmic means. It is one in which the very expressions of agency (likes, dislikes, behavioral patterns, trends in media consumption, and so on) become the medium for the relations of surveillance, which are in turn modulated in conjunction with this data. Wark's observation concerning the waning significance of the "perspective of visibility" is vitally important in this regard, in that it reflects a correlative move away from humanist-based models of seer and seen toward the inorganic.

In these terms, the "everything in view" quality of Struth's images speaks to a "compulsory visibility" in the face of a mode of power which is exercised no longer through enclosure, but through a kind of excessive exposure. It is here that the logic of surveillance overlaps with that of the militarization of the image. As Rey Chow observes, war after World War II would increasingly mean "the production of maximal visibility and illumination for the purpose of maximal destruction."[53] Or, as William Perry, former United States secretary of defense, put it, "If I had to sum up current thinking on precision missiles and saturation weaponry in a single sentence, I'd put it like this: once you can see the target, you can expect to destroy it."[54] Struth's images thus represent the now-familiar proclamation that the modern city has become "a world without hidden sides, a world in which opacity is no longer anything but a momentary interlude."[55] This is made possible not by the eye of the warden, so to speak, but by an omnipresent and algorithmic gaze, which in construing vision as targets makes possible a war that is without spatial or political boundaries. In overlaying the same gaze that accumulates data with that which annihilates the living, the empty cities of Struth and Wesely inadvertently visualize the inner workings of a globalized war on terror of which we are all subjects. Relative to the Cold War context where the city acted as a means to intervene and prevent disaster, the same trope after 9/11 suggests that we are always already at war regardless of space, time, or identity.

IT IS SWEET AND FITTING TO DIE WITH THE
IMAGE: IDENTIFICATION AND ALTERITY

Part of the difficulty faced by any critical project which engages twenty-first-century networked culture is the inherent reflexivity of the structures of power. While this condition may seem to be an anecdote to the lack of transparency of the post-9/11 state, the image's revelation of the processes of its own genesis are in fact precisely the conditions of contemporary spectacular violence. One finds confirmation of this fact in the footage from smart bombs, unmanned drones, or even the Apache helicopter gunsight, all of which produce a self-referential discourse in which the apparatus is not only foregrounded but presented as something of an autopoietic system. Discussing the viewer's experience of the first Gulf War, Lev Manovich writes that

> what we . . . saw were not just images of the war, but endless images by the means of which the war was carried out: video images from an infrared camera mounted on a plane; video images from a camera installed on a weapon guided by a laser sensor; video in its role as "battle damage assessment" where a weapon equipped with an imaging device follows a weapon of destruction and records details of the damage. This was no longer a traditional reporter's view of a battle. . . . More often, in a strange case of identification we witnessed what was "seen" by a machine, a bomb, or a missile.[56]

The reflexive nature of this antispectacle, which tends to forego the climactic explosion or actual assault in favor of a direct identification with the machine, is crucial to cultivating the notion of "humane violence." In marveling at the "surgical precision" of these devices, the audience loses touch with the destruction of human life that these images are implicated in. In this, the "not me" of the image articulates a kind of survival and safety relative to the elsewhere of the actual conflict, which is deferred indefinitely. However, at the same time, this presentation fuels the anxiety regarding what Manuel De Landa describes as the birth of a "machinic phylum." Through this concept, De Landa suggests that the presence of these inorganic agents, which are capable of selecting and destroying their own targets in what often appears to be an autonomous fashion, has reached a kind of critical mass wherein they begin to function as a higher entity.[57] In this way, the visual presentation of contemporary military conflict negotiates a fragile duality of reaffirming a position of safety for the subject while articulating a destruction of the controlling idea of human as origin of the world. Throughout this drama, the experience of military violence as well as spectacular acts of terrorism remain within the domain of the image, becoming, as Paul Virilio insists, a matter of representation, a conflict within and for the logistics of perception.[58]

From Edwin S. Porter's bandit who trains his pistol on the audience in the final shot of *The Great Train Robbery* to Jean-Luc Godard's endlessly reflexive layering in films such as *Contempt,* foregrounding the apparatus in the context of the cinema has historically functioned in terms of a Brechtian distanciation, which undercuts the seductive lure of the image in favor of a more critical reception. However, as the self-referential presentation of contemporary war jettisons the humanist base of this convention it comes to issue a seduction of a different kind, one that is wrapped up with the Freudian death drive. Acknowledging a mode of identification which flows away from rather than toward subject formation, Leo Bersani and Ulysse Dutoit explain,

> The self-protective and self-preservative ego of the Lacanian imaginary . . . should not be conceptualized as intrinsically distinct from the simultaneously self-shattering and self-constitutive ego of primary narcissism. The specular illusion is sustained by the promise of the image being shattered . . . the ecstatic loss of the appropriated identity. The confrontational nature of object-relations is perhaps less the result of the subject's insanely blaming the object for its own inescapable self-alienation, than the pre-condition for that masochistic "sympathy" in which the subject will re-create the jouissance of self-loss.[59]

In the context of virtual war, this masochistic union with the inert is reenacted for the viewer who, in a sense, dies with/as the smart bomb, the detonation of which is announced by the self-annihilation of static or the unmanned surveillance camera which disappears into the rubble of 9/11. While Lyotard's "libidinal economy" or Deleuze's "bodies without organs" stress the masochistic pleasure of the body that joins with the machine/apparatus to produce new formations of immanence, here the return to a primordial state of nondifferentiation becomes entangled with a coherent and legible mode of address. Specifically, the modulated death that it/we endure essentially co-opts the sublime ecstasy of preintegration in order to reiterate the familiar narrative which Horace summarized in the *Odes:* "Dulce et decorum est pro patria mori" ("It is sweet and fitting to die for one's country"). Broughton explains,

> To the extent that there is symbolic identification between the viewing subject and the missile, the subject can die together with the object. There is a brief encounter, a passionate interlude, followed by the classical and dramatic *Liebestod* that is so much a part of the American narrative tradition. . . . Dying anonymously through televisual satellite space [conforms to a] Romantic vision of [wartime heroism].[60]

The capacity of the machine to represent our nonpresence summons a contradiction by which this fantasy becomes possible. In essence, the viewer's exclusion from the image comes to turn upon itself, producing subjectivity by way of a traumatic encounter with the otherness of the apparatus.

While eschewing the reflexivity of photography, post-9/11 cinema discloses a similar logic via the empty city. The picturesque return to wild nature, the seductive beauty of urban ruins, the rat race of New York City frozen in a moment of quiet contemplation – these recurring images promise that a simpler life follows our disappearance. As Mathias Nilges argues, "Unlike Cold War-era representations of destruction that mediated a dominant fear of annihilation, [post-9/11] representations of destruction are beautiful because destruction is in fact an antidote to a world that produces the fears we seek to escape."[61] The disappearance of the city's population that the images of Struth and Wesely visualize can be seen as disclosing the stakes of this mode of spectatorship that the disaster enacts. Rather than an antagonism toward the living, these images reveal the secret of subjectivity in the context of spectacle of war, namely, that the subject springs from his or her absence, an absence that is wrapped up with and, to some degree, produced by the alterity of the machinic gaze.

DISASTER AND THE FUTURE ANTERIOR OF MEMORY

As a spontaneous event whose initial occurrences precluded live coverage, the 9/11 disaster not only opened the door to automated images by way of its reliance upon surveillance footage and webcams, but in turn made possible a kind of autopoietic formation of memory between these image systems and the ensuing inflow of traditional media coverage. The cameras that captured the first hints of the attack did so in a familiar and reflexive visual language, one which actively produced an absence of the human alongside the event itself. Consider the footage of the CCTV camera which recorded the crash of Flight 77 into the Pentagon, or the images of Wolfgang Staehle's webcam which inadvertently captured the collision of the first jet with the North Tower. The stills from these cameras move indiscriminately across the event, frame by tortured frame. Within the prolonged intervals of this succession of images one suddenly makes out an anomalous blur and then an explosion. However, compared to its amateur counterparts which layer shaky handheld sequences over panicked narration, what is startling about this footage is what it doesn't do. The camera does not react. It does not tilt up to capture the full extent of the explosion, as we have come to expect. It does not run toward or away from the disaster or zoom in or out to frame its destruction or climb down from its mount to get a better look, as most cameras do in the face of disaster. Nor does it drop the usual off-camera expletives that seem to accompany every other 9/11 video. Instead the wound simply breathes smoke through the regular intervals of the camera, which remains unfazed by what it records.

As the stutter steps of these extended intervals visualize the uncanny transformation of the event into an image, these operatorless cameras conjure the self-conscious display of the modern "theater weapon." As Virilio notes, such weapons shift the goals of warfare from carnage and physical destruction to a kind of spiritual, psychotropic awe of technological presence.[62] This self-referential presentation, in combination with the naming of the site "Ground Zero," a term which originally served to designate the detonation point for the bomb in World War II, recoded the event in terms of a military conflict rather than an act of terror. In this way, the images of the automated camera projected memory of the disaster forward toward the impending invasion of Iraq. In the process of forging a causal relation to a virtual event, the image articulates the future anterior of memory.

As the second plane slammed into the South Tower on the morning of September 11, the seemingly accidental quality of the first collision

was suddenly recast in a menacing light. Fifteen minutes earlier, the explosion of Flight 11 was assumed to be the product of operator error or systems failure – in short, a freak accident. With a kind a pure bewilderment we watched the baffling, unassimilable footage of this initial crash, not knowing how or why but simply held captive by a remarkable and disturbing image. Now, as the second plane came into view, intentionality came to join these two unimaginable images and perhaps countless others to come as "9/11" officially came into being.

The familiarity of this narrative, which gained momentum as it extended across a network of images, firsthand accounts, personal reflections, and pundits' analysis, belies its lack of truth. Actually, in the network news broadcasts of that day only the second collision was shown. Footage of the first crash would come the following day. Yet, as the results of a recent study confirm, the vast majority of Americans profess to have seen both crashes, one after another on the morning of September 11.[63] The ensuing flow of images had eradicated the absence of the first collision and with it the sheer incomprehensibility of the event. This operation provided the necessary preconditions for the birth of "9/11" as a legible event complete with causality, intention, heroes, and villains. The near universality of this misrecognition, by which images came to redistribute the temporal indices of the event according to a familiar narrative of war, dramatizes Bernard Stiegler's Husserlian reading of the mnemonic power of modern media. By way of repetition of temporal objects, media fuse primary retentions with previous performances of the same event.[64] This coincidence of past performances with present perception allows the image to exert what Mark B. N. Hansen refers to as "a stranglehold over time-consciousness," the end result of which is a vast synchronization of consciousness in which "the world vibrates in unison."[65] Gerry Canavan's analysis of Oliver Stone's *World Trade Center* (2006) confirms this process. In the film, the first attack is immediately understood as a deliberate terrorist attack by the film's major characters. Even the three-minute delay between the collision and the

3.10. A series of stills captured by Wolfgang Staehle's webcam on September 11, 2001. © 2013 Artists Rights Society (ARS), New York / VG Bild-Kunst, Bonn.

coverage of the event by CNN is eradicated as the film's TV reporting begins almost simultaneously with the collision. All of this serves to retroactively "eras[e] the confusion and uncertainty that actually permeated" the early moments of 9/11 so as to reaffirm and secure the narrative of retribution that has since taken hold of the event.[66]

The photographs of Struth and Wesely inadvertently stand as documents of this process by way of the ontological thoroughness with which they envision memory. Rather than present a mnemonic trace to be activated into representation by the spectator, these works visualize a redistribution of the medium's systems of processing and storing of light impressions in relation to an unseen event. In La mémoire saturée, Régine Robin describes the relation of the global autopoietic image system to memory in similar terms. If the work of recollection revolves around the figure of the palimpsest and its operations of "interpolation, alteration, and modification," then, Robin insists, the fullness or "saturation" of the contemporary image means its content is no longer open to the "supplementing [of] these missing aspects" but is rather presented as already remembered.[67] The self-producing nature of this image system in Struth and Wesely is rendered visible for the viewer, for whom the impenetrable quality of the image testifies to its illegible processes of inscription and, more broadly, the presence of a self-sustaining entity which actively produces his or her absence. It is through this relationship that the empty city takes on a dual articulation in the wake of 9/11, whereby a world without humans is envisioned as both the remainder of an unfathomable catastrophe and the media-saturated world of security in which the viewer now lives.

Monuments . . . are . . . born resisting the very premises of their birth.

JAMES E. YOUNG

FOUR

Lights, Camera, Iconoclasm

HOW DO MONUMENTS DIE
AND LIVE TO TELL ABOUT IT?

The World Trade Center was targeted on 9/11 not so much for the number of casualties it would produce or the damage to the infrastructure it would inflict, but rather for the larger symbolic statement that the destruction of this iconic structure would make. As the architectural centerpiece of the economic capital of the world, the triumphant verticality of the Twin Towers succinctly embodied the global reach and self-assuredness of postwar American capitalism. Their unnerving gigantism implicitly guaranteed a future where such structures, though grossly oversized for the present, would eventually be the norm as the fruits of capitalism flowed into U.S. accounts. This narrative was reaffirmed by the fact that the primary residents of the towers were banks, insurance companies, and the leaders of the money market. With their operations running in parallel with the nearby New York Stock Exchange, the towers served as both apparatus and shrine to late capitalism. Fluent in this logic of expansionism and dominance, the terrorists bargained that the destruction of this nexus of power would, if only momentarily, rattle the symbolic stability of this world order.[1] As the editors of *Architecture Week* summarized on September 12, 2001, "The terrorists chose carefully. They discerned those skyscrapers as the cathedrals of our age and aimed at the heart."[2]

In the wake of the disaster, this relationship was repeatedly cast in terms of a familiar rhetorical trope. From Žižek's "high theory" to the editorials of *Time* magazine, the targeting of the World Trade Center was attributed to its status as a "monument" to capitalism. While the association of the structure with excessive commercialism has accompanied the site (and the skyscraper in general) since its inception, the appearance of this particular discursive framing of the monument at this particular time captures something precise about the conditions of 9/11. Most immediately, of course, this pervasive reference reflects a collective desire in the aftermath to transform the public space of the towers into the kind of "hallowed ground" that invites reverence and reflection. However, this association was also deployed in reference to the motivations behind the attacks and as such it simultaneously addresses the everyday functioning of the towers before the disaster. Suspending the disaster between these two trajectories/temporalities, this discourse of the monument, when pushed further, opens onto a larger prospect concerning the visual culture of 9/11, namely, that the symbolic dominance of the skyline and its subsequent eradication are not necessarily opposed, but rather maintain the possibility to act as complementary components of a larger regime of (in)visibility.

Bringing this narrative to light requires revisiting some of the core assumptions regarding monuments, many of which have been recast if not inverted by the dominance of media spectacle. As the last several decades have confirmed, the monument's enduring historical role as target for acts of iconoclasm and destruction is largely overseen by media. In this alliance, the duality of iconoclasm – its tendency to produce images in the process of destroying them – is amplified, giving the monument the capacity to achieve an extraordinary, if only momentary, (negative) presence. In the everyday sphere, this possibility has the inverse effect of exaggerating what can only be called the invisibility of the monument. After all, it has been nearly a century since Robert Musil so skillfully chronicled the ability of the form to elude perception and, despite the undying urge to produce monuments, the vast majority remain bound for a kind of purgatory of the banal. So dominant is this spectacular image in comparison that, in certain contexts, the site comes to exist primarily as a kind of latent presence, a future-oriented possibility of activation.

While the ubiquitous presence and overwhelming size of the towers would seem to contradict the invisibility of the monument, a closer examination of the experience of the site suggests otherwise. From the standpoint of the visitor/inhabitant who made his or her way through this space, the site continually foregrounded its own lack of presence

4.1. The World Trade Center as seen from the Microsoft Flight Simulator (2000).

through spatial play and shifts in proximity. This penchant for invisibility would manifest in the view of the city from the "Top of the World" observation deck, where blockages and blind spots littered the supposedly omniscient image. The recurring dropout within the visual field that the towers produced not only pushed the experience and representation of the site toward the imaginary, but also initiated a symbiotic relationship between the structures and the logic of the camera. Through this union, these absences mirrored the inverse logic of the monument in that they served as the origin of the totalizing image from which the structure's triumphant symbolic statement would come into being. From the 1976 remake of *King Kong,* which replaced the original 1933 film's Empire State Building with the Twin Towers, to the Microsoft Flight Simulator which allowed players to fly their planes into the iconic landmark, the towers have been at the center of an enduring media fantasy of disaster. Reading the site through the lens of the monument extends this familiar narrative beyond the screen to the experience

4.2. Michael J. Fox holds a photograph of his disappearing
family in *Back to the Future* (1985).

of the structures themselves, which, with the help of the image, would
repeatedly materialize this fantasy for their inhabitants.

MONUMENT DEATH AND THE REVERSAL OF PRESENCE

In the film *Back to the Future* (1985), Michael J. Fox is transported to the
1950s where, through a series of coincidences, he inadvertently prevents
his parents from meeting and thereby threatens the future in which he
now lives. Throughout the film, the impending loss of the past is symbol-
ized by the gradual disappearance of Fox and his siblings from a family
snapshot which he keeps in his wallet. As a photographic hourglass, the
vanishing body parts of the image not only provide the ticking time
bomb for the quest to bring his future parents together and return to
the future, but so do they inadvertently dramatize a certain understanding of iconoclasm whereby the loss of physical presence of an image or

object is equated with the death of the past that it represents. As a kind of pure forgetting which compromises not only the historical narrative but, as the plight of Marty McFly suggests, identity itself, the destruction of the monument similarly appears as a wholly negative gesture.

Yet, in the course of the Reformation, the French Revolution, the Soviet cult of personality, and the dissolution of the Eastern Bloc, the cultural position of the monument became inextricably bound to its destruction. This relationship between statue-breaking and history has escalated in recent years to the extent that the unveiling of the monument, and indeed the presence that it obtains thereafter, rarely if ever so fully enters public consciousness as its destruction does.[3] The monument in the context of the post-9/11 "war of images" exemplifies this new status as its capacity to serve as target is recast as its primary role. After all, as W. J. T. Mitchell points out, in addition to the lure of oil and the unfinished business of the second President Bush's father, it was the prominence of monuments and other large-scale historical markers in Iraq compared to Afghanistan which made it a more attractive destination in this war of representation.[4]

In this context, the commemorative function of the monument, let alone its sheer visibility, proves capable of working through a reversal of presence whereby disappearance no longer proves synonymous with forgetting or loss, but rather provides the possibility for otherwise invisible monuments to break through the haze of the everyday. In light of this reversal, it no longer suffices to speak of monuments as casualties of war or revolution. As Robert S. Nelson and Margaret Olin observe, once the monument's "potential for destruction or defacement" becomes "the most meaningful aspect of the monument's existence as an object," its destruction becomes its realization, perhaps even its primary means of signifying.[5] The futurists were perhaps the first to recognize this shift. Describing the "inauguration of the monument" as "rendezvous of uncontrollable hilarity," the artist Umberto Boccioni understood the significance of these sites solely in terms of their destruction.[6] In freeing the present of the burden of the past, these acts of destruction were intended to elevate the experience of the monument to the level of art and in the process reinvite these pulseless sites to once again participate in history.

Sergei Eisenstein dramatized this paradox in the opening sequence of his film *October* (1928), where the revolution is announced by an attack on the statue of the tsar, which is toppled and broken in pieces. Later, as the uprising begins to falter, the same footage is reversed so that the statue is magically restored to its pedestal. The uncanny second life that the monument achieves speaks not only to the threat of the return of the tsarist government, but also to the way in which the initial act of destruction quite literally gives life to a once largely subliminal symbol. The film's presentation of this act of iconoclasm also foregrounds the role of the medium in this transformation of the monument. Showcasing the newfound ability to perform perceptions outside of the everyday human capacity, the camera/projector bends time, reversing the processes of history as if mirroring the revolutionary potential of its proletariat audience. In this, the film illustrates the way in which modern media's penchant for the spectacular resonates with the productive aspect of iconoclasm, bringing the monument into being, so to speak, by way of its negation. This scenario reproduces the larger-than-life media stagings of monument death that have worked their way into the collective imaginary (the destruction of Dzerzhinsky's statue, the Berlin Wall, the Bamiyan Buddhas, and even the World Trade Center), all of which confirm a reversal of presence whereby eradication becomes the primary means for an otherwise invisible form to *take place*. The formative relationship that the monument maintains to its own destruction is driven home by the Iraqi dissident Samir al-Khalil's reaction to the unveiling of Saddam Hussein's Victory Arch in 1989. Upon encountering the work, al-Khalil was prompted not to contemplate the victory over Iran that the site commemorates, but rather to visualize the moment when the statue would be torn down in the same way the statues of King Hussein and General Maude had been before it. In internalizing this historical relation to violence, the monument appears from the beginning directed toward its destruction.

From this perspective, the formal qualities of monumentality articulate a contradictory message.[7] While the impenetrable surfaces of the monument most immediately function to weather the elements and convey a sense of permanence, the stone and bronze facades of these sites serve in equal measure to endure potential violence. Indeed, the successful monument must, according to Lawrence Alloway, be "invulnerable or inaccessible [as well as] . . . have the material strength to resist attack."[8] However, the causality of this relationship is thrown into question by Erika Doss's observation that the increase in memorials in the last several decades has provoked a simultaneous rise in anger and vitriol directed toward these sites. Her use of the term "memorial mania" to convey this "furor and frenzy, agitation and excessive passion" suggests a less passive role for the monument.[9] Robert Musil takes this position one step further by presenting what is typically considered as the monument's *assumption* of violence, its preparation for the *possibility* of attack, in terms of a "vandalism inciting quality" which does not simply presuppose but, as if in response to some longing for (re)activation, actively calls for its own assault.[10]

Representing the *possibility* of such violence as much or more than a present or past reality, the monument embodies a future orientation. Its partial presence marks a deferral, a waiting for a grand activation by which the site will make history rather than passively reflect or preserve it. As such, it is wrapped up with both the representations of media and the fantasy of self-annihilation. This may at first appear to be an odd base from which to approach a work of architecture. After all, the very purpose of the built environment is to shelter, enclose, and ultimately protect. Yet perhaps more than that of any other structure the semiotic currency of the World Trade Center was primarily symbolic. In this realm, the towers, like so American skyscrapers, continually elicited fantasies of destruction.[11] Even before the completion of the site, these fantasies circulated through the discourse surrounding the structure. Exemplary of this phenomenon is Ada Louise Huxtable's eerily prophetic statement in 1966 that "the gamble of triumph or tragedy at this scale – and ultimately it is a gamble – demands an extraordinary payoff. The trade-center towers could be the start of a new skyscraper age or the biggest tombstones in the world."[12] Admittedly, the World Trade Center was certainly not invisible in the same way as the everyday monument. In fact, it was an almost inescapable presence in the iconography of Hollywood and American national identity. Adorning posters, coffee cups, establishing shots, and baseball hats, the towers were undoubtedly one of the most recognizable icons of American architecture. Yet despite their ubiquity in popular media and their overwhelming size, the firsthand experience of the towers presented a self-effacing character which eerily prefigured their destruction. Tracing the specifics of this experience suggests that the towers rehearsed their own eradication on a daily basis, presenting a latent possibility which, like the monument, would draw upon the image of mass media to fully manifest.

DISAPPEARANCE, DEMATERIALIZATION, AND THE BUILDING THAT NEVER WAS

While the iconic panoramic view of the city offered by the South Tower's observatory deck gave the impression of a totalizing, all-encompassing image, it is precisely such a view that the towers themselves resisted. Throughout their design, the structures consistently sabotaged such an image by both engaging the eye in various modes of disappearance and/ or actively ignoring human scale and the limits of vision. The latter is perhaps most prominent in the comparatively miniaturized scale of the facade, which featured 18¾-inch aluminum-clad steel columns separated by 21¼-inch glass panes. As a result of these proportions, beyond a dozen or so stories all detail was lost from view, leaving a nondescript gray surface that seemed to extend indefinitely and without delineation.[13] This in combination with architect Minoru Yamasaki's recession of the telltale modernist grid into the facade, an alteration intended to celebrate the structure's triumphant verticality, meant that the eye had little to latch onto as it was emphatically directed upward.[14]

This breakdown in proximity was not limited to close viewing, as is usually the case for the skyscraper whose sheer scale renders it "too tall to be seen, except at a distance."[15] From remote viewing positions, the majority of the towers' structure was blocked from view by neighboring buildings, a situation which had the effect of severing their top halves from their foundations, leaving the structures to hover uncannily above the city.[16] The result was not simply incomplete representations from both up close and afar that could then be mentally woven together by the viewer to form some sense of the whole, but rather a more generalized negation of vision itself.[17] On account of this adversarial relationship to embodied vision, the towers required the camera to communicate their "true" size and shape and as such only existed in images.

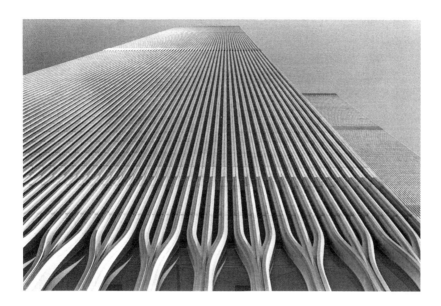

4.3. Richard Kalvar, facade of the World Trade Center, 1976.
By permission of Magnum Photos.

However, the structural properties of architecture cannot be conflated with the experience of space. As Henri Lefebvre famously pointed
out in *The Production of Space,* when the former is conceived of as preceding experience, material assemblages are mistaken for the social practice,
leading to a dominance of abstraction over lived experience. As practice
can often – and in fact, according to Lefebvre, de Certeau, and others, by
definition *does* – exceed these predeterminations, material formations
are only part of the story. When read in the context of this kinetic exchange of practice, the above relations are recast in terms of an active
play between appearance and disappearance. One hears this in, for example, Eric Darton's description of visiting the Twin Towers as bearing
witness to a peculiar "vanishing act." According to Darton,

> to make the Towers disappear . . . is not as difficult as it seems. Nearly anyone
> can do it. You don't have to be a terrorist, a demolition expert, or a photo
> retoucher. You just have to go to the plaza and stand in the right spot. Choose
> either Tower 1 or Tower 2 and walk right up to it – not to one of its broad sides,
> but instead, to one of its narrow, beveled corners. Stand about as close as if you
> were going to have a conversation. Then look straight up. Four million square

feet of office space stacked a quarter mile into New York's skyline have been transformed into a thin gray ribbon of highway, stretching into space. With a subtle shift of perspective, you have caused one of the most massive buildings of the modern era to perform its built-in vanishing act.[18]

While for Darton this desire is spawned by the specific interrelations of form as they relate (or do not relate) to the viewer, for Baudrillard it is grounded in the recurring trope of the multiple, which distorts and despecifies each member of the pair. As two indistinguishable copies of the same structure, the towers pointed not only to an end of "original reference," but more immediately to a visual experience in which the South and North structures slid into one another, becoming indecipherable. According to Baudrillard, this dynamic exchange reinforced a "secret desire to see [the towers] disappear."[19]

This relation is visualized in the photographs of the towers by Josef Koudelka and Dennis Stock, both of whom use wide-angle lenses in order to give the impression that these structures touch just beyond the frame. As if physically connected, the towers appear to be a single structure while at the same time maintaining that degree of autonomy that all skyscrapers seem to embody. This resonance between the two structures eliminates hierarchical relations, leading to a compromise of their individuality and, in a broader sense, their specificity and material presence. According to Baudrillard, the Twin Towers were "not the same breed as other buildings. The glass and steel façades of the Rockefeller buildings still mirrored each other in an endless spectacularity. But the Twin Towers no longer had any façades, any faces."[20] Their lack of singularity, combined with the "featureless" quality constantly bemoaned by critics, further contributed to what Darton describes as a "vanishing act."[21] Accordingly, as this pair of 110-story buildings had "little direct presence" and in fact "tended to disappear," Manfredo Tafuri and Francesco Dal Co have aptly referred to them as "skeletal phantasms" and "transitory happenings."[22]

The experience of invisibility discussed in regard to the visitor's interaction with the facade escalated into an active sabotaging of vision as she made her way through the interior of the structure and up to the observation deck. Once inside, the visitor took either two or three elevators (depending on whether she used the express or the locals)

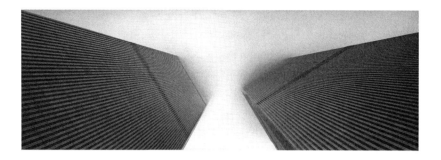

4.4. Josef Koudelka, the Twin Towers as seen from below, 1988.
By permission of Magnum Photos.

to the top. The confined space of the elevator concealed the passing cityscape and in so doing directed the gaze inward. As Mark Wigley explains, as tourists were "rocketed through" the interior space of the towers "in America's largest and fastest elevator," they were "suddenly aware of the inside of their own flesh but oblivious to the spaces and people that surrounded them."[23] Sara Teasdale's poem "From the Woolworth Tower" describes a similar sensation in another skyscraper, as the poet's narrator and her lover "shoot" through "swirling and angry" air via the elevator's "sharp unswerving flight," all the while keenly aware of a "chasm under [them]."[24] The World Trade Center elevator's momentary subordination of the eye to bodily sensations such as the dropping of one's stomach or the popping of the ears both dismantled vision and disconnected the viewer from the streets below. These processes would prove critical to the restructuring of vision that occured atop the observation deck where this newly cleansed eye would be recast in spectacular fashion.

Upon the visitor's arrival at the Top of the World, the pervasive dematerialization of the structure discussed earlier entered into a tension between what Darton refers to as "a panoramic ideal and a structural actuality."[25] Most immediately, this tension refers to the tendency, perhaps inevitability, of the structure to compromise the otherwise panoramic quality of the view with the presence of beams, supports, and other reminders of its material presence. Rather than attempting to minimize the latter and thereby enhance the all-seeing quality of the view (as is the case with, for example, recent additions to the Sears Tower in Chicago), the Twin Towers integrated these spaces of invisibility into the construction of vision, recasting them as productive ellipses. In the following section, I will consider the dynamics of these productive absences in terms of two interrelated trajectories. First, in reproducing the blindness of embodied vision, these interruptions in the field of vision served to elicit a process of identification between visitor and building through which a larger displacement of vision was made possible.[26] Second, by situating these "blind spots" within a larger chain of media that includes television and film, these absences were in turn activated by the viewer, becoming productive breaks within the visual register rather than momentary slips within an otherwise seamless representation.

In its ability to rope the negativity of the visual into larger narratives of power, the World Trade Center embodies what I have argued above is a central trajectory of the modern monument, namely, its existential reliance upon erasure and iconoclasm. After cataloging this relation in the towers, the larger ramifications of this logic will be drawn out in the final section, which focuses on an instance of monument destruction that occurred in Baghdad at the hands of the U.S. Army. This case study will bring together these relations of media and monument so as to disclose the larger political potentiality of these convergences.

MOVING BODIES/MOVING IMAGES: MEDIA MONUMENTS

While the experience of all skyscrapers is inevitably mediated by film, television, and photography, the towers took this relationship one step further. In light of the pervasive drive to invisibility cataloged in the previous section, the structures relied upon the image to an inordinate degree. In fact, it would not be an exaggeration to say they required the image in order to exist as a legible entity. In this relationship, the intervals of absence that characterized the experience of the site elicited the evocative power of media, which in turn provided the structures with a fullness and coherence that eluded direct apprehension. This formative presence of media had the effect of pushing the site into the imaginary, allowing the disaster to circulate through the structure as both fantastic premediation and affective reality, latent possibility and manifest actuality. The structures exemplified the logic of the modern monument not simply by enacting their own disappearance through a pervasive play between presence and absence, but by utilizing media to invert and confound these parameters.

As the elevator doors opened, the visitor experienced an abrupt transition from an enclosed space to the expansive mirrored hallway that led to the observation deck. The confinement of the former and its minimization of the visible suddenly gave way to an excess which would set the stage for the panoramic representation of the city that the visitor was about to encounter. However, the expansiveness of the impending view must be qualified, as even on those days when, weather permitting, the open-air observation deck was available, a substantial portion of the view took place through the slender bays of the facade three stories below. In this space, the recessed grid of the exterior introduced a new horizontality as the lines of the ceiling and floor bisected the strong verticality of the windows.[27] This aggressive framing of the scene served to not only effectively disconnect the observation deck from the previous experience of the facade, but also to initiate a concatenation of media through which "the towers," those triumphant symbols of American capital, would come into being.

Bisected by a forest of fifty-nine equidistant columns, the indoor observatory presented the city through a series of singular slices. The fragmentation produced by the narrow slits of the facade was exaggerated by the fact that the windows of the towers were recessed a full twelve inches from the columns that enclosed them. Forcing the frame into view, this arrangement intensified the sense of a singular image being cut from a more expansive totality.[28] In Sigfried Giedeon's experience of Paris from the observation platform of the Eiffel Tower one hears echoes of these spatial relations: "The landscape enters through the continuously changing snippets. . . . The structure creates views which it then arranges and from which we form a whole."[29] The Twin Towers' longtime critic Ada Louise Huxtable addresses a similar experience in her 1973 *Telegraph* piece entitled "World Trade Center: Daintiest Big Buildings in the World." In it, she similarly bemoans the fact that the "miniaturized modules" of the towers' facade tended to destroy the panoramic quality of the view. However, whereas as Giedeon claimed that the Eiffel Tower reorganized these singular images into a new whole and thereby reaffirmed a modernist drive to totality, according to Huxtable the Twin Towers offered no such gestalt ("No amount of head-dodging from column to column can put that fragmented view together").[30] For many if not most visitors, it would be the camera and the tools of post-production that would reassemble this fragmented view into the kind of omniscient image appropriate to the "Top of the World."

As a quick YouTube search confirms, the camcorder was a fixture atop the observation deck. The quantity and sheer repetitiveness of this footage speaks to the necessary union of this apparatus with the fragmented and partial mode of seeing that the visitor encountered atop the towers. What is striking about this archive of video is its reliance upon a recurring set of codes to negotiate the physicality of the structure in pursuit of the omniscient view. Indeed, one could separate this footage into two formal camps. In the first, one finds very little if any panning, this in the context of a view that would seem to invite an appreciation of its vast horizontal expansion. The reason is of course that the bays created by the facade prohibited such movement. As a result, the videographer is presented with a choice of either staying within the confines of the space delimited by these beams, as is the case with the first body of footage, or, as an alternative, recording the movement of the videographer as he or she moves between discrete positions. In the case of the latter, what Huxtable identified as "pure visual frustration" could be reconciled via desktop montages in which these singular scenes are edited together without the interruption of the columns. However, the more popular option seems to be producing an uninterrupted long take in which the operator simply walks between bays, leaving the steel beams to perform impromptu wipe transitions between views.

Despite the obstacles posed to the camera operator, these interruptions in the visual field would in the end contribute to the sense of omniscience enjoyed by the "all-seeing eye," as they would allow for a larger convergence of media through which the illusion of totality would be born. While the amateur operator was perhaps the first clue of this relationship, cataloging the specifics of this experience atop the observation deck suggests that the possessing camera was not necessarily a prerequisite for this ensuing dialogue between media. Exemplifying what Flusser calls "the atomized, punctuated structure characteristic of all things relating to the [photographic] apparatus," the towers were so permeated by its logic that the actual experience of the site was thoroughly cinematic.[31] This relationship, however, went beyond mere association or reference. Rather, by catalyzing a mode of identification which draws upon the codes and cues of film spectatorship, the visitor/viewer was prompted not only to experience the site in cinematic fashion but to read this experience in conjunction with a series of filmic and televisual presentations that preceded it.

As a result of a renewed historicism, Yamasaki's design for the World Trade Center represented a loosening of his ties to the International Style that had so strongly influenced his earlier work. Perhaps the clearest point of departure was in the decrease in glass relative to the exterior, a significant contrast with Mies van der Rohe's "all-glass" facades. In order to break up the monotony of the surface and create a more interesting visual play of light and shadow, Yamasaki thickened the columns of the exterior. (At least, that was the official explanation; elsewhere Yamasaki claimed that these narrow windows were meant to prevent workers from looking outside and thereby increase productivity.)[32] The result was that whereas the facades of International Style structures were typically composed of around 60 percent glass, Yamasaki's design for the Twin Towers only used 30 percent. His primary justification for this shift was not only to separate his work from that of his mentor, but also to relate this colossal structure to the human scale and to create a firm, solid, secure feel within an otherwise ephemeral, potentially dizzying experience.

As many critics have noted, the twenty-two-inch span of the windows roughly matched the shoulder width of a human figure and thereby invited the viewer to physically enter the frame.[33] According to Angus Kress Gillespie, the effect of this was strangely comforting, as now the viewer could "lean right up against the frame of the windows and look out and down with no fear of falling."[34] A 1972 *New York Times* piece announcing the opening of the observation deck conveys a similar sense of security by mitigating the vertiginous heights of the structure in its description of the resulting image of the city as a "non-aerial aerial view."[35] Despite the recurring antagonism of critics to the overall

4.5. Peter Marlow, the World Trade Center observation deck, 1992.
By permission of Magnum Photos.

structure, Mark Wigley points out that these design features served
to solidify an intimate bond between the towers and their users that
would make the destruction of the former all the more traumatic. Part
of this bond involved a shared visuality, as inhabitants of the towers
were prompted to press "their eyes to the glass between the narrowly
spaced columns, literally putting their heads inside the depth of the
façade to share its view."[36] Mirroring the way in which the viewer takes
on the gaze of the camera as his or her own, the structure reproduced
the narcissistic status of the film spectator. This occurred not simply
through the immersion of the inhabitant into the structure or the reas-
sembly of static images, but also through the relations of invisibility that
followed from this entry.

In discussing the Eiffel Tower, in many ways the progenitor of the
modern skyscraper, Roland Barthes notes an antagonistic relationship
between the objecthood of the structure and the view it produces: "Like
man himself, who is the only one not to know his glance, the Tower . . .

is the blind point of the total optical system of which it is the center."[37] Just as the cinema's claim to realism is contingent upon a repression of the apparatus and the construction of a voyeuristic position of seeing without being seen, Barthes suggests that the ability of a structure to produce the omniscient gaze is tied to a similar logic of negation. While this relationship may be dictated by practical concerns (the perfect view is after all one that is without impediments), the architectural site, like the cinematic apparatus, nonetheless replicates the nature of embodied perception in its attempts to obscure of the source of the gaze. As a result, such sites prompt a familiar mode of identification as these visual *dispotifs* come to appear as prosthetic extensions of "natural" vision rather than assemblages that actively reconstitute the eye.

On the one hand, this was certainly true of the experience of the World Trade Center. As if mimicking Maupassant, who frequently dined at the Eiffel Tower's restaurant because it was the only place in Paris where one could avoid seeing the tower, the tourist who stood atop the World Trade Center effectively erased what was once the centerpiece of one of the world's most famous skylines. This was made possible by the unique play between presence and absence discussed in the previous section as well as by the disembodiment that the spectacular view of the structure seemed to produce. Yet, at the same time, the articulation of vision that occurred at the observation deck reconfigured the apparent conflict between the absences produced by the materiality of the structure and the expectation of a panoramic mode of vision. Reading this relation through a vital third term of the camera suggests that these were no longer mutually exclusive prospects but rather complementary terms. This revision is made possible by an intermedia resonance which culminated atop the Twin Towers, connecting a chain of media frames which in circular fashion would build an implicit promise of visual omniscience that the towers would subsequently fulfill.

One of the earliest examples of these extra-architectural framings came with a 1975 Port Authority commercial for the Top of the World observation deck, which featured a wide-angle view of the tops of the towers, shot from an encircling helicopter. Over this image ran the promotional jingle "It's hard to be down, when you're up," a thinly veiled reference to the city's financial woes of the time.[38] Visually, the piece confounds expectation in that the view that the screen presents hardly foreshadows that which the viewer would expect to encounter upon visiting the site. The audience is positioned well above the observatory deck, so much so that all detail is washed out by the grainy 16mm image. As a result, the Top of the World is left uninhabited by the camera/viewer in both a literal and a figurative sense, appearing more as a vacated roof than the tourist destination that the jingle suggests.

A subsequent commercial from the 1980s appears to solve this problem by coupling aerial shots of the city with the gaze of two onscreen tourists whose awe and excitement clearly mark them as surrogates for the potential visitor watching at home. The spot begins with the couple entering the elevator of the South Tower on the ground floor. As the doors open at the outdoor observation deck, a sense of wonder spreads across the actors' faces. The piece then cuts from the male's pointing finger to a series of shots of the attractions of the city. By connecting the ensuing images with the sight lines of these internal spectators, such sequences would typically serve to collapse the gaze of the audience with those of both the camera and the onscreen performers. Initially, this appears to be the case. However, tucked within this collection of tourist attractions are the Twin Towers themselves, an image which we could not possibly see from the position that the film has established for us. Similarly, the shot of the Statue of Liberty is taken from a rapidly approaching helicopter despite the fact that the source of the gaze, the couple standing on the observation deck, stands stock-still. The impossibility of this spectatorial position disconnects this surrogate gaze from that of the camera, presenting an incomplete, but nonetheless enticing, mode of identification.

Despite their differing contexts and motives, both commercials share an unwillingness to divulge the view itself. In the first instance, this occurs quite literally as the elevated camera fails to connect with the actual experience of the deck, which in turn appears as a distant, almost uninhabitable space. It appears as if it is the soundtrack that is entrusted with selling the view, a reversal of the conventional hierarchy of sound and image that leaves the camera circling the top of the tower aimlessly. However, even the voice-over, though more forthcoming in its attempt to capture the tourist's experience, also ends up reinforcing a logic of deferral. At the conclusion of the ad, the voice-over interjects, "If you think the view from the inside is spectacular, wait until you get outside to the roof – it's breathtaking." With this request to "wait" for the real image, the view of the city that the camera can't possibly provide, the voice suggests that, rather than a failure of representation, the absence of the view functions as a strategic withholding.[39] In the second instance, this withholding occurs via the disconnect of sight lines and traditional modes of cinematic identification. However, it is precisely this disconnect that allows the aerial views of the city's notable landmarks to convey a representation of the affective experience of the deck. Thus, the image withholds the view while at the same time hinting at the pleasures of disembodiment that such a view would bring about. In both cases, the strategic deployment of absence forms something of a "lure," as a recurring deferral of the view itself incites the viewer to complete the chain of images by visiting the actual site.[40]

For the visitor to the towers, the repetition of the cinematic frame in the Gothic bays reinforced the connection of the structure to this preceding progression of images, allowing the absences introduced by the facade to be recuperated as cinematic intervals and, more broadly, the discontinuity of the observation deck to be rewritten in terms of a larger coherence. In this regard, the withholding of the image performed by the string of television commercials for the site reinforced the repression of the visible enacted by the elevators as well as the curious self-effacement of the facade. This served to initiate a transformation through which the towers systematically dematerialized so as to rematerialize around this newly formed spectator at the Top of the World observation deck. In the process, spatial incoherence, discontinuity, and invisibility became the condition of possibility rather than a detriment to a seamless and omniscient image of the city as well as the towers themselves. The confirmation of this process of consolidation was provided by a short film which played in a theater atop the towers.[41] Articulating an all-seeing, omniscient aerial eye, the film took visitors on a virtual helicopter ride through the city before finally yielding the iconic image of the World Trade Center that had up to this point eluded experience. This filmic experience reaffirmed John Tauranac's description of the site in 1979: "For one of the city's most spectacular views, go to the observation deck.

As you see planes fly below you, you will have the feeling that you too are in a plane, one that has magically stalled over the city, providing an undreamed-of panorama."[42] By reproducing an experience of the moving image within an architectural setting, the towers consolidated the trail of media which preceded the experience of the observation deck, making good on its promise of totality and omniscience and in the process producing the symbolic image of American dominance with which we are all familiar.

Built upon the management of absence, erasure, and invisibility, the image of power that the towers articulated was the product of a contradictory logic. Their dominance of the skyline and correlative celebration of American capitalism was reliant upon media supplements which would both push their invisibility toward a symbolic totality and rehearse their destruction. As such, the structures mimicked not only the futural direction of the monument, but also its intimate relation with iconoclasm. As Bruno Latour points out, "The damage done to icons is . . . always a charitable injunction to redirect their attention toward other, newer, fresher, more sacred images: not to do without image."[43] Iconoclasm, in other words, operates not through negation, but rather through the multiplication and revivification of those images that are born out of destruction. It is best understood as a mode of image-making that hinges upon precisely the kind of overseeing of absence and erasure that produced the symbolic power of the Twin Towers.

Yet the destruction of monuments often exceeds the linear causality that Latour ascribes to these acts of erasure. In many cases, these gestures produce an unruly potentiality which is only partially contained by the image. In turning to a rather notorious instance of monument destruction after 9/11, the slippages and missteps that comprise the visual record of this event become vital components in revealing the processes by which the image enfolds acts of erasure and negation into larger narratives of power. Reading the destruction of the World Trade Center in conjunction with these dynamics of iconoclasm reinforces the circular nature of this symbolic relationship whereby acts of defilement can be turned upon themselves, enacting a consolidation or reenclosure of the power relations that were originally targeted.

4.6. The toppling of a statue of Saddam Hussein in Firdos Square, April 2003.

HOW TO FALL A STATUE AND LOOK GOOD DOING IT

On April 9, 2003, U.S. forces attempted to rival the spectacle of 9/11 by orchestrating what was to be an equally cathartic shock to the symbolic order: the toppling of the statue of Saddam Hussein in Firdos Square in real time for an American audience.[44] The effectiveness of this performance was contingent upon not only the sheer display of destruction but, more importantly, the ability of the image to oversee the productive aspects of the (re)activation that followed. Of particular importance to this enterprise was the image's capacity to situate the event in relation to two crucial discursive categories of image destruction: iconoclasm and vandalism. Approaching the event in these terms reveals a convergence between the monument's aspirations toward destruction and the image's desire for spectacle, the interrelationship of which would largely determine the political significance and overall message of the event.

As Dario Gamboni points out, the term "iconoclasm" has historically been used to designate acts of destruction or defilement which are dictated by a coherent set of beliefs. These attacks are the product of forethought and are meticulously executed. Against this neutrality stands "vandalism," a word whose "barbarian" association was used during the French Revolution to "exclude those who continued to attack such objects from the civilized community and to banish their actions from the domain of enlightened, rational behavior."[45] Born out of impulse, the only basis for such actions is nihilism; the only desired result, destruction. While the values attached to these designations remain fairly consistent, the boundary between them is fluid and determined in large part by discourse. Thus, more important than the distinction itself is the capacity of the media presentation to define and assign these categories.[46]

As if realizing the aforementioned fantasies that Saddam's monuments seemed to elicit from their viewers, the crowd that gathered in Firdos Square that day struck the statue's base with sledgehammers, threw stones at its face, beat it with the bottoms of their shoes as it hovered above them, and then rushed the fallen statue as it broke free from its pedestal. Not long after, its severed head was being ridden like a sled by enthusiastic Iraqis. In these images, one seemed to witness what Boris Groys calls "these human masses [which] represent the blind, material forces that covertly govern consciously perceived human history."[47] Despite the infectious spontaneity of these images, however, we now know that the falling of the statue was anything but organic. In fact, the entire event was orchestrated by a "psychological operations team" of the U.S. Army. The sense of immediacy that these images conveyed was strategic, a vehicle for transferring responsibility from the U.S. Army to the Iraqi people. With the exception of one poorly played scene (the covering of the statue's face with an American flag by a U.S. soldier), this presentation was intended to remove the sense of outside intervention, thereby naturalizing the destruction of the statue. While the collective and spontaneous quality of this destruction would seem to associate the event more closely with vandalism than with the more rehearsed and institutionally framed acts of iconoclasm, such a designation contradicts the positive spin these events were given. In this incongruity lies the true force of these images, as the presentation celebrated the event by drawing upon the populist overtones of vandalism while simultaneously maintaining the negative connotation of the term, albeit in indirect and buried form.

Vandalism is short-sighted. It does not think beyond the act itself. Its pleasure is in exercising the power to destroy or in the shock such destruction will deliver to the social body. This exercise of power proceeds without what Anne McClanan describes as iconoclasm's deference to "some theory, however thin and indefinite."[48] Vandalism, in other words, fails to extend beyond the sheer physical act of destruction in any coherent or meaningful way. Thus, staging the event in these terms presented both the euphoria of a populist uprising and the vulnerability of the ensuing power gap. As intoxicating as the collective destruction of repressive symbols may be in the here and now, the lingering ambivalence of the images of Firdos Square reinforced the sense of an utter lack of a future plan.[49] The chaos of the scene, that element which seemed to qualify the jubilance of a new era, was thus intended to function as both the sign of a populist groundswell and a call for intervention, thereby allowing the lawlessness of vandalism to be reframed as a plea for occupation. In practice, however, the incident would convey a much more ambiguous message.

For viewers at home, the images this event produced seemed somehow out of sync with the real-time coverage it attracted.[50] We watched prolonged scenes of the crowd gathering, interspersed with tired dissolves to the monument as news anchors tried to fill the dead air with speculation and hypothetical scenarios. Finally, a chain was placed over the statue's neck and attached to an offscreen Humvee, whereupon the monument slowly began to bend. Hovering over the anxious crowd for almost a full minute as it endured a hailstorm of stones from eager Iraqis, the statue then finally broke at the knees and fell to the ground. Acknowledging the anticlimactic nature of this event, Fox newscasters joked about Saddam "clinging to power" as the demolition vehicle tugged unsuccessfully at the half-fallen dictator. Not surprisingly, the uneventful buildup and the ambiguous moment of Saddam's likeness poised above the crowd were often left out of subsequent airings. In their place was a continuous and cathartic fall from power. In these revisions, the continuity of the falling body becomes synonymous with the establishment of a legible narrative, reinforcing a larger displacement of the struggle of the past onto a struggle with monuments.

Implicit in the image's attempt to establish a smooth and seamless transition is the recognition of a certain danger in this "pregnant moment" where history is suspended, literally just out of reach. Jürgen Habermas describes this image of the hovering statue in Firdos Square as an "optical illusion" which when "looked at long enough, [threatens to] 'flip' into a new form." In this precarious image, one sees the active management of two conflicting perceptions of the event as "the 'shock and awe' inflicted on a helpless and mercilessly bombed population . . . morphed into the image of joyful citizens freed from terror and oppression in the Shiite district of Baghdad [and vice versa]."[51] The ramifications of this instability are visualized in Komar and Melamid's contribution to a 1992 exhibition entitled "Monumental Propaganda." The work presents what was a familiar sight in Russia at the time, a monumental statue balancing precariously above its pedestal by the cables of a crane. However, the legibility of this scene is compromised by an ambiguity as to whether the work presents the installation or demolition of the statue. By suspending this moment the work testifies to an inability or outright refusal to mark the coherent shift from one era to another, leaving history itself unrealized. As the artists explain, the statue is "hanging in the air, ambiguously arresting the moment of dismantling and extending it into eternal retribution."[52] It is this productive illegibility that the lack of speed and spectularity of Firdos Square seemed to invite and which the image struggled to contain.

Clearly, the sheer unexpectedness of 9/11 prohibited the kind of plotting that characterized the presentation of the falling of the Saddam statue. However, both incidents work upon a shared logic by which the dialectic between absence and presence that acts of iconoclasm introduce is utilized to transform acts of erasure into legible images. The lesson of Firdos Square for critical engagement with 9/11 is that the *givenness* of images of spectacular destruction must be scrutinized in a diachronic fashion. This involves questioning not simply the legitimacy of the event that they depict, as in the case of conspiracy theory, but rather the way in which the image retroactively produces the reality that it purports to passively reflect. Such scenarios call for an additional layer of what Latour calls "B type" iconoclasm. This mode of defilement is rooted in a rejection of "freeze-framing," the notion that a singular image extracted from the flow might stop all movement within the event.[53] In this regard, unpacking the naturalness of these displays of destruction necessitates extending the interval of 9/11 beyond the panicked moment of that day and instead positing the event as an ongoing struggle in which the negation of the towers is continually being rewritten and co-opted by new narratives of power. From this perspective, this act of iconoclasm is both a historical event and a horizon, a constellation which collapses the question of what happened that day with the question of what 9/11 will become.[54]

MEMORY, MONUMENT, AND OBLIVION

While reading the World Trade Center as a monument has served as a strategic means to open new modes of inquiry into the destruction of the towers and the images that it produced, this union also reflects back upon the monument itself, suggesting its most immediate cultural function, its relation to memory, might similarly be conditioned by an inverse relation to materiality and presence. To summarize the formative relation to media that this chapter has attempted to ascribe to monuments, one might follow W. J. T. Mitchell's methodology and ask what it is that the contemporary monument wants.[55] The answer appears to be that it wants not only its own destruction, but the kind of spectacular death that only the media can grant. It is, after all, in this confluence that the connection between the monument and history comes into being most fully and in which the monument, that form which is otherwise predisposed to disappearance, finally comes into view. In this relationship, what begins as a kind of blind drive on the part of the monument to self-destruction, a martyrdom to some as-yet-unnamed cause, is transformed by the image into a message.

While the invisibility of the monument is certainly reinforced by this dependence upon the image, this does not mean that such sites exist *only* as latent acts of violence – iconoclasms in waiting – or that this state is an inherently passive one. Even without the cameras of CNN or other mainstream media outlets, the roadside monument, which might appear all but destroyed by what Nathaniel Hawthorne once called the "encrustation of the senses,"[56] nonetheless performs a kind of work through its disappearance. As the necessary correlative to the dominant historical narrative, the monument's invisibility and inevitable entanglement with absence contains a potentiality that mimics the formative relationship that forgetting maintains with memory.[57] From this perspective, the disappearance of the monument, whether performed by everyday perception or physical attack, does not necessarily diminish its role but simply pushes its powers to the side of oblivion, that necessary interlocutor with memory. After all, in order for an event to be perceived as a memory it must be subject to a process by which its fullness or presence is in some way depreciated. This position is reiterated in the classical figure of memory, those impressions or outlines of a missing event, pressed in wax or written in the sand, veiled and yet present in their absence.[58] As an essentially subtractive process, memory involves a selection or loss through which the aura of *pastness* is conjured. As Friedrich A. Kittler observes, "Memory consists in the awareness . . . of the diminished intensity of an impression."[59] Without this founding loss, the past would be indistinguishable from the present that it was, and time itself would cease. It is by way of this interdependence upon forgetting that the performance of memory, in its normative instantiation, is able to establish and maintain a certain distance between the past and present through which it becomes possible to experience the time of history.

As many scholars have noted, the first formalized memory techniques of the Western world sprung in large measure from the story of Simonides, who was paid to deliver a poem in honor of Scopas, a nobleman hosting the banquet.[60] Angered by the poem's praise of Castor and Pollux, Scopas decided to pay the orator only half his due. Not long after, Simonides was informed that two visitors were waiting to see him outside, whereupon he left the hall and mysteriously found no one. At that very moment, the building behind him collapsed, killing everyone inside. The bodies of the deceased were pulverized by the weight of the roof and as such were unrecognizable even to their family members. Luckily, Simonides remembered where the guests were sitting and thus was able to identify their remains. The story is often summoned as a means to illustrate the spatialization of memory or to reinforce the Nietzschean link between memory and trauma. However, it also reminds us that that memory is born out of an absence from perception. The monument's drive to invisibility serves to shape the past from a similar position of absence. Its propensity toward death is the product of this disappearance within sight and the no less active dissolution by discourse and/or violence, both of which inform the monument's claim to the past even as they remove it from view. The site of the World Trade Center, marked initially by a crater of destruction and then by the official production of absence, traffics in these dynamics, presenting absence as a the presymbolic means of memory, while at the same time codifying its cultural function and delimiting its capacity to summon the virtuality of the past.

The extermination of the Jews of Europe is as accessible to both representation and interpretation as any other historical event.

SAUL FRIEDLÄNDER

I do not think that the Holocaust, Final Solution, Shoah, Churban, or German genocide of the Jews is any more unrepresentable than any other event in human history.

HAYDEN WHITE

FIVE

The Failure of the Failure of Images

THE CRISIS OF THE UNREPRESENTABLE FROM
THE GRAPHIC NOVEL TO THE 9/11 MEMORIAL

For the first hundred years of their existence, comics functioned as an art form whose abbreviated shelf life rivaled the ephemerality of modern media such as television or radio.[1] Born out of the nineteenth-century "circulation wars," their serial format was aimed at transforming the casual reader into the regular customer and as such betrayed not only an incompleteness at the level of narrative, but a material disintegration which fueled the urgency of their consumption. However, as the form has gained credence among collectors, scholars, and artists in the last several decades, the planned obsolescence of yellowing newsprint has given way to a new sense of permanency. The emerging "graphic novel" not only jettisoned the serial format (a transformation which can be traced back to the arrival of the comic book in the early 1930s) but also enjoyed high-quality printing (and correlative high prices) alongside a more sophisticated mode of address.[2] Despite the shift from "disposable pulp to acid-free archival paper" that has accompanied the elevation of the art form in recent years, an enduring connection to the medium's prehistory appears to partially determine the medium's cultural position.[3] At least, this seems to be the implication of the unique status that the graphic novel assumed in the wake of 9/11.

Posed somewhere between the immediacy of news and the afterwardness of art, the graphic novel in the wake of 9/11 appeared to offer an intermediary or safe space in which those as-yet-unresolved questions of representation could safely be worked out. Indeed, while Hollywood and the major television networks observed an extended taboo against representing the event, this heterochronic medium seemed all but preoccupied with the disaster.[4] In the months following 9/11, a veritable wave of graphic novels on the disaster hit the shelves. These included *9-11: Emergency Relief; Heroes: The World's Greatest Super Hero Creators Honor the World's Greatest Heroes, 9-11-2001;* and Dark Horse and DC Comics' release of a two-volume set about 9/11 which featured some of the most prominent artists working in the field.[5] Born out of what Thierry Groensteen describes as an "art without memory," a self-effacing medium which "happily cultivates amnesia," the mnemonic function of these works could not contrast more starkly with the permanency and timelessness of the more officially sanctioned cultural form of the memorial.[6] Yet, as the following analysis will suggest, it is this opposition which allows these two disparate media to form virtual bookends to the period of iconoclasm that followed 9/11. As such, the progression instantiated by this unusual pairing charts a broader trajectory within the visual culture of the disaster, which effectively bridges the gap between an unthinkable image and a permanent installation.

Of the graphic novels created in response to the event, none is as exemplary of the impasses of representation that this unique position afforded the medium as Art Spiegelman's *In the Shadow of No Towers* (2004). Marianne Hirsch has described Spiegelman's work in terms of a larger trajectory of the visual culture of 9/11 which encapsulates both the "impossibility of seeing and the impossibility of not looking."[7] This paradox manifests in the text in terms of a confusion between firsthand experience and the mediated memories of the mass media, an unstable relationship between textual and visual elements as well as a pervasive play between presence and absence which informs the graphic aspect of the work. The challenges that these elements pose to the artist/narrator are presented in such a way that merges the creative process with the disaster itself. As such, the dystopia presented in *In the Shadow of No Towers* concerns not only the event and its aftermath, but also the author's struggle to translate his experience of the disaster into graphic narrative form. The conflict that Spiegelman chronicles is twofold: the encroaching images of the media which serve to confuse the boundaries of personal and collective experience, and the unavailability of the "unrepresentable" as a viable visual strategy in the twenty-first century.

Interestingly, it is precisely this entanglement that would materialize in the 9/11 memorial almost a decade later.

Drawing upon what Graham Bader identifies as an increasingly "standard tactic" to represent the "inconceivable atrocit[ies]" of the past century, Michael Arad's memorial *Reflecting Absence* not only establishes absence as its central design feature, but presents this idiom in terms of an undetermined and neutral space whose lack of material presence eschews symbolic coding.[8] Couching these assumptions within the discourse of therapy, transparency, and participation, *Reflecting Absence* co-opts the utopian promise of an all-inclusive populism and in the process safely conceals its larger intervention. As such, the work escalates the conflict of Spiegelman's drama as individual testimony proves not simply diminished or untenable but actively caught up in and absorbed by systems of representation and their corresponding power relations. Ultimately, the conflict that structures the graphic novel in the wake of the disaster is assimilated into the memorial's mode of subjectivity as the latter elicits personal experience as a means to reaffirm a narrative of aggression and violence. From this perspective, *In the Shadow of No Towers* serves as a cautionary tale that warns of precisely the kind of operation that would materialize in the memorial.

EXPERIENCE BECOMES IMAGE:
THE ARTIST AS SPECTATOR

That trauma studies would prove to be a primary lens through which scholars have read Spiegelman's work is hardly unexpected. Not only does each new disaster seem to breathe life into this critical idiom, but so does the work's specific character (its abrupt shifts in location, point of view, and style; atavistic reexperience of the past; and overall ontological rootlessness) bear all the classic symptoms of the Freudian constellation. This knee-jerk reaction, though productive in its own right and even indirectly referenced by the work itself, has nonetheless served to deemphasize the reflexive character of the text and thereby obscure a crucial discourse. Taking into consideration what can only be called the work's obsession with its own creation, an obsession that at times takes on the dimensions of the disaster itself, suggests that these same attributes might just as easily be read as the product of a historically specific conflict of representation. From this perspective, the threat to the stability of the symbolic order that structures the work is issued not only by the unassimilability of the disaster itself, but perhaps more pressing from the standpoint of the creative process, the absorption, even co-opting of the experience of the event by the images of the media. As this latter process shares many of the same surface features as trauma, its relative scarcity in scholarship is understandable. As *In the Shadow of No Towers* suggests, both dynamics are engaged in absorbing the utter incomprehensibility of firsthand experience and in the process undermine the first-person perspective of the witness.

On the first page of the work, Spiegelman establishes the narrator's perspective of the events of 9/11 as the structuring agent of the work: "I live on the outskirts of Ground Zero and first saw it all live – unmediated."[9] However, with the television keeping the narrator awake at night with conspiracy theories and camera crews swarming his Manhattan neighborhood, it is not long before the reader senses a slippage in the authenticity of this perspective. On the following page, the author reiterates his intent to "sort out the fragments of what I'd experienced from the media that threatened to engulf what I actually saw."[10] However, this text bubble is positioned underneath a static laced image whose 4:3 aspect ratio conjures an anachronistic televisual frame at the same time that the untenable viewing position of the image betrays the presence of a zoom lens. As Patrick M. Bray describes, the grid-like quality of the image's static also bears the influence of a more contemporary regime of images. He explains,

> The computerized illustration, which repeats dozens of times throughout the book, calls attention to itself as visually different from the surrounding hand-drawn comics. At the same time, within the image itself, its own status as the representation of a lived memory is undermined by the exaggerated size of its pixels, which guarantee the readability of the image's technological origin. The fleeting memory of the moment just before the collapse of the north tower, a memory threatened by the devastating force of media images, can only be represented by an image that … offers a vision of disintegration (of the tower and of memory).[11]

Reaffirming the contamination of the narrator's "unmediated" access, two frames later we see the author sitting mesmerized in front of a television as an airplane smashes into the side of the screen. The cathartic blending of lived experience and image (two realms that the author has promised to keep separate) that this scene visualizes is echoed in the work's recurring dynamic of materialization whereby nonvisible and/ or unrepresentable phenomena are mobilized by the media's images of the event. As the seeming immateriality and instability of memory give way to a static and legible narrative in these instances, the work, as Anne Whitehead puts it, "make[s] visible the inscription of 9/11 into state-organized acts of commemoration and the rhetoric of war."[12]

Describing the scene in which Spiegelman confesses to not actually seeing but hearing the jet collide with the World Trade Center, Marianne Hirsch notes "the word-image 'roarrrrrrrr!!' almost covers the statement about not seeing, occluding it to the point of near illegibility. *Not seeing* becomes *visible* and even *audible,* as graphic as the absent towers." Following the logic of trauma, Hirsch regards this transformation as a reflection of the way in which "words, images, and word-images work together to enact the impossibility of seeing and the impossibility of not looking."[13] However, at the same time, so much of the work seems to suggest the exact opposite trajectory, namely, the uncanny ability of experience to succumb to the visible and manifest in graphic form. Rather than a negation of the image, this manifestation of the nonvisible within the frame speaks to its hypervisualization, a process by which even nonvisible sensation achieves visual form. The dystopic position of the narrator/artist comes about as a result of the intersection of the unrepresentability of the disaster and the quest to somehow preserve this quality in the graphic novel itself with the hypervisualization of the same event which occurs at the hands of the media.

The intrusion of this process of becoming-image into Spiegelman's project is driven home by the objectification of what is usually an invisible aspect of the image: the frame. At the top of page 2, as the author describes the sensation of trauma ("Time stands still . . . I see that awesome tower, glowing as it collapses"), the frames gradually turn as the eye moves from left to right, eventually forming two burning towers at the end of the sequence. As the incomprehensibility of this reactivated moment transmogrifies into an iconic image, the impossibility of the traumatic experience literally takes shape. Katalin Orbán understands this emphasis on materiality in terms of Alois Riegl's notion of the "memory of tactile surface."[14] By foregrounding the object quality of a memory, such phenomena essentially introduce a material trigger which instantiates the "near" of subjective experience so as to banish the more abstract "distant view" that is to some degree inherent to the illusionistic plane of images. However, in the context of *In the Shadow of No Towers* this process does not return sensory experience, but rather speaks to its reification by the image.

Historically, the frame, as a materialization of Alberti's famous theorization of the image as a "window onto a world," turns upon invisibility. Yet, in the context of the graphic novel, the seriality of images is often interrupted by actions and words which bleed outside the frame in order to signify intensity and/or create nonlinear chronologies. In short, the frame is both an invisible cue whose presence precludes the outside and thereby bolsters the fictitious world inside, and a boundary to be transgressed, often to mark the subjectivity of experience. The closing of the frame illustrated by the above sequence demonstrates a larger unavailability of the event to inscription. It is telling in this respect that often the end result of this transformation in the context of Spiegelman's work is canonical images of the event whose impersonal and "objective" quality gives them the air of history at the same time that they preclude the narrator's own experience of the event.

This opposition between material presence as both the domain of subjective experience and the residue of the ossifying tendency of the historical record manifests most immediately in the design of the book itself. Certainly, the tangible presence of the book does prompt an individual experience and, as Orbán points out, the images themselves reinforce this quality through their play with depth and texture.[15] Frames are stacked on top of one another as the text layers on top of the entire layout. Indeed, on page 4 the entire layout almost mimics a table upon which photographs and handwritten notes have been spread. While these attributes might serve to reinterject the here and now of reading so as to foreground the subjectivity of such an experience, the sheer girth of the work seems to almost parody such interventions. Despite the book's having only seventeen full-page plates, the exceptionally thick pages create the impression of a much larger work. Turning the page for the first time, the reader feels as if she is the butt of a joke, as the book she holds more closely resembles a clandestine "hollow book," whose pages have been cut out to hide valuables or incriminating evidence, than a graphic novel.

Throughout this exchange, the opposition between incomprehensible subjective experience and legible narrative is tilted toward the latter. As this "intrusion" appears to displace experiential knowledge of the event, the self-assuredness of the author's initial declaration gives way to an admission of non-seeing. Eventually, he describes being "haunted now by images he didn't witness . . . images of people tumbling to the streets below . . . especially one man (according to a neighbor) who executed a graceful Olympic dive as his last living act."[16] As Katalin Orbán points out, it is telling that Spiegelman does not "fabricate the visual record" of this event and instead relies upon a verbal description which is based only on hearsay.[17] Rather than the unassimilability of trauma, this non-seeing is the remainder of the media's translation of memory into narrative, a presentation of the event which has destabilized the parameters of image, memory, and rememberer. Accordingly, the original distinction that the narrator makes between "his" events and those presented on television no longer holds, as memory now appears always already prosthetic. The dystopia that this realization presents for the artist who continually seeks to rescue lived experience from the image is further magnified by his recourse to the unrepresentable, a constellation which once served to summon an outside to representation but which now proves untenable for the artist/narrator.

THE OUTSIDE AND THE IMAGE: THE UNREPRESENTABLE AS HISTORICAL TROPE

The cover of *In the Shadow of No Towers* presents one of the earliest artistic interpretations of 9/11. Originally published on the cover of the *New Yorker* magazine on September 24, 2001, the image features what at first glance seems to be a monochromatic black surface. Only by tilting the work ever so slightly or by placing it in bright light do the shadows of the two towers reveal themselves. Most immediately, this play between presence and absence visualizes the lingering afterimage of the towers that the Manhattan skyline and indeed the collective imaginary itself now seemed to contain. At the same time, the image signaled what would soon become a resurgence of the unrepresentable. From Hollywood's unofficial ban on disaster films to the art world's self-imposed silence, the "most photographed disaster in history" most often appeared in the aftermath of the event as a silent but reverent non-image. As Patrick Bray points out, Spiegelman's cover "crystallizes the [ensuing] tension between the overwhelming presence of media images [from that day] and the absence revealed by a shadow image."[18]

Gauging the depth of this internal opposition within both the visual culture in the wake of 9/11 and Spiegelman's own work requires that the unrepresentable be understood as a historically specific constellation rather than a transcendental outside to representation. While in the aftermath of the Holocaust illustrating the inadequacy of representation may have appeared to preserve the unfathomability of the event, such a strategy has undergone a radical transformation in recent years. Suffice it to say that Theodor Adorno's original prohibition on poetry and the expectation of a necessary failure of the image it engendered has largely been undermined by popular culture. From *Sophie's Choice* (1982) to *Schindler's List* (1993), Hollywood has not only sidestepped the taboo but has in fact wed the event to the image in intimate fashion, especially for those born after the war. Recognizing that the unassimilable quality of the event does not necessarily preclude representation in the contemporary sphere, scholars such as Hayden White, Saul Friedländer, and Andreas Huyssen have recently declared the Holocaust to no longer be unrepresentable.[19]

As Derrida's critique of the void in Daniel Libeskind's Jewish Museum suggests, recourse to absence as an aesthetic strategy can no longer be considered in terms of a contemplation of the ineffable, but rather seems to introduce a kind of nostalgic emptiness that lacks the productivity ascribed to its postwar instantiation.[20] Derrida illustrates this shift by comparing architectural articulation of absence in Libeskind's museum with the refusal of closure that one finds in the Platonic *chora*. Whereas the latter functions as "a place that precedes history and the inscription of Forms," Libeskind's evocation of a historically determined visual trope presents a space which is already "circumscribed" by the history it claims to destabilize.[21]

The contradictory status of this motif in the contemporary sphere is illustrated on page 3 of *In the Shadow of No Towers* as the narrator describes his father's attempts to convey the horrors of Auschwitz. In recounting this event (itself a representation), the narrator suddenly appears as a character from Spiegelman's *Maus*, all the while his cigarette and first-person narration retain the figure's identity as Spiegelman. The transformation is emblematic of a larger chain of associations which have come to destabilize the image: the smoke from the concentration camp merges with the toxic air of lower Manhattan, which in turn slips into the cigarette smoke that fills the frame. Overseeing this chain of causal associations is the originary trauma, which Spiegelman tells us his father could only describe as "indescribable" and which subsequently appears as shadows of the present event. Such sequences illustrate what Kristiaan Versluys describes as the text's "transmission of trauma . . . far beyond the immediate circumstances."[22] At the same time, they evoke the paradox of this trope as it resurfaces in contemporary visual culture. They embody the fragmentary perceptions of an event that exceeds representation while simultaneously establishing the event as wholly representable, one which can be conjured by a well-established back history of images which in this case the author himself has helped to establish. However, it is not simply the author's previous work which creates this latter dynamic, but also Spiegelman's pervasive references to Cold War sci-fi films of the 1950s and '60s, gas mask public service announcements, and billboards for Hollywood disaster films, all of which present the unrepresentable as anything but.

This unending flow of historical images undercuts the linearity of the narrative and in this way reproduces the dislocation that occurs with trauma's reactivation of past events.[23] The subsequent collapse of time whereby the original event returns "without having lost any of its freshness" is in fact referenced throughout the text itself ("Time stands still at the moment of trauma . . . trauma piles on trauma").[24] To this extent, the work continues a trajectory begun in *Maus*, which in recounting the father's tale of the Holocaust presents the past's intrusion on the present in terms of what Andreas Huyssen describes as a "cross-cutting of past and present [which] points . . . to how this past holds the present captive, independently of whether this knotting of past into present is being talked about or repressed."[25] However, aside from the creative impasse it creates, this reactivation seems safely contained within the image in the more recent work. Indeed, the fact that trauma itself appears as one of the cultural references that the author resorts to in order to convey the anxiety of the event and its aftermath suggests a kind of assimilation into symbolic discourse. From this perspective, the suddenness and lack of explanation that accompany the appearance of these images from the past testify as much to the iconic quality of the author's earlier work as to the Freudian reactivation of the past.

The artist's goal of conveying the incomprehensibility of the event is in some sense sabotaged by the realization of the historical determined-ness of this category. Rather than a pure outside, which safely suspends the symbolic, such a trope has been thoroughly coded and as such inter-nalized by the image. The work thus forms the very shadow that the title references. The sense of remove built into the word "shadow" combined with the "no" forms a double negative, which reiterates the visual pres-ence of this missing thing, a presence that is canonized and historically specific. The unrepresentable as a transcendental category therefore proves unavailable in the midst of this hypervisualization, a fate which ensures the absorption of the narrator's very work into the narrative that it so desperately seeks to evade. Spiegelman's attempts to preserve the incomprehensibility of the event end only in anxiety and frustra-tion ("despair slows me down") which ultimately render the artist pas-sive. We eventually find him asleep at his drawing table, while Bush and Osama bin Laden battle it out in the foreground. Confirming the utter passiveness of the artist in the face of this political struggle, a missing poster for Spiegelman's brain hangs in the background.

The issues that occupy Spiegelman's confessionary tale would re-surface almost a decade later in Michael Arad's 9/11 memorial. While articulating less a personal testimony than a space of collective mourn-ing, the memorial nonetheless sought to lay claim to an outside of the of-ficial record in much the same way as the narrator of In the Shadow of No Towers did. In foregrounding the negative presentation of the towers' empty footprints, Arad's Reflecting Absence would appear to sidestep the impasse of Spiegelman's project by working outside rather than within representation. Yet a closer look at the design, selection process, and conceptual backdrop of the work suggests that this enterprise is not immune to the historical burdens and official narratives that threaten to overwhelm the preceding graphic novel. Plagued by an overdetermined visual strategy and a contradictory discourse of participation, the memorial would in fact fall victim to the very top-down articulation of the past that it sought to circumvent.

THE MEMORIAL AS THERAPY:
MICHAEL ARAD'S *REFLECTING ABSENCE*

With its disavowal of presence, antiverticality, and articulation of the past as multiple and fluid, Michael Arad's *Reflecting Absence* (2011) is in many ways the inheritor of the now-established postwar trope of the counter-monument. In the shadow of the Final Solution, the power relationships that undergird official narratives of history came to embody the same fascistic tendencies that made possible the horrors of the past. With this abiding link between the means of articulating history and an abhorrent past, the very notion of the monument appeared untenable in postwar Germany. In response to this impasse, a handful of works attempted to dramatize this impossibility by way of a refusal or even an active negation of presence. By utilizing strategies of self-sabotage such as disappearance, destruction, and sheer invisibility, these interventions sought to deconstruct the notion of a singular narrative of the past and thereby free the monument from its "*demagogical* rigidity and certainty of history" (emphasis mine).[26] James E. Young coined the term "counter-monuments" to describe the way in which the self-effacing quality of these works not only places the act of memory in the hands of the beholder but also undermines the basic assumptions of the monument itself in the process.

While reiterating many of the basic assumptions of this mode, *Reflecting Absence* redirects the ends of this project from overtly political, collective, and utopian aspirations toward individual processes of healing and reflection. Using the terms of Alain Badiou, Joel McKim claims that the memorial exemplifies the classical model in which the Aristotelian dictum that art concern catharsis rather than knowledge acquisition or revelation structures the work and its reception.[27] As such, the

5.1. Detail of one of the "voids" of *Reflecting Absence*. Photograph
by Wally Gobetz. By permission of the photographer.

memorial eschews the impasse of truth claims or symbolic meaning and
instead measures its functions in terms of a "utility for the treatment
of the affectations of the soul."[28] This sentiment is succinctly summarized by the jury statement's insistence that "memory belongs primarily
to the individual: the unique and personal remembrance of someone
deeply loved, of shared lives, of unspeakable grief and longing."[29]

At the center of this "therapeutic" function of the 9/11 memorial,
which necessarily undermines the didactic and static quality that has
historically accompanied the form, is the jury's insistence upon (and
Arad's subsequent acquiescence to) the integration of the footprints
of the towers in the memorial design. According to the Lower Manhattan Development Corporation's (LMDC) website for the memorial, in
the context of the completed memorial these two large voids serve as
a "space that *resonates with* [rather than represents] the feelings of loss
and absence that were generated by the destruction of the World Trade
Center" (emphasis mine), functioning as what Michael Arad and Peter Walker describe as a "mediating space."[30] The implication of these

statements is that the formlessness of these empty spaces subverts the top-down quality of the conventional memorial, lending the experience an individual and indeterminate quality that allows personal reflection to take precedence over the historical record and its codified memory. Confirming historian John Gillis's claim that "the era of collective memorialization is over," *Reflecting Absence* presents the events of that day as both the product of and prescription for an activated user rather than as "objective" representation.[31]

This transfer of agency is articulated through not only the work's lack of physical presence, but also its intimate and enclosed spaces. As running water pours into a central opening in each of the empty bases, a private and enclosed interior counterbalances the grandeur of the "wounds" outside. This interior space literally positions the individual at the base of the monument, but also confuses sensory experience in such a way that undercuts narrative. The viewer can "sense . . . what is beyond this curtain of water" but cannot see it.[32] The sound of the city, already buffered by the museum and cultural buildings around the memorial's exterior, is now effectively washed away by the falling water as the visitor descends into relative darkness. Through this experience, the past is posited as an internalized domain, subject to the same indeterminate sensory connections that structure memory. A similar logic informs the list of names, which wraps around the exterior of the voids in no apparent order.[33] The intent, according to the artist, is to refrain from "impos[ing] meaning through physical adjacency" or "impos[ing] order upon this suffering."[34] Unburdened by such symbolic coding, the absences of these dual voids become activated, creating what Arad describes as an "inexplicable sense" rather than a predefined narrative to be passively absorbed by the visitor. Thus, the memorial's apparent refusal of overt narrative combined with a foregrounding of individual experience posits memory as an internal formulation, which is indeterminate, anti-hierarchical, and largely immaterial. In this way, the work utilizes the visual vocabulary and underlying conceptual base of the countermonument so as to allow the individual to come to terms with his or her own unique experience of the event.

However, probing the work further suggests that the memorial's therapeutic quality might reiterate a process which Adorno observes in postwar Germany whereby the discourse and practice of therapy (in this case psychoanalysis) was itself co-opted by the collective psyche. Overtaken by the logic of repression, the Freudian constellation of "seriously working upon the past ... through a lucid consciousness [in order to break] its power to fascinate" was actively reconfigured in popular discourse of the time as a justification for forgetting and "clos[ing] the books on the past."[35] Beyond a simple misunderstanding, Adorno suggests that this misreading bore witness to the infiltration of analysis by the ego which had effectively shielded the self and in turn the culture at large from the difficult task of truly working through the past. As the aspirations of Arad's memorial are at least partially born out of the conflicts of representation from this same context, it is only logical to ask whether a similar process might be taking shape in the context of Lower Manhattan. Reading the site in these terms suggests that the work utilizes not only the discourse of therapy but also the populist connotations of participation as a means to similarly smooth over what is at base an imposition of power.[36]

In this, *Reflecting Absence* echoes a larger cultural shift which from Web 2.0 to the museum places the agency of the user at the center of a mode of cultural consumption based in modulated and diffuse modes of power.[37] As such, the following analysis of the 9/11 memorial will resonate with recent critiques from media studies and art history which seek to problematize the "empowerment" that these artifacts appear to bestow upon their subjects. While in the last decade the online sphere and its failed promise of a free and open space of connectivity have become the epicenter of this debate, the growing skepticism toward once-celebrated models of interactivity in the art world is especially instructive for the discussion of the memorial. Without getting too bogged down in the complexities of this reappraisal, I would like to briefly touch upon the paradoxes and shortcomings that manifest in the context of contemporary interactive art in order to more successfully frame the specific deployment of participation that manifests at the memorial.

Describing a trend in the work of European artists at the end of the twentieth century, Nicolas Bourriaud famously coined the phrase "relational aesthetics" to denote a mode of practice that "takes as its theoretical horizon the realm of human interactions and its social context, rather than the assertion of an independent and private symbolic space."[38] Examples include Rirkrit Tiravanija's hybrid installation/performances in which the artist transformed numerous galleries and museums into kitchens and cooked meals for visitors, or Liam Gillick's *Prototype Erasmus Table #2,* which featured a large table which the artist envisioned he might use to complete his book *Erasmus Is Late,* but which was also open to visitors to use as they wished. Like the counter-monument, such work sought to eschew historical hierarchies between artist, audience, and museum by not only foregrounding the constructive process and overall indeterminacy of the work, but also allowing the audience to determine the particular form and shape of these designations. By presenting what Gillick calls interactive "scenarios" rather than already complete objects these pieces undercut the expectation of a static art object by taking the social sphere itself as their primary subject. Through these strategies, Bourriaud claimed, the work of art would itself be the creation and experience of a utopian community, forged and maintained by the agency of a free and willing subject.

In hindsight, such work clearly foreshadowed the twenty-first-century position of the museum, which pursues monumental spectacle and a "have it your way" consumerist logic with a zeal that rivals more visible institutions of late capitalism such as the shopping mall or mobile device. Yet, even at the time of their inception, the conviviality and sheer "feel-good" quality of these performances led one to wonder if the radical potentiality assigned to these gestures by Bourriaud and others might be something of a smokescreen for an infinitely marketable but ultimately undisruptive form of entertainment. These suspicions were confirmed with Claire Bishop's 2004 biting critique of relational aesthetics in the journal *October.* Bishop proposed that, unlike the confrontational works of Santiago Sierra or Thomas Hirschhorn which utilized a kind of transformative antagonism in their mode of interaction, the festive, populist feel of these works betrayed a larger inability to engage with the conditions of their own genesis. Furthermore, as this failure was couched in the rhetoric of the open possibilities of participation and the formation of an ideal democratic community, it effectively conflated the call for participation with a powerful mode of interpellation.

At the heart of this critique is Bishop's observation of a disconcerting symmetry between Bourriaud's concept (and the work that he cites as exemplary of its logic) and the "dominant economic model of globalization."[39] Not only does interactive art often bolster the marketing potential of these works in the "experience economy," but so do its claims to democratic relations rest upon a troubling oversimplification of subjectivity. Starting from an autonomous, fully formed subject, these models of participation eradicate the critical precondition for the democratic commons, which Bishop defines in terms of Ernesto LaClau and Chantal Moffe's concept of "antagonism." Recognizing a Lacanian decentered subject, antagonism is understood not in terms of the interaction of two fully formed subjects, but as the productive encounter between partially externalized beings.[40] While Bourriaud posits participation as *tout court* emancipatory and democratic, LaClau and Moffe warn that "without antagonism there is only the imposed consensus of authoritarian order."[41] Framed by this free and willing subject, relational aesthetics not only fails to bring the conditions of its existence into view, but also denies the conditions for a truly transformative aesthetic experience.

Brian Massumi explains that the sheer inquisition to interact is not enough for a work of art: "More and more things in our lives are saying that.... If 'please interact' were enough to define a category, it would be gaming, not art."[42] Instead, such a work must understand interactivity in terms of Gilbert Simondon's characterization of technical invention as "emergent relational potential."[43] Art becomes political for Massumi the moment it pushes reality toward the "indeterminate but relationally potentialized fringes of existing situations, beyond the limits of current framings or regulatory principles."[44] In contrast, Bishop observes that "even the most 'open-ended' [work of the genre] determines in advance the depth of participation that the viewer may have with it."[45] Steeped in predetermined parameters of memory and illusory modes of agency, the 9/11 memorial would exemplify the contradiction that the discourse of participation articulated in the context of the museum. In the process, the memory of the event would be directed toward a predetermined future, all the while operating under the guise of the freedom of the individual to manifest and commune with his or her singular creation of memory.

From the beginning, the LMDC's publicity material portrayed the openness of the selection and design process as intimately connected to the broader goals of the memorial itself. Hailed as the largest event of its kind, the inclusive and transparent nature of the competition was intended to both illustrate the "unbounded faith in humanity...that transcends nationality and geography" and reaffirm "the democratic values that came under attack on September 11."[46] To this end, all submissions were made available for public scrutiny online via the LMDC's website. Certainly, the public forums that preceded the competition featured passionate debates, and the monument itself continues to have its critics (perhaps most notably former mayor Rudy Giuliani, who after seeing Arad's design suggested that the committee should "start over"). However, for the most part the memorial process was completed without serious controversy and in reasonable time, at least relative to the master plan for the site, which has been mired in infighting and bureaucracy from the beginning.[47] While the success of this process may appear to be the result of its apparent transparency, a closer look into the specifics of the process and the memorial's design casts this efficiency in a disconcerting light.

The design proposals were subject to a number of restrictions which limited and contained their possibilities. Most immediately, the jury stipulated that the names of all victims be included in the memorial and that the footprints of the towers be integrated into its final design. At the same time, Daniel Libeskind's master plan effectively predetermined the dimensions of the memorial itself. Just as these strictures served to inhibit a truly creative process, so did the process prove less open than its public campaign would suggest. Not only were members of the jury asked to sign confidentiality agreements which prohibited them from either discussing the competition with the press until the final design was selected or making negative comments about designs until the end of 2005, but so were the notes from the proceedings kept under lock and key each night.[48]

In addition to this lack of transparency, it is undeniable that the winning design reflected the tastes of jury members Maya Lin and James E.

Young in its minimalist reflective surfaces and overall concern with absence. In fact, as Philip Nobel reports, Lin had once sketched a design which featured twin reflecting pools in the footprints of the towers for Herbert Muschamp's "Masters' Plan." That Arad would essentially win the contest with the same design suggests that the shortcomings of the selection process spoke not simply to the perils of "art by committee" or the pervasive conservatism that followed 9/11. Rather, as McKim contends, this redundancy reflects the establishment of a "creative, institutional and critical consensus concerning the aesthetics of such a memorial" which had effectively "predesigned" the memorial under the auspices of a participatory model.[49] In this regard, it is not surprising that, despite LMDC interim president Kevin Rampe's appeal to designers to "above all else, be daring, be bold, be unconventional," many critics noted an overly conventional and staid quality in the finalists' submissions. As Nobel puts it, the process was "largely predetermined by the strict guidelines of the LMDC brief and the restrictions of Daniel Libeskind's master plan," both of which meant that "Michael Arad [gave] back to the process that which it had already made."[50] This is not to suggest that the LMDC or the jury members consciously sabotaged the process. Rather, these shortcomings are the result of an ahistorical collapse of absence with neutrality and inclusiveness, which undergirds the memorial's claims. While the democratic nature of the monument was to simply emanate from the memorial's antimonumental character, its formlessness, and, most importantly, its apparent refusal to predetermine or contain the event, one need only pursue the history of the counter-monument discussed above in order to find that participation and the refusal of form do not necessarily preclude institutional power.

The transformation of Arad's design during the selection process exemplifies the larger consequences of these assumptions. Initially, Arad had hoped to place the two voids in the Hudson River itself. As the water would continually flow into these absences, the work would materialize as a break within the surface. While this sense of an immaterial presence may have been carried over to the final design, the jurors' insistence upon a shift in location from the Hudson to Ground Zero itself would utterly transform the associations it provoked. Because of this relocation, the empty spaces of the site became wrapped up with the violence of the

5.2. Vietnam Veterans Memorial, Washington, DC. Photograph by Eva Sanchez-Turro. By permission of the photographer.

attacks in direct fashion. Accordingly, the voids functioned as remnants of the recently destroyed, closer to the empty plinths of Eastern Europe or Iraq than to the beyond of representation that the counter-monument and indeed Arad's own vision appeared to draw upon. Acknowledging the "contamination" of this motif of absence by a reminder of destruction and aggression, Anthony Gardner, spokesperson for the Coalition of 9/11 Families, complained that "these footprints evoke what was lost." The site's indexical reference to the events of that day serves to reinforce the act of aggression behind the disaster and in the process allows the absence of the site to turn into its heroic, commemorative other. Curiously, James E. Young argues that "to the extent that we leave this site as a festering wound in our cityscape or concentrate only on the destruction, we invite memory to disable life in the city, not to nourish it."[51] It is precisely this sabotaging of memory that the collapse of the voids with the actual footprints of the towers encouraged.

The empty foundations of the memorial effectively outline the missing structures, at the same time that they project the optimism and promise of rebuilding (an association that is reinforced by the perpetual status of Ground Zero as construction site). This future orientation is amplified by the surrounding city, which as Michel de Certeau observes has "never learned the art of growing old by playing on all its pasts." Unlike its European counterparts which actively materialize their history alongside the now, Manhattan lives within a "present [that] invents itself, from hour to hour, in the act of . . . challenging the future."[52] In this environment, the conspicuously empty footprints of the memorial inevitably prompt the viewer to mentally reconstruct the missing towers. This connection is the basis for a recurring criticism of the site, which in "so lovingly recording the towers' outlines" seemed to function first and foremost as a memorial to the buildings themselves.[53]

In "recording" rather than remembering, the memorial recasts the experience of the event from an act of creative exchange to the reiteration of an established and foreseeable narrative. This exchange not only immobilizes the past, but also bolsters a larger trajectory of post-9/11 visual culture. W. J. T. Mitchell notes the establishment of a pervasive logic of symmetry in the aftermath of the disaster whereby, in almost Biblical prefiguration, the specifics of the attacks are echoed in future events of the Iraq invasion through almost uncanny visual homology. For example, the falling of the Saddam statue in Firdos Square (discussed in chapter 4) "counter[s] the destruction of the headless twin icons of global capitalism," a connection that was almost ritualistically solidified by the controversial draping of the head of the statue with the American flag which flew over the Pentagon.[54] Seen from this perspective, the reiterative structure of memory that the memorial elicits serves as a mobilization of the discourse of rebuilding, a means to push this deterministic logic toward the realm of retribution.

This virtual reconstruction of the symbolic center of global capitalism reaffirms a larger worldview by essentially repairing the causal relations and overall coherence of the historical narrative, which was placed under assault by the attacks. In this, the individual and cathartic base of the therapeutic model, which traffics in sensory impressions and an engagement with the immaterial, is co-opted as *dispotif* around which the logic of mnemonic symmetry is built. Recognizing a temporal "unevenness" which undergirds the irreversible and homogenous time of capitalism and its articulation of history, Harry Harootunian describes the post-9/11 moment as one in which

> [a] specter – in the figure of noncontemporaneous contemporaneity – that has come back to haunt the present in the incarnate form of explosive fundamentalism fusing the archaic and the modern, the past and the present, recalling for us a historical déjà vu and welding together different modes of existence aimed at overcoming the unevenness of lives endlessly reproduced.[55]

While this atavistic presence of the past may have forced the time of progress to suddenly reveal the conditions for its own articulation, the causal and deterministic underpinnings of the memorial disavow and prohibit an engagement with this "collision of temporalities." It is precisely this lost opportunity that Slavoj Žižek mourns in *Welcome to the Desert of the Real*. In the aftermath of the event the opposition between fundamentalism and capitalism ("Jihad vs. McWorld") was recast in terms of an external threat rather the condition of possibility for Western dominance. Žižek understands this disavowal as the basis for the West's fascination with, even desire for, disaster, as such events reinforce the false consciousness of the other, keeping it at the necessary distance through which legible and coherent identity comes into focus. From this perspective, the virtual reconstruction of the towers serves as an eradication of temporal difference, as the subject flattens out the "thickened present" introduced by the attacks. Herein lies the duality of violence that the site invokes. Not only does the indexical presence of the footprints tether memory to a prior act of aggression, but so does the site's prompt to reconstruct the object of violence serve to reinstate a dominant worldview in which the presence of these temporalities and their representative cultures are negated.

Far from the kind of pure beyond that the jurors seem to ascribe to them, the footprints were always already filled with meaning. Not only did they bear the inscription of the supposedly open process of selection and design, but so too did they serve as a reminder of a violence performed against the city, which the viewer was effectively asked to displace onto a future event by mentally reproducing the missing towers. The memorial process and eventual design thus materialized Derrida's claim that the outside of representation is anything but, as absence remains a historically determined category that is just as prone to the stasis

5.3. The names surrounding the "voids" of *Reflecting Absence*.
Photograph by Wally Gobetz. By permission of the photographer.

of narrative or symbolic trappings as the memorial's heroic conventions. Yet jury member Maya Lin continued to suggest that in "let[ting] the footprints be the memorial" *Reflecting Absence* presents a space without "extra aesthetic form" or "arbitrary and additional meaning."[56] These views were in turn reproduced by Arad himself, who described his memorial as "allowing absence to speak for itself."[57] Summarizing the effect of this adulation of absence and the corruption of the competition on the memorial itself, Nobel states,

> The list of names, the healing waters, the sanctity of the footprints, the faith in architectural salvation – these things were well established before Arad arrived. . . . It wasn't a critical work, leaning toward some future understanding; it was a summary of what was known. . . . The process had stopped short of investigating the limits, and perhaps even discovering the opportunities, of the site's peculiarly compromised sanctity.[58]

He also suggests a more appropriate memorial form by asking whether "the best the process could do was to provide those two empty vessels and wait for them to fill up with meaning."[59] However, the physical absences which would come to undergird the memorial's design would in the end function as a projection of an already remembered past which actively repressed the creative aspects of memory as much as it reinforced existing narratives of history.

THE STOCK UNREPRESENTABLE; OR, THE
UNREPRESENTABLE BECOMES THE INACCESSIBLE

The visual strategy of Thomas Ruff's *jpeg ny02* (2004), an appropriated digital image of the smoking World Trade Center, might best be described as a twenty-first-century version of pointillism. With its large but lo-fi image engulfed by pixels in the close view, the unyielding grid relinquishes nothing of the event except for the illegible substrate of the image itself. The scene only comes into focus when the viewer walks away from the work, thereby breaking the immediacy and intimacy of physical proximity. The image's scale and lack of resolution renders the experience of the image closer to that of a billboard or advertisement for some overly theatrical film than a gateway to the reexperience of that day. Robert Storr describes Gerhard Richter's *September* (2009), a photograph of the collision of the jet with the South Tower that has been partially painted over by the artist, in similar terms. The intricate layering of these opposing media effectively buries the event underneath the materiality of the new image, creating a "muffling" effect, which places the "gratification of any desire to see and thereby seize death pictorially beyond the viewer's reach."[60] These works testify to a fundamental inaccessibility of the event, a feature which would in turn saturate the visual culture of the disaster with shadows, specters, and empty placeholders.

From Ad Reinhardt's black canvases to the young lovers in Resnais's *Hiroshima mon amour* (1959) who endlessly negate one another's claims to "have seen" the disaster, such breakdowns were emblematic of the political reckoning of representation in the wake of World War II.[61] In these instances, the interstice between the event and its representation was mired in *mise-en-abyme*, thus allowing the "text" to speak only through its failures and inadequacies. In the last several decades, however, the Holocaust, in many ways the center point of this discourse, has

5.4. Thomas Ruff, *jpeg ny02*, 2004. © 2013 Artists Rights
Society (ARS), New York / VG Bild-Kunst, Bonn.

moved from a position of unrepresentability epitomized by Adorno's
prohibition on poetry and the crisis of representation in postwar art
to a recognizable visual trope. The newfound representability of the
atrocity speaks to a larger transformation whereby events which were
once deemed outside the confines of representation have proven less re-
sistant to the image under the "visual turn." This shift was reinforced by
9/11, the reception of which, though incomprehensible at almost every
level of the experience, could certainly not be described in terms of the
same melancholic acknowledgment of the failure of representation that
characterized the experience of the Holocaust or Hiroshima. Rather,
the event was from the beginning saturated with presence, as images
endlessly presented the collisions and subsequent collapse of the towers from almost every imaginable angle. Indeed, to speak of the failure
of the image in such a context is not only to disregard the hypermedia-
tion of the disaster, but to overlook a primary intent of the attack, which,

as the work of Ruff and Richter suggests, was itself directed at and made for the image.

As this excessive mediation effectively divorces the motif of absence from its metaphysical and reflexive associations, the presence of the latter in the visual record of 9/11 comes to represent a space for the intervention of power as much as for a contemplation of the ineffable. Indeed, these interstices within the visual experience in many cases allow for the inscription of narrative and the eradication of the outside of the spectacle. Exemplary of this process is Spiegelman's *In the Shadow of No Towers*, which illustrates the way in which the immediate transformation of the event into a "national trauma" served as the prerequisite for mobilizing the general public for war. The dissolution of the singular perspective that the work dramatizes not only illustrates the always already prosthetic quality of media and its relation to memory, but subtly suggests the ways in which this formative power can be used to produce collective experiences. Summarizing this progression, E. Ann Kaplan explains that "trauma produces new subjects . . . the political-ideological context within which traumatic events occur shapes their impact . . . [and in the end] it is hard to separate individual and collective trauma."[62] Registering an encroaching objectification of the image and a correlative unsustainability of an outside to representation, Spiegelman's work conveys the drama of resistance and assimilation to the narrative of "9/11" which was formed within and by the image. The dystopia of the event bleeds into the process of representation in such a way that both acknowledges the limitlessness of the image and at the same time exposes its vulnerability.

In like fashion, the centrality of absence in Michael Arad's *Reflecting Absence* stands at the center of larger process of co-option whereby the site utilizes the discourse of transparency, participation, and personal healing to solidify what is at base an exercise of power. These dynamics flow from a larger institutionalization of memory that is wrapped up with an understanding of absence as free from historical baggage and/or ideological trappings rather than as a historically burdened trope open to the influence of power. However, in practice the negativity of *Reflecting Absence*, its continual disappearance from view and general weariness of presence, not only failed to materialize as a future-oriented poten-

tiality, but rather comes to illustrate what Leo Bersani calls "the sus-
ceptibility of all potential being to nothingness – as if potentiality could
itself *fail to take place* . . . could tilt the universe backward into the void."[63]
It is this "tilting backward" which in turn accounts for the circular nature
of Spiegelman's tortured images, their struggle to come into being in the
shadows cast by a missing referent. As Lisa Saltzman observes, "There
is no shadow without the towers. And there are, after the events of the
morning of September 11, 2001, no towers. Spiegelman's shadow fully
gives way to its essential nonessence; it is dematerialized into the void
that it always already was."[64] These shadows and absences which fill the
post-9/11 visual culture prove capable of absorbing firsthand experience,
leaving a kind of dead spot in the visual register, a place where power
has intervened and left only a faint residue of what Deleuze refers to as
a "thought of the outside."

These are the days after.

DON DELILLO,
Falling Man

Terrorism and the "war on terror" are parts of [the] new media
regime, but they are not its basis, not even its primary focus. At most,
they are catalysts: they intensify and speed up the emergence of new
media forms, and of their corresponding new modes of subjectivity.

STEVEN SHAVIRO,
Post-Cinematic Affect

Conclusion

DISASTER(S) WITHOUT CONTENT

While the immediate aftermath of 9/11 saw Hollywood pull virtually anything from distribution that vaguely resembled the experience of that day, five years later in 2006 the event would be front and center in films such as *United 93* and *World Trade Center*. Writing in February of the same year, Julian Stallabrass noted, "There is . . . a vast outpouring of 9-11 merchandise that surely seeks to heal the image wound: posters of heroic firemen against the backdrop of the fallen towers, badges, caps, T-shirts, magnets and memorial candles."[1] The cries of "too soon" seemed to have rescinded and the concomitant return of the image appeared to form something of a bookend to the reconstitution of the visible that took place in the wake of the disaster. As W. J. T. Mitchell observes, "the spectre of 9-11" was supplanted by the global financial crisis and the killing of Osama bin Laden. For Mitchell, the latter is especially important, as the sense of closure it enacted was the product of a kind of double negative within the spectacle which canceled out the power of invisibility: "It is significant that the War on Terror that began with a massive spectacle of erasure on 9-11 should end with the erased image of someone who had been reduced to little more than a hollow icon of a widely discredited movement."[2] In these terms, the killing of bin Laden not only redresses the constellations of invisibility outlined in this book, but also recuperates an earlier image of absence which would mark the beginning of the "war on terror."[3] A similar symbolic transference was performed in almost ritualistic fashion in a press conference held on the eve of the invasion of Iraq.

On February 5, 2003, as Colin Powell urged the United Nations to support a U.S.-led attack on Iraq, an eerily familiar image was deployed as a backdrop. While a tapestry reproduction of Picasso's *Guernica* has traditionally provided the backdrop for press briefings, on this day arrangements were made for the work to be covered by a large blue curtain in front of which would stand the flags of the United Nations. While UN spokesman Fred Eckhard explained that the action was taken in order to provide an "appropriate background for the cameras," the public's interpretation of this gesture was not surprisingly as an act of concealment, manipulation, and censorship. Such sentiments were summarized by Maureen Dowd, whose *New York Times* column stated, "Mr. Powell can't very well seduce the world into bombing Iraq surrounded on camera by shrieking and mutilated women, men, children, bulls and horses."[4] This performance enacted a displacement of the logic of absence from the attacks of 9/11 to the war on terror and in the process announced an ensuing campaign of the veiled, the covered, and the invisible that would define wartime experience.

Laura U. Marks describes the ensuing war on terror as a "struggle to define the terms of invisibility." This struggle, according to Marks, is apparent in the persistent attempt to control the meaning of not only the clandestine (cave) networks of the Taliban, but perhaps more importantly, the empty skyline of Manhattan. Through the concept of "enfolding" – the containment of information within an image in such a way that renders it latent, "coiled up like vipers or jacks-in-the-box" – Marks describes a process in which invisibility extends to media themselves. This situation is without predetermined ideological valence, as "invisible media" can lie behind both momentary breakdowns in the hegemonic image and the active concealment of "concrete events" under the cover of "information" (the camera footage of the smart bomb, for example).[5] Absence in these media formulations echoes the trajectory established by this book in that it serves as both the site of a potential coming into being of an alternate mode of representation and the struggle of the existing visual order to maintain its global dominance. Consider the portrayal of Ground Zero in Spike Lee's *25th Hour* (2002) in relation to Joel Meyerowitz's photographs of the cleanup effort. While presenting

C.1. Ground Zero in Spike Lee's *25th Hour* (2002).

the same space, these works conceptualize absence in ways that serve dramatically different ends.

In *25th Hour*, the ominous pit (along with the "Tribute in Light" memorial featured in the introductory sequence of the film) appears abruptly within the filmic diegesis. Its presence during a particularly poignant conversation in the film is entirely without explicit narrative justification. Indeed, one can say that from a dramatic standpoint the scene is hardly successful, as the space threatens to overwhelm the significance of this conversation. This tension is dramatized by the camera's own sudden sense of futility, as the supposed omniscience of the aerial shot is undercut by the unsettling presence of the wound of 9/11. However, from the standpoint of memorialization, the scene is exceptionally well played, as the suddenness of its appearance, its inability to be contained within the narrative, and its overall destabilizing presence maintain a certain fidelity to the traumatic experience itself. Additionally, as it is unclear whether the workers are removing debris or beginning to fill the absence with a new structure, the labor that is depicted comes to take place somewhere between destruction and construction and, as such, places the towers once again in the realm of the in-between. The absence of Ground Zero refuses to come into being in any legible manner and yet insists upon the frame with undeniable urgency.

Around the same time that Lee was filming *25th Hour*, photographer Joel Meyerowitz was trudging around the wreckage with his camera, documenting the cleanup efforts for the city of New York. The images that came out of this study couldn't be more opposed to those of Lee's film. While the sheer size and scale of these works drive home the magnitude of the disaster, the cleanup effort is recast by Meyerowitz's camera in terms of perseverance in the face of adversity, brotherhood (a concept which tended to function as a thinly veiled version of "nationhood" in post-9/11 discourse), and, more generally, the familiar rhetoric of the indestructibility of the spirit. The removal of debris, a project which resonates with the post-9/11 mantra of "getting back to work," becomes a rather heavy-handed metaphor in these photographs for the reestablishing of national identity and the healing of this collective wound. More fundamentally, the aestheticization of the scene via its association with the "ruin" serves to contain and categorize what is otherwise an incomprehensible event. In this way, the work of the camera doubles the cleanup effort in that both actions are about the (re)making of meaning in the face of an event which threatened to shatter our most basic grasp of reality. The presence of absence in these two disparate works by Meyerowitz and Lee illustrates Geoffrey Batchen's description of Ground Zero as a "blank spot which told you everything and nothing."[6]

As 9/11 became the lifeblood of the war on terror, the logic of absence which defined its visual culture was co-opted by the global counterinsurgency. In the process of this displacement, the unsteady duality between the formative possibilities of these visual constructs and the static iteration of power was increasingly stalled within the dominant image as potentiality congealed into ideology. The resulting sense of both continuation and break that would define the transition between the disaster and the war on terror is at the root of the challenges involved in grasping the historical specificity of the particular constellations outlined in this book, as well as the study of September 11 more broadly. James Elkins was perhaps the first to acknowledge the slippery parameters of this issue. Admitting to a nagging suspicion that the majority of readings of the event in its immediate aftermath (including his own initial responses) could feasibly have been written about a whole host of other modern disasters, Elkins found himself at an impasse in the

C.2. Joel Meyerowitz, *Smoke Rising in Sunlight*, 2002. By permission of the photographer.

wake of 9/11. Scholarship in the aftermath appeared bound to simply replay or amplify the event through familiar discourses of spectacle, simulacra, and the hyperreal (and, on the Anglo-American side, trauma studies). This was not simply a matter of the universal tendency to read traumatic events in terms of prior catastrophes. Rather, the impasse

Elkins identified was wrapped up with a more incestuous relation between the disaster and the methodology of its interpretations or readings. In light of this relationship, analysis seemed destined to run in
parallel and be somehow redundant with the disaster, forcing Elkins to
wonder if 9/11 needed visual studies in any significant or meaningful
way. While this book obviously forms something of a retort to Elkins's
skepticism, the larger point behind his anxiety is crucial to gauging the
ramifications of its thesis.

The introduction to this book chronicled the various ways in which
recent transformations in the spectacle shifted the category of content
beyond the stasis of the image and toward a kind of primary or essential
movement based in dynamics of flow and spatial montage. This transformation empowered the "negative" as it leveled the hierarchy between
presence and absence that has historically characterized media. While
these relations may have been the technological precondition for the
activation of the images of absence chronicled in this book, Elkins's remarks speak to an additional consequence of this scenario. Specifically,
this new status of absence and the correlative move beyond representation which makes it possible is complicit in establishing the unique
temporality of the disaster. It fuels a particular state that might be called
"living with the disaster," whereby the event spreads, or better yet "thick-
ens," beyond its historical moment. 9/11 draws its power to transform and
migrate into the present in part from the confusion of historical referents these formations generate, as well as from the enduring association
of absence with a lack of specificity (an association I have challenged in
chapter 5). In this regard, these formations are crucial to the capacity
of the disaster to continue as present, to serve as the active ground from
which our supposedly "post"-9/11 condition is forged.

Read in this light, the knee-jerk reaction to contain the event within
the past, as the "bookend model" posed above attempts to do, threatens
to bolster a disconcerting discourse of the disaster as a turning point
or watershed event. We often speak of the "post-9/11" world as if the disaster were complete, informing the present only indirectly from some
stable position in the past. This rhetoric contributes to the elision of an
underlying power dynamic through which the disaster is rendered ongoing and perpetual so as to be used for various ends. Like the wars that

it spawned, 9/11 has, in the last decade, proven to be without temporal parameters, let alone geographic specificity. Pronouncements of the disaster as a watershed occurrence repress the dual nature of this event and with it the interplay between the potentiality of the past and the present which it inflected.

This notion of living *after* 9/11 is also inadequate for the simple recognition of the way in which so many things have not changed since the disaster.[7] In many respects, we seem to have simply witnessed a reentrenchment of the very dynamics which contributed to the event. As Žižek and others have noted, the opportunity of the event to reconsider America's identity and its relation to the Other was quickly elided by a narrative of aggression and patriotism, and as such now seems a distant memory in the face of the global culture of counterinsurgency in which we all live. In this regard, to describe the event as a turning point is to overlook this path untaken, and perhaps even to ensconce the event in a hermeneutic frame which renders this virtual potentiality unreachable. This discourse of disaster and its correlative "state of exception" exemplify the kind of utilization of instability that Marx described in *The Eighteenth Brumaire of Louis Napoleon,* and which more recently manifests in Naomi Klein's notion of "disaster capitalism," whereby the uncertainty of disaster reaffirms if not escalates the hold of existing power structures. As warrantless searches, the execution of American citizens by executive order, and the once-temporary measures of the Patriot Act have all become permanent conditions of subjectivity, a history of 9/11 must necessarily refuse closure or risk reaffirming the kind of global exercise of power across history that we are witnessing today. Rather than working ahistorically, as Elkins fears, such a project must acknowledge the disaster's movement *through* history. Paradoxically, historical specificity must rest in the acknowledgment that the event maintains an almost uncanny ability to be used and conjured within the present.

No doubt, this rhetorical framing of the post-9/11 world is a layover from the midcentury, a moment which is, with some justification, often described as the postwar period. The processes of coming to terms with the capacity of technology for human annihilation, the possibility of genocide within a so-called "advanced society," and the catastrophic loss of life during the war are events that many around the world continue to grapple with and make sense of. So too do these events directly shape reality in the now, even for those of us who did not live through them. Yet in the aftermath of 9/11 we are living with the disaster in a different way. Even while the practicalities of the events of that day slowly fade from the public sphere, we continue, consciously or unconsciously, to live the event as present, as a historical event without historical distance. It constitutes the emergency of the now from which suspension of law, the eradication of privacy, and covert wars are waged. From the unchecked power of the NSA to perpetual drone attacks launched overseas, September 11 is the structuring absence of our current political situation, the other ear on the line or the U.S. missile fired into a crowded bus depot.[8] Tethered to wars that eschew beginning, middle, or end, the disaster is a condition rather than an occurrence or historical event.

It is inevitable that, like Benjamin's angel of history which accumulates all past disasters in a single image, these formations of the invisible resurrect a historical iconography of disaster and, in turn, resurface in future events beyond the confines of 9/11. It is also all too easy to confuse the backward trajectory of the disaster as something more than the retroactive revisions to history that follow all events of significance. Yet, more than a decade after the disaster, it is clear that 9/11 refuses to enter history. It has, in effect, not yet passed. Despite the fact that its images may have begun to fade from collective memory, it persists as a subterranean affective and political constellation. The critique of the image of absence, as a site of redefinition, a becoming-image that teeters between legible content and prerepresentational flux, offers a way back to the openness and sheer confusion of the event. It is a means to reimagine the disaster as a truly watershed event which might still produce a world which would be unrecognizable relative to today's heightened security and virtually limitless exercise of power.

Notes

INTRODUCTION

1. This is not to say that the towers were not destroyed and lives were not lost; nor is it to suggest that images of the event did not prompt real human emotions. Rather, it is to acknowledge the fact that the experience of the disaster was such that the image was bound up with the violence of the event at some base level.

2. Charles Paul Freund, "The Art of Terror," *San Francisco Chronicle,* October 6, 2002, http://www.sfgate.com/opinion /article/The-art-of-terror-2764708.php.

3. Giovanna Borradori and Jacques Derrida, *Philosophy in a Time of Terror: Dialogues with Jürgen Habermas and Jacques Derrida* (Chicago: University of Chicago Press, 2003), 107–108.

4. Samuel Weber, "War, Terrorism, and Spectacle: On Towers and Caves," *South Atlantic Quarterly* 101, no. 3 (Summer 2002): 449–458.

5. Katalin Orbán, "Trauma and Visuality: Art Spiegelman's *Maus* and *In the Shadow of No Towers*," *Representations* 97, no. 77 (Winter 2007): 59.

6. As Barbie Zelizer points out, the only possible exception to this general rule were the photos of a severed hand and a dead chaplain being removed from the towers; both photos were published in the *New York Post.* Barbie Zelizer, *About to Die: How Images Move the Public* (New York: Oxford University Press, 2010), 115.

7. Jacques Rancière, "Are Some Things Unrepresentable?," in *The Future of the Image,* trans. Gregory Elliott (London: Verso, 2007), 109.

8. Marie-José Mondzain, "Can Images Kill?," *Critical Inquiry* 36, no. 1 (2009): 20–21.

9. "Hollywood Caught in a Quandary," Fox News, September 27, 2001, http:// www.foxnews.com/story/2001/09/27 /hollywood-caught-in-quandary/.

10. Despite or perhaps because of the explicitly visual character of the disaster, the novel would take on 9/11 in full force in this same period. See David Wyatt, "*September 11* and Postmodern Memory," *Arizona Quarterly* 65, no. 4 (Winter 2009): 139–161.

11. Tyler Green, "9/11 Wrap-Up with Paul Schimmel," *Blouin Artinfo,* September 2007, http://de.blouinartinfo.com /blog/tyler-green-modern-art-notes /911-wrap-up-with-paul-schimmel.

12. Hal Foster, "September 11th," *Art-Forum,* January 2012, 210–211.

13. In this, I reiterate Jill Bennett's insistence that 9/11 be understood as a *casus* or "point of orientation in relation

to which method is shaped." Jill Bennett, *Practical Aesthetics: Events, Affects and Art after 9/11* (London: I B. Tauris, 2012): 13–15.

14. In light of the enduring fashionability of Debord and the Situationists, it is easy to forget that as early as the 1970s, critical theory began to display a healthy skepticism regarding the validity of the concept of spectacle in diagnosing the late twentieth-century condition. Foucault declared in *Discipline and Punish* that "our society is not one of spectacle, but of surveillance; under the surface of images one invests bodies in depth." The panoptic model he proposed in the place of the Marxist "repressive hypothesis" articulated an automatic and diffuse mode of power which located invisibility as the focal point of larger processes of subject formation and discipline. Drawing from McLuhan, Jean Baudrillard observed in *The Precession of the Simulacra* that the disappearance of contemporary media into their content led to the dissolution of the boundaries through which what Debord described as "the impoverishment, enslavement and negation of real life" was believed to take place. The violence of media, according to Baudrillard, is therefore an "illegible" one as the very terms of representation come to collapse within the image. As a result, Debord's famous declaration that "all was once lived directly has now become mere representation" proves no longer fathomable only a decade later, leading Baudrillard to declare, "We are no longer in the society of spectacle that the Situationists talked about, nor in the specific kinds of alienation and repression that it implied." Michel Foucault, *Discipline and Punish: The Birth of the Prison* (New York: Vintage Books, 1995): 217; Jean Baudrillard, *Simulacra and Simulation,* trans. Sheila Faria

Glaser (Ann Arbor: University of Michigan Press, 1995): 30.

15. Guy Debord, *Society of the Spectacle* (Detroit: Black & Red, 2000): 14.

16. The Situationist collective Retort, for example, describes these instances as lapses which serve as evidence of a larger "wound" in the skin of Empire, the fatal nature of which was confirmed by the subsequent taboo placed upon images of the attack. However, Hal Foster rightfully questioned the sheer predictability of the spectacle, which would allow this kind of calculation on the part of the terrorists, not to mention the all-encompassing nature of the visual which it assumes. Drawing upon a psychoanalytic base, Julian Stallabrass also cautions that Retort's association of the absence of images (as well as images of absence) with a failure or death of the spectacle is perhaps too hasty, as this condition might simply reference a period of mourning. In which case, it is entirely feasible that the integrity of the visible would remain while the spectacle is simply suspended in order to return at a later date. Indeed, the reversion to regularly scheduled programming that followed the live coverage of the event, as well as President George W. Bush's call for the American people to begin consuming again, would seem to suggest just that. These misgivings reflect a larger problem of deploying this critical rubric in the context of 9/11, which this project seeks to rectify. Retort, *Afflicted Powers: Capital and Spectacle in a New Age of War* (London: Verso, 2005): 25, 34; Hal Foster et al., "An Exchange on *Afflicted Powers: Capital and Spectacle in a New Age of War,*" *October,* no. 115 (Winter 2006): 5; Julian Stallabrass, "Spectacle and Terror," *New Left Review* 37 (January–February 2006): 87–106.

17. Jonathan Crary, "Eclipse of the Spectacle," in *Art after Modernism: Re-*

thinking Representation, ed. Brian Wallis (New York: New Museum of Contemporary Art, 1984), 287.

18. Ibid. Crary's position is representative of larger discourse that is intimately connected to the vitalism of Gilles Deleuze. In *The Logic of Sensation,* Deleuze chronicles invisible and insensible forces within the paintings of Francis Bacon which "scramble every spectacle." This asignifying capacity of media is perhaps most legible in his writings on cinema, where processes of deterritorialization, immanence, and becoming overtake the unity of representation, articulating images of the creative capacity of "pure time."

19. Raymond Williams, "Programming as Sequence or Flow," in *Television: Technology and Cultural Form* (London: Fontana, 1974), 86–96. 142–147.

20. Lev Manovich, "Macrocinema: Spatial Montage," 2001, http://manovich.net/macrocinema.doc. In the graphical user interface (GUI), the web browser, and digital culture in general, Lev Manovich sees a resurfacing of an "aesthetics of density." Drawing from northern baroque painting and Russian formalist film, this spatialized aesthetic works upon a simultaneity within rather than between frames.

21. Ibid.

22. Steven Shaviro, *Post-Cinematic Affect* (London: Zero Books, 2010), 71.

23. Quoted in Manovich, "Macrocinema."

24. Crary, "Eclipse of the Spectacle," 289.

25. Leslie Kan, "Spectacle," University of Chicago: Theories of Media; Keywords Glossary, accessed November 13, 2013, http://csmt.uchicago.edu/glossary2004/spectacle.htm.

26. As Wark puts it, the spectator of this antispectacle spectacle watches "the withering away of the old order . . . down

to near nothingness" without ever leaving the power relations which comprise it. Mc-Kenzie Wark, *The Spectacle of Disintegration: Situationist Passages out of the Twentieth Century* (London: Verso, 2013), 3.

27. Guy Debord, *The Society of the Spectacle,* trans. Fredy Perlman and Jon Supak (Detroit: Black & Red, 1970), par. 10.

28. Mondzain, "Can Images Kill?," 29.

29. Marie-José Mondzain, "Iconic Space and the Rule of Lands," *Hypatia* 15, no. 4 (Autumn 2000): 65.

30. Mondzain, "Can Images Kill?," 22.

31. Mondzain observes that we have reached the point where "the process of globalizing the image [and with it imperial power] across the world has begun." Mondzain, "Can Images Kill?," 162.

32. Marie-José Mondzain, *Image, Icon, Economy: The Byzantine Origins of the Contemporary Imaginary* (Palo Alto, CA: Stanford University Press, 2004), 223.

33. Susan Buck-Morss. "Visual Empire," *Diacritics* 37, nos. 2–3 (2007): 183.

34. Mondzain, "Can Images Kill?," 21.

35. Meaghan Morris, "Banality in Cultural Studies," *Discourse: Journal for Theoretical Studies in Media and Culture* 10, no. 2 (1988): 17.

36. Mimi White, "Site Unseen: An Analysis of CNN's War in the Gulf," in *Seeing through the Media: The Persian Gulf War,* eds. Susan Jeffords and Lauren Rabinovitz (New Brunswick, NJ: Rutgers University Press, 1994), 138.

37. Ibid.

38. As the church's response to iconoclasm succinctly illustrates, it is this relationship of the visible to the invisible that is overseen and, to some degree, produced by an external body. The effect of this triad between visible, invisible, and the gaze (the organization of the relation of the previous two by an external "authority") is summarized by Mondzain in the following

terms: "[This] apparatus which, giving its flesh and its form to something, the very essence of which is a withdrawal, invisibly takes possession of all earthly, visible things. . . . By virtue of the economic unity of the system, the operation of an uninterrupted pathway between the spiritual and temporal worlds was made possible . . . they are one and the same world. . . . No power without image." This process of "taking possession," a phrase surely meant to be read in a dual sense of both inhabitation of spirit and a forcible taking, appears in Hegel's aesthetics in reference to a similar discussion of the relation between the universal and the particular in Christian imagery. Hegel cites this duality as the center point for a "spreading abroad" of the divine, a process meant to describe the movement of spirit from the unrepresentable to the singular presence, but which, in light of Mondzain's reframing, might also be read in terms of the powers of conversion embedded in Christian theology and its images.

> For in so far as it is God, who, though in Himself universal, still appears in human form, this reality is, nevertheless, not limited to particular immediate existence in the form of Christ, but unfolds itself in all humanity in which the Divine Spirit becomes ever present, and in this actuality remains one with itself. The spreading abroad [in humanity] of this self-contemplation, of this independent and self-sufficing existence (*In-sich-und-bei-sich-sein*) of the spirit, is the peace, the reconciliation of the spirit with itself in its objectivity. It constitutes a divine world-a kingdom of God-in which the Divine, from the center outward, possesses the reconciliation of its reality with its idea, completes

itself in this reconciliation, and thus attains to independent existence.

Mondzain, "Iconic Space and the Rule of Land," 58; Georg Hegel, *The Philosophy of Art: Being the Second Part of Hegel's Aesthetik, in which are Unfolded Historically the Three Great Fundamental Phases of the Art-Activity of the World* (New York: Appleton, 1879), 89.

39. Marianne Hirsch, "Collateral Damage," *PMLA* 119, no. 4 (2004): 1213.

40. Commenting on the transitory monument, W. J. T. Mitchell describes these structures as "phantasmic, ghostly spectacles of resurrection." W. J. T. Mitchell, *What Do Pictures Want? The Lives and Loves of Images* (Chicago: University of Chicago Press, 2004), 22.

41. "About the WTC: Memorial and Museum; Design," World Trade Center, accessed March 25, 2014, http://www .wtc.com/about/memorial-and-museum -design.

42. These sentiments were later echoed in the San Francisco–based collective Retort's *Afflicted Powers*.

43. E. Ann Kaplan, *Trauma Culture: The Politics of Terror and Loss in Media and Literature* (New Brunswick, NJ: Rutgers University Press, 2005), 15.

44. Ibid.

45. Whitney Davis, *A General Theory of Visual Culture* (Princeton, NJ: Princeton University Press, 2011), 9.

46. W. J. T. Mitchell, "The Pictorial Turn," *Artforum* 30, no. 7 (March 1992): 90–94.

47. Nicholas Mirzoeff, "The Subject of Visual Culture," in *The Visual Culture Reader*, ed. Nicholas Mirzoeff (New York: Routledge, 2012), 3.

48. In pursuing these issues, this chapter also attempts to revise the position of trauma studies with regard to the role

of the invisible in relation to representation. This interrelation of the visible and
its other has been understood by trauma
studies as mirroring the psyche's internal
division between the coherence of the ego
and the potential rupture which manifests
as an "unassimilable" event. From this perspective, the invisible mimics the psyche's
own inability or unwillingness to fully experience an event. While such breaks often
create communities around the image and
safeguard the incomprehensibility of the
event from the ideologies of representation, the absent remains beyond presence,
safely shielded.

49. George H. Douglas, *Skyscrapers:
A Social History of the Very Tall Building*
(Jefferson, NC: McFarland, 2004), 169.

50. Thierry Groensteen, *La bande
dessinée: Un objet culturel non identifié*
(Mouthiers-sur-Boëme: Éditions de
l'An 2, 2006).

51. Irit Rogoff, "Studying Visual
Culture," in Mirzoeff, *The Visual Culture
Reader*, 26.

1. FROM LATENT TO LIVE

1. Jeffrey Melnick, *9/11 Culture:
America under Construction* (New York:
Wiley-Blackwell, 2009), 66. I use the
phrase "digital turn" with some reserva-
tions. As the following analysis will suggest, the implication of an irreversible and
smooth transition between the analog and
its apparent successor fails to capture the
often heterochronic temporalities of "new"
media.

2. John Roberts, "Photography and
the Photograph: Event, Archive and the
Non-Symbolic," *Oxford Art Journal* 32,
no. 2 (2009), 289–290. Exemplary of this
phenomenon is the work of photographer
Luc Delahaye, who sacrificed his early
practice in photojournalism for extremely
large and highly aestheticized portrayals

of contemporary events such as the war
in Afghanistan or the trial of Slobodan
Milosevic. These works often depict scenes
that are far from the front lines and lack
the immediacy of photojournalism in their
posed and overall highly constructed feel.
As Mark Durden observes, "In opposition
to the quick image capture and instantaneous global distribution associated with
the contemporary news media, Delahaye's
pictures entail a slow record of newsworthy
and historical moments." Mark Durden,
"Documentary Pictorial," in *Picturing
Atrocity: Photography in Crisis*, ed. Geoffrey
Batchen, Mick Gidley, Nancy K. Miller,
and Jay Prosser (London: Reaktion Books,
2012), 242.

3. David Campany, "Safety in Numbness: Some Remarks on Problems of Late
Photography," in *The Cinematic* (Cambridge, MA: MIT Press, 2007), 185–194.

4. Dana Heller, *The Selling of 9/11:
How a National Tragedy Became a Commodity* (New York: Palgrave Macmillan,
2005), 8.

5. A photograph of the possessions of
Bill Biggart, an independent photojournal-
ist who died covering 9/11, eerily encapsulates this unique status of photography at
the time of the event. It shows several bat-
tered cameras, misshapen and melted film
rolls, and a handful of seared press passes,
all of which are spilling out of a Ziploc bag
stamped "Property of New York City Police Department." In reflexive fashion, the
image collapses the death of the photographer with that of a medium, memorializ-
ing analog practice as yet another casualty
of the disaster. In this, it reiterates the
sentiments of Wendy Doremus, Biggart's
widow, who after claiming her husband's
personal belongings at the morgue observed, "September 11th became the watershed day. After that, photographers went
digital." At the same time, the charred film

rolls bear witness through an undeniable indexicality which confirms not only their presence at the scene but their internalization of a now-unreachable disaster. The ambiguity of this picture is further complicated by the official police record of Biggart's possessions. Positing an almost impossible simultaneity of practice, it lists two film cameras which produced one roll of color negative film and six rolls of color transparency film, and a digital camera whose memory card contained 154 images. David Friend, *Watching the World Change: The Stories behind the Images of 9/11* (New York: Picador, 2011), 19.

6. E. Ann Kaplan, "A Camera and a Catastrophe: Reflections on Trauma and the Twin Towers," in *Trauma at Home: After 9/11*, ed. Judith Greenberg (Lincoln: University of Nebraska Press, 2003), 95.

7. Friend, *Watching the World Change*, xi.

8. Barbie Zelizer, "Photography, Journalism, and Trauma," in *Journalism after September 11*, ed. Barbie Zelizer and Stuart Allan (London: Routledge, 2002), 60. Citing a recycling of the Holocaust "template" which used internal spectators to convey a sense of "bearing witness," Zelizer attributes this sudden rise of photography to the medium's ability to restore the sense of community that was broken by the traumatic event. Because of its ability to forge order in the place of chaos, the photograph "emerged as a powerful and effective way of visually encountering the horrific event."

9. Susan Sontag, *On Photography* (New York: Farrar, Straus and Giroux, 1977), 11–12. Bob Adelman's *Birmingham, Alabama 1963* illustrates this inescapable binary between action and observation that undergirds photographic practice in the context of traumatic events. While at first glance the female in the center of the triplet of figures to the left appears to gaze directly at us, it doesn't take long for the viewer to realize that the desperation on her face is in fact addressed to the photographer. Given the context of the civil rights movement, it is significant that on the other side of the lens is a white male, a figure who would seem to wield the very power that the subject herself lacks. More recently, *Eagle Tribune* photographer Marc Halevi took pictures of a woman standing dangerously close to the sea during Hurricane Bill in 2009. Halevi intended to capture the human scale of the highest tide that Plumb Island, Massachusetts, had experienced in more than sixty years. However, while he was peering through his viewfinder, a wave struck the wall of earth upon which she was standing, sending her into the violent waters. The woman drowned and the photograph now operates as a token of that disconcerting choice. I offer these examples not as indictments of unethical operators. Rather, as this chapter will suggest, these stories dramatize the paralyzing disconnect that emanates from the apparatus itself.

10. Jane Gallop has pointed out that Sontag's position "mistakes the moment for eternity," claiming that "the person who intervenes *can* record; the person who is recording *can* intervene-just not at the same moment." The binary between action and inaction that Sontag works within is, in other words, better understood as positions which the operator continually oscillates between. Yet Gallop arrives at such a conclusion after discussing a photograph taken in the midst of an argument with her husband, after which the camera was put down and the operator was able to console his disheartened subject. Jane Gallop, *Living with His Camera* (Durham, NC: Duke University Press, 2003), 73.

11. Frank Rich, "Whatever Happened to the America of 9/12?," *New York Times*, September 10, 2006.

12. Ibid.

13. Walter Sipser, "It's Me in That 9/11 Photo," *Slate*, September 12, 2006, http://www.slate.com/articles/news_and_poli tics/culturebox/2006/09/its_me_in_that _911_photo.html.

14. Margaret Olin, *Touching Photographs* (Chicago: University of Chicago Press, 2012), 172–173.

15. Robert Cumins, a photographer for *Black Star*, explains that throughout the process of photographing the collision, "I never thought about the plane I had seen. It just wasn't in my mind." Robert Cumins, *Running toward Danger: Stories Behind the Breaking News of 9/11* (New York: Rowman & Littlefield, 2002), 42.

16. Friend, *Watching the World Change*, 13.

17. Vilém Flusser, *Towards a Philosophy of Photography*, trans. Anthony Mathews (London: Reaktion Books, 1983), 58.

18. Walter Benjamin, "A Small History of Photography," in *One-Way Street and Other Writings*, trans. Edmund Jephcott and Kingsley Shorter (London: New Left Books, 1979 [1931]), 251.

19. Sylviane Agacinski, *Time Passing: Modernity and Nostalgia* (New York: Columbia University Press, 2003), 91.

20. Ariel Goldberg, "Letters to Robert Gober and Ehren Tool," *Very Small Kitchen Sink*, March 28, 2012, http://verysmall kitchen.com/2012/03/28/vsk-project-ariel -goldberg-letters-to-gober-and-tool/.

21. Roland Barthes, *Camera Lucida: Reflections on Photography*, trans. Richard Howard (New York: Farrar, Straus and Giroux, 1982), 47.

22. Italo Calvino, "The Adventures of a Photographer," in *Difficult Loves* (New York: Mariner Books, 1985), 220.

23. Ibid.

24. Ulrich Baer, *Spectral Evidence: The Photography of Trauma* (Cambridge, MA: MIT Press, 2002), 9.

25. Bob Rogers, "Photography and the Photographic Image," *Art Journal* 38, no. 1 (Autumn 1978): 29–35.

26. Just weeks after the events of 9/11, a report was released by the InfoTrends research group that showed low-end digital cameras comprising 21 percent of international camera sales. As Jeffrey Melnick points out, revenue from digital camera sales topped that of film cameras for the first time in 2000. In addition to 9/11's being the "most photographed disaster in history," one could say with some certainty that it was one of the first global, catastrophic events recorded in significant numbers in digital form. InfoTrends, "Digital Camera Sales Capture 21% of Worldwide Camera Market in 2001," September 25, 2001, http://www.capv.com /public/Content/Press/2001/09.25.2001 .html; Melnick, *9/11 Culture*, 66.

27. Nicholas Mirzoeff, *An Introduction to Visual Culture* (New York: Routledge, 2009), 258.

28. Pavel Büchler, "Live View," *Philosophy of Photography* 1, no. 1 (2010): 14–17.

29. Admittedly, online photo sharing may reintroduce this futural aspect as the image becomes tied to the imagination of a future use. However, one could argue that the instant transmission of contemporary cameras (some of which even have Facebook buttons) collapses the interval between taking and sharing as well.

30. Johanna Drucker, "Temporal Photography," *Philosophy of Photography* 1, no. 1 (2010): 23.

31. Upon feeling himself "observed by the lens," Barthes describes an almost involuntary reaction, which prefigures

the ensuing still image. He explains, "I constitute myself in the process of 'posing,' I instantaneously make another body for myself, I transform myself in advance into an image." Barthes, *Camera Lucida*, 10–11.

32. This new live quality of the still image is dramatized by a JVC ad from early 2001 which features a stylish and chic young woman preparing for a night out on the town. With the city waiting in the background, she applies her lipstick using the camera's live preview screen as a mirror.

33. Cumins, *Running toward Danger*, 124.

34. According to David Friend, many of those who took pictures of the event chose to put off processing or never process the film from that day. Similarly, theorist Jean Baudrillard notes multiple experiences whereby "the developed film produces no image" or "the roll of film mysteriously disappear[s] in the photographer's apartment." Jean Baudrillard, "The Art of Disappearance," in *Art and Artefact*, ed. Nicholas Zurbrugg (London: Sage, 1997), 29.

35. Being characterized by the presence of *both* pleasure and displeasure, the sublime initiates a movement between these polarities that is circular and simultaneous; the mind is both "attracted and repelled" simultaneously. Displeasure results from the frustration or confusion over the experiences of an object that exceeds our comprehension, as in the mathematically sublime, or from the fear that characterizes the dynamically sublime. The pleasure in both instances is the reassurance of reason that is produced from this initial displeasure.

36. A similar relationship is found in the dynamically sublime, where Kant claims that the subject both acknowledges an object as "fearful" and yet is not afraid of it.

37. Flusser, *Towards a Philosophy of Photography*, 90.

38. Ibid., 35.

39. Max Horkheimer and Theodor W. Adorno, "The Culture Industry: Enlightenment," in *Dialectic of Enlightenment* (New York: Continuum, 1998), 124.

40. This expansion in the understanding of the ideological function of media from content to the means of delivery has proven to be one of the last half-century's most valuable contributions of the culture industry argument for media studies. However, it is clear that some account for agency must be made in the context of image producers, which unlike the passive spectator of the culture industry engage the means of production.

41. Flusser, *Towards a Philosophy of Photography*, 35.

42. Paul Crowther, *The Kantian Sublime: From Morality to Art* (New York: Oxford University Press, 1989), 79.

43. Flusser acknowledges the ability of photographer artists to manipulate these categories, but understands such "meta-programming" as beyond the act of photographing in which the apparatus acts as a given.

44. To put this in Flusser's terms, the disaster prompts a breakdown in the "symmetry between the function of the photographer and that of the camera, [in which the] apparatus functions as a function of the photographer's intention, this intention itself functions as a function of the camera's program." Flusser, *Towards a Philosophy of Photography*, 35.

45. Guy Debord, *The Society of the Spectacle*, trans. Donald Nicholson-Smith (New York: Zone Books, 1994), 7.

46. Martin Heidegger, *The Question concerning Technology and Other Essays* (New York: Harper Torch Books, 1982), 129.

47. Hans Berten, *The Idea of the Postmodern: A History* (New York: Routledge, 1994), 133.

48. Don DeLillo, *White Noise* (New York: Penguin, 1999), 12–13.

49. Damian Sutton, "Real Photography," in *The State of the Real: Aesthetics in the Digital Age*, ed. Damian Sutton, Susan Brind, and Ray McKenzie (London: I. B. Tauris, 2007), 168.

50. Flusser, *Towards a Philosophy of Photography*, 34.

51. Christine Battersby, "Terror, Terrorism and the Sublime: Rethinking the Sublime after 1789 and 2001," *Postcolonial Studies* 6, no. 1 (April 2003): 67.

52. Ibid.

2. ORIGINS OF AFFECT

1. Karen Blumenthal, *Six Days in October: The Stock Market Crash of 1929* (New York: Atheneum Books for Young Readers, 2002), 15.

2. José Clemente Orozco, *José Clemente Orozco: An Autobiography* (Austin: University of Texas Press, 1962) 135.

3. Will Rogers, "Daily Telegram #1013," October 4, 1929; Eddie Cantor, *Caught Short! A Saga of Wailing Wall Street* (Whitefish, MT: Kessinger, 2003), 12.

4. Interestingly, Magritte himself was devastated by the crash. With the collapse of the art market his dealer folded and the painter was forced to go back to Brussels to work as a commercial artist to make ends meet.

5. Nina Rastogi, "Wall Street Suicides," *Slate*, September 22, 2008, http://www.slate.com/id/2200633/.

6. Blumenthal, *Six Days in October*, 15.

7. Winston S. Churchill, *The Great Republic: A History of America* (New York: Modern Library, 2000), 276.

8. Albeit on less pervasive scale, the image of the falling body reappeared in response to the more recent financial collapse. Michael Ramirez's 2008 cartoon for the *New York Post*, for example, depicts an executive from an investment firm sprawled out on the sidewalk beneath a skyscraper. A dialogue bubble emanating from the body reads, "It's ok, I landed on a taxpayer." While the trauma of the original event is shown to be safely dissipated by government intervention, the cartoon suggests that this action is not without a price of its own.

9. Douglas, *Skyscrapers*, 169.

10. D. Gunnell and M. Nowers, "Suicide by Jumping," *Acta Psychiatrica Scandinavica* 96, no. 1 (July 1997): 2.

11. For a history of New York's ordinances see http://www.nyc.gov/html/dcp/html/zone/zonehis.shtml.

12. After being open only eighteen months, the Empire State Building, a favorite destination for leapers at one time, saw its first suicide, thereby setting off a ten-year period in which sixteen people would leap from the observatory deck before a protective fence was erected in 1947 (Gunnell and Nowers, "Suicide by Jumping," 2). On April 13, 2007, Moshe Kanovsky, a thirty-one-year-old lawyer from Brooklyn, jumped from the sixty-ninth floor of the Empire State Building, only to be caught by the thirtieth-floor landing. Prior to that, Dovid Abramowitz leaped from the sixty-sixth floor on February 2, 2006, before landing on the sixth-floor ledge. In fact, the very first leap from the Empire State Building began from the open observation deck when Fred Eckert jumped from the 103rd floor before coming to rest on the setback on the 87th floor. All of this is made almost farcical by the case of Elvita Adams, who in 1979 leaped from the same observation deck only to break her hip on the eighty-fifth-floor setback as a gust of wind pushed her back against the

building once she left her feet. Douglas, *Skyscrapers,* 173.

13. Filming in the Trade Center lobby, documentary filmmakers Jules and Gedeon Naudet inadvertently captured the chilling thud of these bodies as they struck ground outside. While they avoided direct visual representation, the bewilderment on the faces of the firefighters and police officers as they came to understand the source of the sound, combined with the ominous thud of the soundtrack itself, nonetheless hinted at the horror occurring outside. Their documentary, *9/11,* aired on CBS in March 2002.

14. The falling bodies of 9/11 have variously been referred to as leapers, jumpers, and even flyers. Each designation carries its own insinuations of agency and victimhood. While recognizing this not-unimportant distinction, it is all but impossible to universalize the varied situations that led to the deaths of these individuals. For this reason, I will use these terms interchangeably when describing the event as a whole. However, when describing specific situations I will try as much as possible to reflect the unique experiences of these individuals with the appropriate word choice.

15. Sigmund Freud, *The Interpretation of Dreams* (New York: Basic Books, 2010), 270–272, 393–394.

16. Ibid., 271.

17. As Griffith Edwards points out, London was an avid reader of Freud and Jung, especially in his later years. Edwards, "Jack London," *Alcohol and Alcoholism* 2, no. 1 (1965): 28.

18. Freud admittedly flirts with the idea of a "phylogentic heritage" throughout his work, but remains inconsistent in his stance and never really formulates a position. As is well known, his fallout with Carl Jung was based in part on their disagreement on this issue.

19. One can't help but think that the common belief that if one hits the ground in a dream, one is dead, might have some connection to this phenomenon. Jack London, *Before Adam* (North Hollywood, CA: Aegypan, 1906), 1–5.

20. Freud, *The Interpretation of Dreams,* 271.

21. The discussion that follows is based largely on D.W. Winnicott, *The Maturational Processes and the Facilitating Environment: Studies in the Theory of Emotional Development* (London: Hogarth, 1965).

22. Ibid., 59–63.

23. I place "the mother" in quotation marks because there is some question as to whether the figure is gender-specific in Winnicott's writing.

24. Winnicott, *The Maturational Processes,* 59–63.

25. Winnicott, *The Maturational Processes,* 58.

26. Ibid., 48–60.

27. Mary Jacobus, *The Poetics of Psychoanalysis: In the Wake of Klein* (New York: Oxford University Press, 2006), 197.

28. Walter Benjamin, "The Work of Art in the Age of Mechanical Reproducibility," in *Illuminations: Essays and Reflections,* ed. Hannah Arendt, trans. Harry Zohn (New York: Harcourt Brace & World, 1968), 234.

29. I thank Tom Gunning for bringing these latter two examples to my attention.

30. Gary Morris, "Crossing the Bridge," *Bright Lights,* August 2005, http://www .brightlightsfilm.com/49/joy.php.

31. Friedrich Kittler, *Optical Media,* trans. Anthony Enns (Cambridge: Polity, 2009), 35.

32. London, *Before Adam,* 1.

33. On Paz's work, see Donald Bertrand, "New Furor Sparked by Falling-Bodies Art," *New York Daily News,* September 21, 2002, http://www.nydailynews

.com/archives/news/new-furor-sparked
-falling-bodies-art-article-1.512008; for a
discussion of the *Mad Men* ad campaign,
see Rebecca Martin, "New Mad Men
Poster Sparks 9/11 Controversy: Is the Ad
Insensitive?," *Wetpaint,* January 19, 2012,
http://www.wetpaint.com/news/articles
/new-mad-men-poster-sparks-911-contro
versy-is-the-ad-insensitive-.

34. "My fall creates the abyss; in no
way is the abyss the cause of my fall."
Gaston Bachelard, *Air and Dreams,* trans.
Edith Farell and Frederick Farell (Dallas,
TX: Dallas Institute Publications, 1988),
95. According to Bachelard, when Milton,
for example, tells us that the angel fell for
nine days, he presents the fallen angel
as an object that is merely tossed out of
heaven and thereby misses the qualitative
"overwhelming becoming" of the pure fall.
On the other hand, in turning to a passage
by Thomas de Quincy, Bachelard finds
that by measuring the fall in relation to
a change in qualitative state, in this case
despair, rather than quantitative time or
space, the fall is transformed. See Gaston
Bachelard, "The Imaginary Fall," in *Air
and Dreams,* trans. Edith Farell and Frederick Farell (Dallas, TX: Dallas Institute
Publications, 1988), 95–110.

35. Bachelard, "The Imaginary Fall," 92.

36. Ada Louise Huxtable, "Big but Not
So Bold: Trade Center Towers Are Tallest,
but Architecture Is Smaller Scale," *New
York Times,* April 5, 1973.

37. Henri Cartier-Bresson, *The Decisive
Moment* (New York: Simon & Schuster,
1952), unpaginated.

38. Liz Wells, *Photography: A Critical Introduction* (New York: Routledge, 2004), 73.

39. Cartier-Bresson, *The Decisive
Moment.*

40. Ibid.

41. It is for this reason, according to
Lessing, that the famous Hellenistic sculp-

ture Laocoön does not scream despite
Virgil's insistence upon the priest's "roar"
and "loud bellowing." Breaking with his
contemporary Winckelmann, who explained the lack of a scream in terms of a
general refusal to depict suffering on the
part of the ancients, Lessing claimed that
the work gives us only a sigh so as to allow
the impending scream to take place in the
imagination. In this, *Laocoön* illustrates
Lessing's larger point that, while poetry
is able to present sequential moments in
order to convey narrative, the stasis of the
work of art necessitates the use of representative transitional moments in order
to prompt the viewer's imagination to
extend the action beyond the represented
moment. Summarizing the intended result
of this scenario, David Bate explains that
"the viewer of the picture can run their
imagination back and forth across the time
before and after the depicted action to
imagine the sequence of events constitut-
ing the story." Bate, *Photography: The Key
Concepts* (New York: Berg, 2009), 58.

42. David Wellbery, *Lessing's Laocoon:
Semiotics and Aesthetics in the Age of Reason*
(Cambridge: Cambridge University Press,
2009), 169.

43. Roy Quan, "Photography and the
Creation of Meaning," *Art Education* 32,
no. 2 (February 1979): 6.

44. Cartier-Bresson, *The Decisive
Moment.*

45. Peter Wollen, "Fire and Ice," *Photographies* 4 (March 1984): 118–120.

46. Cartier-Bresson, *The Decisive
Moment.*

47. Wollen, "Fire and Ice," 78.

48. Roland Barthes, "Diderot, Brecht,
Eisenstein," *Screen* 15, no. 2 (1974): 73.

49. William Shepherd, "Eyewitness at
the Triangle," Remembering the 1911 Triangle Factory Fire, accessed May 14, 2014,
http://www.ilr.cornell.edu/trianglefire

/primary/testimonials/ootss_william shepherd.html.

50. This might seem unusual since we are used to photographers' snapping a series of images within a short period of time. However, Terence Wright claims that Sorgi was most likely using a Graflex Speed Graphic camera, which, unlike a 35mm camera, requires that the photographer take out the 4 × 5 sheet negative and insert another between each shot. In a situation such as this, where the action of interest would be complete in a matter of seconds, the photographer must exercise an incredible restraint. As a result, the very process of taking the photograph is itself tied to a discrete moment, no longer connected in any meaningful way to the previous image captured, as the often cathartic contact prints of 35mm photography suggest. Summarizing this allegiance to the instant that occurs both at the moment of production and at the moment subsequently represented by the internal organization of the image, the title of the story that ran on the front page of the *Courier Express* the next day was "Camera Catches Death Leap in Mid-Air." Here the image's apparent ability to arrest time is equated with a spatial integrity that preserves the body within perspectival space. Terence Wright, *The Photography Handbook* (New York: Routledge, 1999), 95.

51. While the temptation is to align this privileging of "the pose," which often appears random and off the cuff, with a kind of openness or instability of narrative that preserves the inherent complexity of reality, in the case of the fall the exact opposite seems to be the case more often than not.

52. "Suicide Leaps from Twenty-First Story," *New York Times*, April 2, 1904.

53. Ibid.

54. N. R. Kleinfield, "A Creeping Horror," *New York Times*, September 12, 2001.

55. Tim Lott, "She Killed Herself, I Didn't: Why?" *Times* (London), January 6, 2006.

56. "It all came right after 9/11 for me, and one of the key influences-though not the only one-were those images of people falling from the World Trade Center towers," Misrach says. "These people were in this horrific situation, but they were falling through space with such haunting grace and ambiguity." Misrach kept three small prints of World Trade Center jumpers on his studio wall for the four years he worked on *On the Beach*. "On one level or another," he says, "they inspired the whole project." Richard Misrach, interview by Robert Ayers, *Blouin ArtInfo*, January 30, 2008, http://www.artinfo.com/news /story/26514/richard-misrach/.

57. This condition can only be exacerbated with time, given that the connection to 9/11 will only become more tenuous as the event fades from collective memory.

58. This dissolution of the subject is reproduced by the spectator, as the sheer size of the prints (6 × 10 feet) in combination with the minuscule sunbathers who populate them invites viewers to similarly lose themselves in the pursuit of the figure.

59. Barbara Rosenblum, *Photographers at Work: A Sociology of Photographic Styles* (Teaneck, NJ: Holmes & Meier, 1978), 14.

60. Misrach has said in public talks that the size of the images was meant to replicate history paintings and that this reference was intended to work against the newspaper image, which is small in size and, more importantly, ephemeral. He was attempting to make something longlasting, something that could be looked at in the future as a record of our times.

61. Gilles Deleuze, *Francis Bacon: The Logic of Sensation* (Minneapolis: University of Minnesota Press, 2005), 16–18.

62. Giorgio Agamben, *Homo Sacer: Sovereign Power and Bare Life*, trans. Daniel Heller-Roazen (Palo Alto, CA: Stanford University Press, 1998).

63. Henry A. Giroux, *Beyond the Spectacle of Terrorism: Global Uncertainty and the Challenge of the New Media* (St. Paul, MN: Paradigm, 2006), 30.

64. However, rather than a straightforward process of "othering" whereby the establishment of identity serves in equal measure to identify the "not us," the work utilizes the familiar motif of the melting pot in order to visualize what Carmen Luke regards as the Hegelian "contradiction" of global citizenship. While acknowledging the presence of an increasingly "global village," Luke maintains that the new mode of subjectivity is not synonymous with the death of the nation-state and its ability to mobilize group identifiers, but rather turns upon a dialectic or "perpetual tension . . . around difference and sameness, heterogeneity and homogeneity." In these terms what appears as the suspension of global identity in the context of terror is in reality simply the shifting of a dynamic constellation. This dialectical quality of global subjectivity manifests in the statue as a heterogeneous yet recognizable national identity, a simultaneously pluralistic and singular articulation of Americanness which supports the "us-them" discourse of the Cold War at the same time that it articulates the intimate connectedness of a shared experience. The sudden sensitivity to inclusiveness that the statue seemed to materialize was part and parcel of militarizing the conflict, a shifting of this dynamic of global citizenship so as to transform the event from an isolated act of terrorism to an attack. Carmen Luke, "As Seen on TV or Was That My Phone? 'New' Media Literacy," in *Media/Cultural Studies: Critical Approaches*, ed.

Rhonda Hammer and Douglas Kellner (Bern: Peter Lang, 2009), 200.

65. Interestingly, only 2.7 percent percent of the firefighters killed were African American and 3.2 percent were Hispanic. While this in itself does not somehow preclude their representation, it is interesting to note that Hispanics comprise 11.6 percent of the military and African Americans around 18 percent. John F. Schmidt, "Imaginary History," January 20, 2001, http://www.conservativetruth.org/archives/johnschmidt/01–20–02.shtml.

66. Susan Willis, *Portents of the Real: A Primer for Post-9/11 America* (London: Verso, 2005), 14.

67. Indeed, this latter transformation was made literal as the same flag from Ground Zero was shipped to Afghanistan, where it was raised over the Kandahar International Airport. Ibid., 15.

68. Maurice Blanchot, *The Writing of the Disaster*, trans. Ann Smock (Lincoln: University of Nebraska Press, 1995), 66.

69. Ibid.

70. In "Fear of Breakdown," Winnicott definitively states, "It [the prior experience of depersonalization] is a fact that is carried round hidden away in the unconscious." D. W. Winnicott, *Psycho-Analytic Explorations*, ed. Clare Winnicott, Ray Sheperd, and Madeleine Davis (Cambridge, MA: Harvard University Press, 1992), 90.

71. Despite David Simpson's description of the unofficial ban of this image as an attempt to "write [the leapers] out of the visual and official memories of the event," the exclusion of censorship functions in a dialectical manner which can never be reduced to a pure act of negation. In fact, as the above argument has implied, the rise of this motif is to some degree made possible by the disappearance of the image at the hands of censorship. David

Simpson, *9/11: The Culture of Commemoration* (Chicago: University of Chicago Press, 2006), 49.

3. REMEMBERING-IMAGES

1. Roland Barthes, "The Eiffel Tower," in *The Barthes Reader,* trans. Richard Howard (New York: Hill & Wang, 1983), 238.

2. Le Corbusier's experience of the city from atop the Empire State Building illustrates this sense of visual mastery that the image of the depopulated city produces. Having traveled to New York for the sole purpose of gazing down upon the city from this precipice, the architect describes seeing Manhattan as a set of empty building blocks, an image which Max Page claims "crystallized his vision for violently remaking the city." However, from Henri Lefebvre's *The Production of Space* (1974) to Rosalyn Deutsche's *Evictions* (1996) to Michel de Certeau's *The Practice of Everyday Life* (1980), this transformation from "living" entity to anonymous and empty abstraction has in recent years been regarded as the centerpiece of a larger ideological operation through which the discourses of urban planning and social reform repress the "practice" of the city by its users.

3. Vivian Sobchack, "Cities on the Edge of Time: The Urban Science-Fiction Film," in *Alien Zone II: The Spaces of Science Fiction Cinema,* ed. Annette Kuhn (London: Verso, 1999), 132.

4. Susan Sontag, "The Imagination of Disaster," *Commentary,* October 1965, 42.

5. Gilles Deleuze, *Cinema 1: The Movement-Image,* trans. Hugh Tomlinson and Barbara Habberjam (Minneapolis: University of Minnesota Press, 1986), 141.

6. For example in Elia Kazan's *America, America* (1962) a series of singular action-reaction sequences (the protagonist's entry into America is blocked→he assumes the identity of a deceased passenger→he must work as a shoeshine boy without pay in order to compensate his benefactor) collectively establish the SAS' logic at the macro level, i.e., to escape Anatolia (s) for New York (s').

7. Carl Abbott, "The Light on the Horizon: Imagining the Death of American Cities," *Journal of Urban History* 32, no. 2 (2006): 177.

8. Sobchack, "Cities on the Edge of Time," 132.

9. Abbott, "The Light on the Horizon," 177. The only viable means to reinvigorate the movement of the film is to essentially repopulate the city, a dynamic that from Ruttmann to Vertov is frequently employed by the "symphony of the city" genre of early cinema.

10. Laura Mulvey explains, "There are three different looks associated with cinema: that of the camera as it records the pro-filmic event, that of the audience as it watches the final product, and that of the characters at each other within the screen illusion. The conventions of narrative film deny the first two and subordinate them to the third, the conscious aim being always to eliminate intrusive camera presence and prevent a distancing awareness in the audience." Laura Mulvey, "Visual Pleasure and Narrative Cinema," in *Visual and Other Pleasures (Theories of Representation and Difference)* (Bloomington: Indiana University Press, 1989), 26.

11. The building seen in Yoshida's film is the Hiroshima Prefecture Industrial Promotion Hall. Since it was located at the hypocenter of the explosion it was the only thing that was at all intact after the explosion. The building has come to be known as "the A-bomb dome" and was left in its decomposed state as a reminder of the event. In the late 1960s it was even "restored" to its "original" skeleton.

12. Robert C. Cumbow, "Survivors: The Day after Doomsday," in *Omni's Screen Flights, Screen Fantasies: The Future According to Science Fiction Cinema*, ed. Danny Peary (Garden City, NJ: Doubleday, 1984), 36.

13. A similar scenario was utilized in Steichen's *Family of Man* exhibit, which placed a mushroom cloud at the end of an exhaustive compilation of the world's people, as if to prompt viewers to action to preserve the harmonious worldview they had just taken in.

14. David L. Altheide, "Fear, Terrorism and Popular Culture," in *Reframing 9/11: Film, Popular Culture and the "War on Terror,"* ed. Jeff Birkenstein, Anna Froula, and Karen Randell (New York: Continuum, 2010), 17.

15. Mulvey, "Visual Pleasure and Narrative Cinema," 26.

16. David Harvey, *A Brief History of Neoliberalism* (New York: Oxford University Press, 2007), 6–7.

17. Barthes, *Camera Lucida*, 77.

18. John Berger, "Understanding a Photograph," in *Classic Essays on Photography*, ed. Alan Trachtenberg (Stony Creek, CT: Leete's Island Books, 1980), 292. Similarly, as Susan Sontag observes, "the identification of the subject of a photograph always dominates our perception of it." Sontag, *On Photography*, 92.

19. Michael Sapir, "The Impossible Photograph: Hippolyte Bayard's Self-Portrait as a Drowned Man," *Modern Fiction Studies* 40, no. 3 (1994): 619.

20. Maria Morris Hambourg and Douglas Eklund, "The Space of History," in *Thomas Struth: 1977–2002*, by Douglas Eklund, Ann Goldstein, Maria Morris Hambourg, and Charles Wylie (New Haven, CT: Yale University Press, 2002), 157.

21. Carole Naggar, "Thomas Struth, 1977–2002," *Aperture* 173 (Fall 2003): 8.

22. Ibid.

23. This dynamic is also legible in the photographer's museum project, which chronicles the interaction between canonical works of art and their viewers. In images such as *Louvre IV, Paris* (1989), the spectators arrange themselves in such a way so as to mimic the organization of the figures in the frame, becoming a kind of *tableau vivant* of the painting that they stand in rapture of. As the frame in the image becomes less an impermeable boundary than a site of exchange, the viewing present slides into that of the image and vice versa. The photograph of this interaction acts as a reflexive document of a certain mode of spectatorship whereby the "shuttl[ing] back and forth between 1819, 1989 and . . . the present of the viewer" is complicit in the destabilization of time. Similarly, in the photograph of Veronese's *The Feast in the House of Levi* in the Gallerie dell'Accademia in Venice, the festivities of the painting spill out into the crowd which surrounds it. The majority of the visitors refuse the fetishizing gaze of the typical museum-goer, which would have them freeze before the image. Instead, they stroll or linger, huddle into groups, and, in general, behave as if partaking in the festivities. In contrast to the rest of the visitors, those figures closest to us are blurred, as if we are visualizing both this transitional state between modes of representation and the temporal collapse that this relation makes possible.

24. Charles Wylie, "A History of Now: The Art of Thomas Struth," in Eklund, Goldstein, Hambourg, and Wylie, *Thomas Struth*, 147.

25. Charles W. Haxthausen, review of *Thomas Struth: Dallas and Los Angeles*, *Burlington Magazine* 144, no. 1194 (September 2002): 586.

26. Situating these images in the larger cinematic history from which they draw will reveal a connection between these temporalities of the empty city and traumatic memory. Indeed, Struth himself has referred to his photographs as "film stills" and has even worked in the moving image format in, for example, his Times Square video portrait series. The influence of the medium is seen in the spectral, luminous quality of his photographs, which are laminated directly to the Plexiglas rather than onto backing material, as well as in their grand scale (many of these works span over nine feet wide), both of which reinforce the connection to a cinematic past where the image of the empty city looms large.

27. Michael Fried, *Why Photography Matters as Art as Never Before* (New Haven, CT: Yale University Press, 2008), 277.

28. Slavoj Žižek, *The Sublime Object of Ideology* (London: Verso, 1989), 65. Bringing to light these contradictory relations (an operation which mirrors the interruption of the disembodied eye of Sartre's voyeur in *Being and Nothingness,* which is suddenly and violently reembodied as an object of another's gaze) engenders a "going-through the fantasy," a process in which "we experience how this fantasy-object (the 'secret') . . . materializes the void of our desire . . . a hole at the center of the symbolic order." In the case of Chernobyl, it is the realization that the condition of "untouched" nature is in fact the product of a uniquely human event (nuclear disaster). By "mirroring" the viewer's absence, the empty city maintains a similar capacity to reveal the underlying conditions of disaster subjectivity which the conventional image and its processes of misrecognition conceal. See also Michel Foucault's discussion of *Las Meninas* in Foucault, *The Order of Things: An Archaeology of the Hu-*

man Sciences (New York: Vintage Books, 1994), 3–16.

29. Ann Goldstein, "Portraits of Self-Reflection," in Eklund, Goldstein, Hambourg, and Wylie, *Thomas Struth,* 169.

30. Ibid.

31. Laura Mulvey, *Death 24x a Second: Stillness and the Moving Image* (London: Reaktion Books, 2006), 57.

32. Noting the diachronic experience that the city prompts in its inhabitants, Andreas Huyssen describes how the urban imaginary often overlays the material city with "memories of what was there before, imagined alternatives to what there is. The strong marks of present space merge in the imaginary with traces of the past, erasures, losses and heterotopias." Huyssen, *Present Pasts: Urban Palimpsests and the Politics of Memory* (Palo Alto, CA: Stanford University Press, 2003), 7.

33. Flusser, *Towards a Philosophy of Photography,* 8–9.

34. Michael Wesely, *Open Shutter* (New York: Museum of Modern Art, 2004), 13.

35. Interestingly, the series was shown at the Queens Museum in New York only months before 9/11.

36. Walter Benjamin, "Little History of Photography," in *Walter Benjamin: Selected Writings; Volume 2; Part 2, 1931–1934,* ed. Michael W. Jennings, Howard Eiland, and Gary Smith (Cambridge, MA: Belknap Press of Harvard University Press, 2005), 527.

37. Wesely is currently photographing the reconstruction of the World Trade Center.

38. Printed underneath the image is a poem which reads, "And from his dream he [the photographer] then arises / The works of art, the camera comprises / Yea, verily Eden is now at hand / Nature works even while we dream of slumberland." The shift of agency from photographer to

camera to nature dramatizes the forfeiture that is made palpable in the interval of the long exposure as well as the naturalizing tendency of the power that follows this operation.

39. See, for example, Lady Eastlake, "A Review in the London Quarterly Review: 1857," in *Photography in Print: Writings from 1816 to the Present*, ed. Vicki Goldberg (Albuquerque: University of New Mexico Press, 1981), 88–99.

40. André Bazin, "The Ontology of the Photographic Image," in *What is Cinema? Volume 1*, ed. and trans. Hugh Gray (Berkeley: University of California Press, 1967), 13.

41. Stanley Cavell, *The World Viewed: Reflections on the Ontology of Film* (Cambridge, MA: Harvard University Press, 1979), 21.

42. Gary Snyder, "What Happens by Itself in Photography?," in *Pursuits of Reason: Essays in Honor of Stanley Cavell*, ed. Ted Cohen, Paul Guyer, and Hilary Putnam (Lubbock: Texas Tech University Press, 1993), 365.

43. For an in-depth discussion of the complexity and the intellectual history of automation and photography, see Diarmuid Costello and Dawn M. Phillips, "Automatism, Causality and Realism: Foundational Problems in the Philosophy of Photography," *Philosophy Compass* 4, no. 1 (January 2009): 1–21. Also see the Summer 2012 special issue of *Critical Inquiry* dedicated to the subject.

44. Nicholas Mirzoeff, *The Right to Look: A Counterhistory of Visuality* (Durham, NC: Duke University Press, 2011), 20.

45. John Johnston, "Machinic Vision," *Critical Inquiry* 26 (Autumn 1999): 27.

46. Samuel Weber, *Targets of Opportunity: On the Militarization of Thinking* (Bronx, NY: Fordham University Press, 2005), 4.

47. Ibid., 5.

48. John Broughton, "The Bomb's-Eye View: Smart Weapons and Military TV," in *Technoscience and Cyberculture*, ed. Stanley Aronowitz, Barbara Martinsons, and Michael Menser, with Jennifer Rich (New York: Routledge, 1995), 140.

49. James Der Derian, "9.11: Before, After, and In Between," accessed April 2, 2014, http://essays.ssrc.org/sept11/essays /der_derian.htm.

50. Nicholas Mirzoeff, *Watching Babylon: The War in Iraq and Global Visual Culture* (New York: Routledge, 2005), 77.

51. Greg Elmer, "A Diagram of Panoptic Surveillance," *New Media & Society* 5, no. 2 (June 2003): 233.

52. Andrew Iliadis, "Interview with McKenzie Wark," *Figure/Ground*, December 15, 2012, http://figureground.org /interview-with-mckenzie-wark/.

53. Rey Chow, *The Age of the World Target: Self-Referentiality in War, Theory, and Comparative Work* (Durham, NC: Duke University Press, 2006), 31.

54. Quoted in Ibid.

55. Quoted in Anton Kaes, "The Cold Gaze: Notes on Mobilization and Modernity," *New German Critique* 59 (Spring–Summer 1993): 106.

56. Lev Manovich, "The Mapping of Space: Perspective, Radar, and 3-D Computer Graphics," accessed April 2, 2014, http://manovich.net/TEXT/mapping .html.

57. Manuel De Landa, *War in the Age of Intelligent Machines* (Cambridge, MA: Zone Books, 1991), 20.

58. Paul Virilio, *War and Cinema: The Logistics of Perception*, trans. Patrick Camiller (London: Verso, 1997).

59. Leo Bersani and Ulysse Dutoit, *Arts of Impoverishment: Beckett, Rothko, Resnais* (Cambridge, MA: Harvard University Press, 1993), 156.

60. Broughton, "The Bomb's-Eye View," 153.

61. Mathias Nilges, "The Aesthetics of Destruction: Contemporary US Cinema and T V Culture," in *Reframing 9/11: Film, Popular Culture and the "War on Terror,"* ed. Jeff Birkenstein, Anna Froula, and Karen Randell (New York: Continuum, 2010), 24. These sentiments are echoed in Fredric Jameson's discussion of *Deliverance* (1972):

> This particular future-history convention, the disappearance of civilization after a historic catastrophe, the reversion to Neolithic life, or feudalism, or isolated food-gathering tribal units, is not necessarily the unalloyed nightmare it may at first seem. It relieves us, indeed, of the obligations of civilization as well, of the burden of repression inherent in the latter, of which Freud's *Civilization and its Discontents* is the classic statement. The end of the world is also the end of this particular world of U.S. monopoly capitalism. As such, the possibility can be just as much a wish fulfillment as a source of alarm; in the event, I think, are both at once, in the unity of a single complex and ambivalent fantasy line.

Fredric Jameson, "History and the Death Wish: *Zardoz* as Open Form," *Jump Cut* 3 (1974): 5–8.

62. Virilio, *War and Cinema*, 10.

63. Greg Miller, "How Our Brains Make Memories," *Smithsonian,* May 2010, http://www.smithsonianmag.com/ science-nature/How-Our-Brains-Make-Memories.html.

64. Bernard Stiegler, *Technics and Time, 3: Cinematic Time and the Question of Malaise,* trans. Stephen Barker (Palo Alto, CA: Stanford University Press, 2010), 8–34.

65. Mark B. N. Hansen, *New Philosophy for New Media* (Cambridge, MA: MIT Press, 2009), 256.

66. Gerry Canavan, "Terror and Mismemory: Resignifying September 11 in *World Trade Center* and *United 93*," in *Portraying 9/11: Essays on Representations in Comics, Literature, Film and Theatre,* ed. Véronique Bragard, Christophe Dony, and Warren Rosenberg (Jefferson, NC: McFarland, 2011), 126–127.

67. Quoted in Alison Rice, *Time Signatures: Contextualizing Contemporary Francophone Autobiographical Writing from the Maghreb* (New York: Lexington Books, 2006), 170.

4. LIGHTS, CAMERA, ICONOCLASM

1. By virtue of this symbolic meaning, Slavoj Žižek regarded the attacks as a shattering of the distinction between the digitized, virtual capitalism of the "first world" and material relations of labor of the "third world" market. Breeching this gap reintroduced the material component into a virtualized sphere of global capital. He explains, "If there is any symbolism in the collapse of the W T C towers, it is not so much the old-fashioned notion of the 'center of financial capitalism,' but, rather, the notion that the two W T C towers stood for the center of the VIRTUAL capitalism, of financial speculations disconnected from the sphere of material production. The shattering impact of the bombings can only be accounted for against the background of the borderline which today separates the digitalized First World from the Third World 'desert of the Real.'" Slavoj Žižek, "Reflections on W T C," October 7, 2001, http://www.lacan.com /reflections.htm.

2. Kevin Matthews and B. J. Novitski, "World Trade Center Destroyed," *Architecture Week,* September 12, 2001, http://

www.architectureweek.com/2001/0912 /today.html.

3. Albert Boime, "Perestroika and the Destabilization of the Soviet Monuments," *ARS*, nos. 2–3 (1993): 211.

4. W. J. T. Mitchell, *Cloning Terror: The War of Images, 9/11 to the Present* (Chicago: University of Chicago Press, 2011), 3.

5. Richard S. Nelson and Margaret Olin, eds., *Monuments and Memory, Made and Unmade*, 205.

6. Umberto Boccioni, "Technical Manifesto of Futurist Sculpture," in *Modern Artists on Art*, ed. Robert L. Herbert (Mineola, NY: Dover, 1999), 45.

7. In his novel *The Marble Faun*, Nathaniel Hawthorne's fictional sculptor bemoans this invincibility, declaring it to be "awful thing . . . this endless endurance, this almost indestructibility." He goes on to explain that the ephemeral quality of life is parodied by this quest for immortality in stone, which is so often not warranted by the life represented. More disconcerting for the sculptor is the way in which the very form prompts a second death of the sitter, as inevitably the future beholder will someday "take our nose between their thumb and fingers (as we have seen men do by Caesar's), and infallibly break it off if they can do so without detection!" Nathaniel Hawthorne, *The Marble Faun; or, The Romance of Monte Beni* (New York: Digireads, 2007), 57.

8. Lawrence Alloway, "The Public Sculpture Problem," *Studio International* 184, no. 948 (1972): 124.

9. Erika Doss, *Memorial Mania: Public Feeling in America* (Chicago: University of Chicago Press, 2010), 316.

10. Robert Musil, "Monuments," in *Posthumous Papers of a Living Author*, trans. Peter Wortsman (Brooklyn, NY: Archipelago Books, 2006), 62. One sees the relationship between the formal properties of permanence and the monument's call to violence in Kanan Makiya's reaction to Saddam Hussein's building campaign of the 1990s. Rather than a meditation on history, the encounter with these statues elicits a fantasy of destruction from the viewer, whose primary reaction is to note the fact that they are supported by "cavernous layers of reinforced concrete buried deep under the ground [and as such] will take more than rope and eager hearts to [be torn down]." Samir al-Khalil, *The Monument: Art, Vulgarity and Responsibility in Iraq* (Berkeley: University of California Press, 1991), 130.

11. See Max Page's *The City's End* for more on the cultural obsession with visualizing the destruction of New York.

12. Ada Louise Huxtable, "Who's Afraid of the Big, Bad Buildings?," *New York Times*, May 29, 1966.

13. Contrast this with, for example, the Woolworth Building, which, in the words of architecture critic Montgomery Schuyler, allowed those on the ground access to the intricate details of its uppermost stories in all their "distinctness and sharpness," despite being the tallest building in the world from 1913 to 1930. Montgomery Schuyler, "The Towers of Manhattan and Notes on the Woolworth Building," *Architectural Record* 33 (February 1913): 111.

14. Lauren Kogod and Michael Osman, "Girding the Grid: Abstraction and Figuration at Ground Zero," *Grey Room* 13 (Autumn 2003): 108–221.

15. David I. Grossvogel, *Scenes in the City: Film Visions of Manhattan before 9/11* (New York: Peter Lang, 2003), 1.

16. As Terry Smith observes, this lack of an ideal or even consistent viewing position in combination with their unprecedented height pushed the towers "beyond scale into immeasurability." Smith, *The*

Architecture of Aftermath (Chicago: University of Chicago Press, 2006), 105.

17. David Simpson claims that the towers "refused the spectator's absorptive gaze." Simpson, *9/11*, 58–59.

18. Eric Darton, *Divided We Stand: A Biography of New York's World Trade Center* (New York: Basic Books, 1999), 4.

19. Jean Baudrillard, *The Spirit of Terrorism*, trans. Chris Turner (London: Verso, 2003), 31.

20. Ibid., 42–43.

21. Echoing these sentiments, Terry Smith describes the towers as "a bland, featureless structure-two of them, in fact, side by side, each of the eight sides being the same as the others-opaque to the external gaze, so basic in shape that they could be any other equally basic shape, so generic in form that anything could occur with them, they could serve any function, all functions being equally abstracted, removed from the life flows around them." Smith, *The Architecture of Aftermath*, 139.

22. Baudrillard, *The Spirit of Terrorism*, 18; Manfredo Tafuri and Francesco Dal Co, *Modern Architecture*, trans. Robert Erich Wolf (New York: Harry N. Abrams, 1979), 366.

23. Mark Wigley, "Insecurity by Design," in *After the World Trade Center: Rethinking New York City*, ed. Michael Sorkin and Sharon Zukin (New York: Routledge, 2002), 78. For most commuters, the lack of visibility that was in some sense built into the facade of the towers would be made literal, as arriving via the subway or PATH train, the more popular means of access, meant entering the structure through the concourse level beneath the ground. Here the concealment of the facade's physicality was simultaneous to a concealment of the city itself. This sabotaging of the viewer's visual hold on the structure then occurred for both modes of approaching the towers, either with the "invisibility" that an encounter with the facade produced, or with the literal concealment that the approach from underground brought with it. In both cases, this operation was continued by the enclosed space of the elevator and the disorientation with regard to the outside that its flight to the 110th story brought with it.

24. Quoted in John Timberman Newcomb, "The Footprint of the Twentieth Century: American Skyscrapers and Modernist Poems," *Modernism/Modernity* 10, no. 1 (2003): 111.

25. Darton, *Divided We Stand*, 149.

26. Ibid.

27. As the visitor left the enclosed space of the elevator, the pressing question was, "Where am I, exactly?" The most obvious way to answer this question was to relate one's position to the facade seen from the ground moments before; however, the visitor could not easily connect his or her current viewing position with the structure as seen from the ground. The elevation and structural solidity of the platform the visitor occupied was, as a result, compromised by this disconnect from the frame of reference established by the streets below.

The John Hancock Center in Chicago offers an interesting contrast here, as the building's signature Xs reappear in the interior view of the observation deck and restaurant, allowing viewers to mentally position themselves with regard to the facade they had taken in moments before. With their exceptional uniformity, the Twin Towers allowed no such frame of reference.

28. Darton, *Divided We Stand*, 149.

29. Sigfried Giedion, *Building in France, Building in Iron, Building in Ferroconcrete*, trans. J. Duncan Berry (Santa Monica, CA: Getty Center for the History of Art and the Humanities, 1995), 91.

30. Ada Louise Huxtable, "World Trade Center: Daintiest Big Buildings in the World," *Telegraph,* April 17, 1973.

31. Flusser, *Towards a Philosophy of Photography,* 67.

32. Angus Kress Gillespie, *Twin Towers: The Life of New York City's World Trade Center* (New Brunswick, NJ: Rutgers University Press, 1999), 165.

33. A trip to Europe, India, and Japan in 1954 had renewed Yamasaki's interest in historical forms, and brought with it a willingness to experiment with ornament.

34. Gillespie, *Twin Towers,* 165.

35. Paul J. C. Friedlander, "The Traveler's World: New York's New View from the Top," *New York Times,* April 9, 1972.

36. Wigley, "Insecurity by Design," 73–74.

37. Roland Barthes, *The Eiffel Tower and Other Mythologies,* trans. Richard Howard (Berkeley: University of California Press, 1997), 237. Skyscrapers such as the Sears Tower, the Empire State Building, and even the World Trade Center were made possible by the system of steel-beam construction. While the Eiffel Tower did not introduce the system, it was certainly one of its most prominent examples.

38. This slogan was repeated in radio campaigns and used in the signage of the observation deck itself.

39. It is interesting to note that many have commented that the sound and smell of the city disappeared atop the tower, while sight remained (albeit radically transformed). In this regard, the use of sound in this commercial is consistent with this logic of deferral, as its representation of the view of the city did not give away the actual experience, whereas it is plausible that a visual representation might.

40. Victor Burgin discusses promotional material generated by mainstream films in terms of partial images that entice

but can only be granted closure by the film itself. Historically, one of the most attractive of these lures has been the film still, an image whose drawing power works upon a scintillating tension between movement and stillness. Echoing an early practice of beginning the film with a frozen image that is then granted movement, the film still draws the spectator to the theater by pointing to a narrative that it cannot provide itself. Similarly, the Port Authority's promotional ads for the observation deck convey the gravity, the qualitative and affective delight of such an experience, without fully presenting the experience itself, as only an actual visit to the Top of the World can provide that. Victor Burgin, *The Remembered Film* (London: Reaktion Books, 2004).

41. Interestingly, plans were made in 1978 for New York Airways to conduct helicopter transport from the roof of the Twin Towers.

42. Quoted in Kari Haskell, "Before & After; Talking of the Towers," *New York Times,* September 16, 2001, http://www.nytimes.com/2001/09/16/weekinreview/before-after-talking-of-the-towers.html.

43. Bruno Latour, "What Is Iconoclash? Or Is There a World beyond the Image Wars?," in *Iconoclash: Beyond the Image Wars in Science, Religion, and Art,* ed. Bruno Latour and Peter Weibel (Cambridge, MA: MIT Press, 2002), 27.

44. The reach of CNN is obviously global. However, rather than universalize the American experience I have chosen to err on the side of caution by limiting the discussion to the stateside audience. It is also important to note that, not coincidentally, Firdos Square was located directly in front of the Palestine Hotel where the journalists had been quartered.

45. Dario Gamboni, "Image to Destroy, Indestructible Image," in Latour and Weibel, *Iconoclash,* 93.

46. Consider, for example, two recent assaults upon a favorite target of contemporary image-breakers: statues of Christopher Columbus. The first involved Russell Means, a Native American activist, who during a protest of the 1989 Columbus Day parade in Denver doused a statue of the explorer in "blood." In the second instance, residents of Providence, Rhode Island, awoke to find that a local statue of the explorer had similarly been covered with red paint in the dead of night and draped with a sign that read "murderer." Not only was Means's desecration performed amidst all of the signs of a formal protest (the bullhorn, the battle cry, the handwritten signs) and by a figure who carried with him a considerable history of activism, but so was its reception colored in large measure by the release of a statement which summarized the reasoning behind his actions. In contrast, the anonymity of the gesture in Providence, combined with its lack of discursive staging, led local newscasters to frame the act in terms of vandalism. Even those residents interviewed who "understood the meaning" and "believed in freedom of expression" were obliged to disapprove of the means by which the message was conveyed. The end result was that Means was acquitted of any charges, based on the First Amendment, and his work was even referred to as a "conceptual art piece"; while police continue to pursue the perpetrators of the act in Providence on charges of "malicious injury to property vandalism." While the destruction of the statue serves as an "incitement to discourse" which to a large degree determines the meaning of the gesture, the image which presents this destruction does much in establishing the terms of the discussion.

47. Boris Groys, *Art Power* (Cambridge, MA: MIT Press, 2008), 75.

48. Anne McClanan and Jeffrey Johnson, "Introduction: 'O for a muse of fire . . . ,'" in *Negating the Image: Case Studies in Iconoclasm,* ed. Anne McClanan and Jeffrey Johnson (Aldershot, UK: Ashgate, 2005), 3.

49. Indeed, the coverage of the event repeatedly suggested that the destructive fervor in Firdos Square, while validating the military action of the United States, threatened to spill out from the square. Lara Logan's report for CBS, for example, juxtaposed the falling of the statues with footage of local Iraqis firing against U.S. troops, reminding the viewer that the city "is still not secure." This connection was reinforced by the tendency of many broadcasts to couch coverage of the incident within reports of the looting of ancient artifacts. All of this suggested that the work of the vandal might contain a nihilistic potentiality which once unleashed might not be so easy to contain.

50. In its entirety, the Firdos Square event lasted a full two hours.

51. Jürgen Habermas, "Interpreting the Fall of a Monument," *Constellations* 10, no. 3 (2003): 364.

52. Quoted in Gamboni, "Image to Destroy, Indestructible Image," 102.

53. Latour, "What Is Iconoclash?," 24n4.

54. Jaś Elsner, "Iconoclasm and the Preservation of Memory," in Nelson and Olin, *Monuments and Memory,* 210. Commenting on the defacement of sculpture that occurred as a result of the Roman practice of *damnatio memoriae,* Elsner describes the surviving work in terms of a "two-directional" quality, which "signals both its predamaged state-a different past, with potentially different cultural, political, and social meanings-and its new or altered state." The concatenation of past and present that the destruction and/or

defacement of these sites invokes is succinctly illustrated by a recent protest in
Venezuela where Hugo Chavez supporters
seized a statue of Columbus, pulling it off
its base with ropes latched around its neck.
Upon being removed from its pedestal,
the statue was tried and found guilty of
initiating the saga "imperialist genocide"
that continues to plague Venezuelans today. On the empty plinth of the statue was
etched a simple equation that summarizes
the historical resonance from which iconoclasm is born: "Bush=Columbus. Out!" In
similar terms, the destruction of the World
Trade Center opens the past to the present, enacting a bifurcation in time through
which contradicting possibilities manifest.
Iconoclasm, in other words, introduces
immanence, a circling of time through
which temporal markers are reevaluated
and reassigned. Yet, as the incident in Firdos Square suggests, this dynamic is itself
often co-opted by and reinscribed within
the same forces that were targeted in the
initial act of destruction.

55. Mitchell, *What Do Pictures Want?*

56. Hawthorne, *The Marble Faun*, 187.

57. As Marc Augé writes, oblivion is
"the life force of memory and remembrance is its product." The most basic
function that memory's correlative other
performs involves making space for new
memories. In the absence of this house-
keeping function, the sheer weight of
the past threatens to overwhelm the rememberer, becoming an exhaustive but
unmanageable archive. More importantly,
in the absence of forgetting, the necessary
selective function of memory is paralyzed.
All of the past is equally accessible without
distinction, creating a maddening simultaneity which Jorge Luis Borges describes
in his short story "Funes, His Memory,"
about the victim of a "perfect" memory:
"The present was so rich, so clear, that it

was almost unbearable, as were his oldest
and even his most trivial memories." As
Funes remembers not only every tree he
had ever seen but every leaf of every tree
and every perception he had of them, he
attempts to whittle down his memory bank
to a mere seventy thousand recollections,
but fails. Marc Augé, *Oblivion*, trans. Marjolijn de Jager (Minneapolis: University
of Minnesota Press, 2004), 5; Jorge Luis
Borges, "Funes, His Memory," in *Collected
Fictions*, trans. Andrew Hurley (New York:
Penguin, 1999), 131–137.

58. Aristotle, for example, describes
recollection as the apprehension of an
outline of a past perception or idea which
has been rendered passive by virtue of its
non-inclusion in the present. Following
Plato's metaphor of wax in *Theaetetus*, the
impression that is presented to the mind in
recollection, according to Aristotle, is not
unlike the indistinct image produced by a
ring pressed into a tablet of wax. Aristotle,
*On the Soul and On Memory and Recol-
lection*, trans. Joe Sachs (Santa Fe, NM:
Green Lion Press, 2001), 170; Plato, *Plato's
Theaetetus with Introduction & Analysis*,
trans. Benjamin Jowett (Rockville, MD:
Serenity, 2008), 157.

59. Friedrich A. Kittler, *Gramophone,
Film, Typewriter*, trans. Geoffrey Winthrop-
Young and Michael Wutz (Palo Alto, CA:
Stanford University Press, 1999), 31.

60. Frances A. Yates, *The Art of Memory*
(Chicago: University of Chicago Press,
2001), 1–2.

5. THE FAILURE OF THE FAILURE OF IMAGES

1. As Rebecca Zurier observes,
"Most accounts trace the invention of the
modern comic strip to the Sunday humor
sections, which were developed as ammu-
nition in the circulation wars waged in the
1890s by the American newspaper tycoons

Joseph Pulitzer and William Randolph Hearst. Entertaining characters, reappearing each Sunday, ensured that loyal readers would buy the paper week after week, providing a steady audience for advertisers." Rebecca Zurier, "Classy Comics," *Art Journal* 50, no. 3 (1991): 98.

2. While there is a great deal of uncertainty as to when the first graphic novel was published, the first self-described works of the genre appeared in the mid-1970s. Examples include Richard Corben's *Bloodstar* (1976) and Jim Steranko's *Red Tide* (1976).

3. Douglas Wolk, *Reading Comics: How Graphic Novels Work and What They Mean* (Boston: Da Capo, 2007), 10.

4. As Spiegelman explains, "The only cultural artifacts that could get past my defenses to flood my eyes and brain with something other than images of burning towers were old comic strips; vital, unpretentious ephemera from the optimistic dawn of the 20th century." Quoted in Kristiaan Versluys, *Out of the Blue: September 11 and the Novel* (New York: Columbia University Press, 2009), 64.

5. This preoccupation continued in the years that followed, as works such as *The 9/11 Report* (2006) and *American Widow* (2008) continued this head-on look at the traumatic events of that day.

6. Groensteen, *La bande dessinée: Un objet non identifié.*

7. Hirsch, "Collateral Damage," 1212.

8. Graham Bader, "Honored in the Breach: Graham Bader on Absence as Memorial," *Artforum* 50 (April 2012): 81–82.

9. Art Spiegelman, *In the Shadow of No Towers* (New York: Pantheon, 2004), 1.

10. Ibid., 2.

11. Patrick M. Bray, "Aesthetics in the Shadow of No Towers: Reading Virilio in the Twenty-First Century," *Yale French Studies* 114 (2008): 15.

12. Anne Whitehead, "Trauma and Resistance in Art Spiegelman's *In the Shadow of No Towers*," in *The Future of Memory*, ed. Richard Crownshaw, Jane Kilby, and Antony Rowland (New York: Berghahn Books, 2010), 234.

13. Hirsch, "Collateral Damage," 1213.

14. Orbán, "Trauma and Visuality," 76.

15. Ibid., 75.

16. Spiegelman, *In the Shadow of No Towers*, 6.

17. Orbán, "Trauma and Visuality," 73.

18. Bray, "Aesthetics in the Shadow of No Towers," 15.

19. Andreas Huyssen, "Of Mice and Mimesis," *New German Critique* 81 (Autumn 2000): 66.

20. Citing a pervasive fear of "aesthetic pollution" that pervades postwar art and architecture, Brett Ashley Kaplan points out that even the initial connection between monumentality and fascism was shaky at best. Not only did the conception of, for example, Speers's monumental architecture predate the Nazi regime by at least a century, but so was there considerable disagreement within the party over the proper form of Nazi art. In fact, many, including Goebbels, were sympathetic to modernist designs despite modernism's eventual demonization in the Degenerate Art Exhibition and other venues. Nonetheless, as Kaplan observes, postwar visual culture continues to operate from the assumption that monumentality is inherently fascistic and for this reason often sabotages its own attempts at history in the process. Brett Ashley Kaplan, *Unwanted Beauty: Aesthetic Pleasure in Holocaust Representation* (Champaign: University of Illinois Press, 2007).

21. Jacques Derrida, "Response to Daniel Libeskind," *Research in Phenomenology* 22 (1992): 92.

22. Kristiaan Versluys, "Art Spiegelman's *In the Shadow of No Towers: 9/11* and the Representation of Trauma," *MFS Modern Fiction Studies* 52, no. 4 (2006): 983.

23. See E. Ann Kaplan's discussion of the way in which 9/11 dredged up memories of the air raids in London during World War II, in her introduction to *Trauma Culture.*

24. Spiegelman, *In the Shadow of No Towers,* 2, 5.

25. Huyssen, "Of Mice and Mimesis," 71.

26. James E. Young, "Memory/Monument," in *Critical Terms for Art History,* ed. Robert S. Nelson and Richard Schiff (Chicago: University of Chicago Press, 2003), 239.

27. Joel McKim, "Agamben at Ground Zero: A Memorial without Content," *Theory, Culture & Society* 25, no. 5 (2008): 87–88.

28. Badiou, *Handbook of Inaesthetics,* trans. Alberto Toscano (Palo Alto, CA: Stanford University Press, 2005), 4–5.

29. Lower Manhattan Development Corporation, "WTC Memorial Jury Statement for Winning Design," January 13, 2004, http://www.wtcsitememorial.org /about_jury_txt.html.

30. "Design Competition," 9/11 Memorial website, accessed April 5, 2014, http:// www.911memorial.org/design-competition.

31. Fred Bernstein, "At the Pentagon, Visions of 184 Pieces for the Missing," *New York Times,* December 22, 2002.

32. Lower Manhattan Development Corporation, "Reflecting Absence," accessed April 6, 2014, http://www.wtcsite memorial.org/fin7.html.

33. Arad does arrange names according to "meaningful adjacencies," but this strategy is not visible to the everyday visitor.

34. Lower Manhattan Development Corporation, "Reflecting Absence."

35. Theodor W. Adorno, "The Meaning of Working through the Past," in *Critical Models: Interventions and Catchwords,* trans. Henry W. Pickford (New York: Columbia University Press, 1998), 89.

36. For a critique of the counter-monument, see Thomas Stubblefield, "Do Disappearing Monuments Simply Disappear? The Counter-Monument in Revision," *Future Anterior* 8, no. 2 (Winter 2011): 1–11.

37. For a broader discussion of the role of the discourse of participation in contemporary art and culture, see Robert Atkins et al., *The Art of Participation;* Claire Bishop, *Artificial Hells: Participatory Art and the Politics of Spectatorship;* Joke Brouwer and Arjen Mulder, eds., *Interact or Die!;* Markus Miessen, *The Nightmare of Participation.*

38. Nicolas Bourriaud, *Relational Aesthetics,* trans. Simon Pleasance and Fronza Woods, with Mathieu Copeland (Dijon-Quetigny: Les presses du réel, 2002), 14.

39. Claire Bishop, "Antagonism and Relational Aesthetics," *October,* no. 110 (Fall 2004): 58.

40. Contrary to Lacan's fully externalized model of subjectivity, Laclau and Mouffe posit more of a middle ground in which the subject exists as a "failed structure" or partial identity.

41. Bishop, "Antagonism and Relational Aesthetics," 66.

42. Brian Massumi, "The Thinking-Feeling of What Happens: A Semblance of a Conversation," in *Interact or Die!,* ed. Joke Brouwer and Arjen Mulder (Rotterdam: NAi, 2007), 77.

43. Ibid., 72.

44. Ibid.

45. Bishop, "Antagonism and Relational Aesthetics," 78.

46. Lower Manhattan Development Corporation, "Virtual Exhibit of All 5,201 Submissions from around the World

Opens," accessed April 6, 2014, http://
www.wtcsitememorial.org/submissions
.html; Lower Manhattan Development
Corporation, "About Us," accessed April 6,
2014, http://www.renewnyc.com/About
Us/index.asp.

47. The 9/11 memorial jury included a
representative of the victims' families, two
political appointees, artists, civic leaders,
and specialists in public art. Among them
were Maya Lin, designer of the Vietnam
Veterans Memorial in Washington, DC,
and former Brown University president
Vartan Gregorian, who now heads the
Carnegie Corporation.

48. Lynne B. Sagalyn, "The Politics of
Planning the World's Most Visible Urban
Redevelopment Project," in *Contentious
City: The Politics of Recovery in New York
City,* ed. John Mollenkopf (New York:
Russell Sage, 2005), 52.

49. McKim, "Agamben at Ground
Zero," 84. Echoing these sentiments,
John Mollenkopf describes the site as
"predesigned."

50. Philip Nobel, *Sixteen Acres: Architecture and the Outrageous Struggle for the
Future of Ground Zero* (New York: Metropolitan Books, 2005), 252.

51. James E. Young, "The Memorial
Process: A Juror's Report from Ground
Zero," in Mollenkopf, *Contentious City,* 161.

52. Michel de Certeau, "Walking in
the City," in *The Practice of Everyday Life,*
trans. Steven Rendall (Berkeley: University of California Press, 1984), 91.

53. Nobel, *Sixteen Acres,* 254.

54. Mitchell, *Cloning Terror,* 90–92.

55. Marie-José Mondzain, "Remembering the Historical Present," *Critical
Inquiry* 33, no. 3 (Spring 2007): 471–494.

56. Nobel, *Sixteen Acres,* 254.

57. "Design Competition."

58. Nobel, *Sixteen Acres,* 252.

59. Ibid.

60. Robert Storr, *September: A History
Painting by Gerhard Richter* (London: Tate,
2011), 52.

61. Going back further to modernism
and the work of Yves Klein and Barnett
Newman, these breaks in representation
were understood in terms of a Kantian
"negative presentation," in many ways
the layover of the romantic sublime. Such
fissures in the image acted as the channel
through which an unrepresentable beyond
was allowed to speak.

62. Kaplan, *Trauma Culture,* 1.

63. Leo Bersani, "Psychoanalysis and
the Aesthetic Subject," *Critical Inquiry*
32, no. 2 (Winter 2006): 173. This failure
to historicize both the category of the
unrepresentable and the conception of
monumentality that it is counterposed
against leads to a contradiction with regard to the origins of the aesthetic strategy
of Jochen Gerz and Esther Shalev-Gerz's
Monument against Fascism (1983). This
work attempted to defy the conventions
of the monument by slowly disappearing
into the ground and by integrating the
residents into its composition. The surface
of the vertical stele was coated with soft
lead as a stylus positioned nearby invited
inscription. When the surface was filled
with markings, the piece was lowered
into the ground to reveal a new surface.
This process continued until the monument disappeared into the ground in 1993.
Ironically, the counter-monument owes its
inception to none other than Lenin, whose
monumental program from 1918 to 1922
called for a "people's art" which would utilize ephemeral, disappearing monuments
as a means to undermine existing tsarist
works. As Albert Boime explains, Lenin
employed this strategy to "liberate monuments from their supernatural look of

frozen solemnity and activate them as humanly accessible agencies advancing the progress of the revolution. Not designed for eternity but for eventual self-destruction." This counterintuitive historical lineage reinforces the formative relation that discourse maintains to the monument, as an almost identical aesthetic strategy can serve opposing ends at different moments in history depending on the way in which its conceptual underpinnings are articulated. Boime, "Perestroika and the Destabilization of the Soviet Monuments," 218.

64. Lisa Saltzman, *Making Memory Matter: Strategies of Remembrance in Contemporary Art* (Chicago: University of Chicago Press, 2006), 20.

CONCLUSION

1. Stallabrass, "Spectacle and Terror," 92.

2. W. J. T. Mitchell, "Poetic Justice: 9-11 to Now," *Critical Inquiry* 38, no. 2 (Winter 2012): 242.

3. Describing this new relation, Slavoj Žižek explains, "The omnipresent invisible threat of terror legitimises the all-too-visible protective measures of defence." Slavoj Žižek, "On 9/11, New Yorkers Faced the Fire in the Minds of Men," *Guardian*, September 10, 2006.

4. Maureen Dowd, "Powell without Picasso," *New York Times*, February 5, 2003.

5. Laura U. Marks, "Invisible Media," in *New Media: Theories and Practices of Digitextuality*, ed. Anna Everett and John T. Caldwell (New York: Routledge, 2003), 34. See also Marks, "Getting Things Unfolded," in *Enfoldment and Infinity: An Islamic Genealogy of New Media Art* (Cambridge, MA: MIT Press, 2010), 1–35.

6. Geoffrey Batchen, "Requiem," *Afterimage*, January/February 2002, 5.

7. On these grounds, Marilyn B. Young claims that "September 11th did not change the world; but it has enabled the Bush administration to pursue, with less opposition and greater violence, policies that might otherwise have appeared too aggressive." Marilyn B. Young, "Ground Zero: Enduring War," in *September 11 in History: A Watershed Moment?*, ed. Mary L. Dudziak (Durham, NC: Duke University Press, 2003), 18. The *September 11 in History* anthology provides a balanced assessment of the question of whether or not 9/11 should be seen as a pivotal transformative moment in history.

8. On March 17, 2011, a U.S. drone struck the Nomada bus station in Pakistan. The Pakistani military estimates that forty-two innocent people were killed.

Bibliography

Abbott, Carl. "The Light on the Horizon: Imagining the Death of American Cities." *Journal of Urban History* 32, no. 2 (2006): 175–196.

"About the wTc: Memorial and Museum; Design." World Trade Center. Accessed March 25, 2014. http://www.wtc .com/about/memorial-and-museum -design.

Adorno, Theodor W. "The Meaning of Working through the Past." In *Critical Models: Interventions and Catchwords*, translated by Henry W. Pickford, 89–122. New York: Columbia University Press, 1998.

Agacinski, Sylviane. *Time Passing: Modernity and Nostalgia*. New York: Columbia University Press, 2003.

Agamben, Giorgio. *Homo Sacer: Sovereign Power and Bare Life*. Translated by Daniel Heller-Roazen. Palo Alto, CA: Stanford University Press, 1998.

Alloway, Lawrence. "The Public Sculpture Problem." *Studio International* 184, no. 948 (1972): 122–125.

Altheide, David L. "Fear, Terrorism and Popular Culture." In *Reframing 9/11: Film, Popular Culture and the "War on Terror,"* edited by Jeff Birkenstein, Anna Froula, and Karen Randell, 11–22. New York: Continuum, 2010.

Aristotle. *On the Soul and On Memory and Recollection*. Translated by Joe Sachs. Santa Fe, NM: Green Lion Press, 2001.

Atkins, Robert, Rudolf Frieling, Boris Groys, and Lev Manovich. *The Art of Participation*. London: Thames & Hudson, 2008.

Augé, Marc. *Oblivion*. Translated by Marjolijn de Jager. Minneapolis: University of Minnesota Press, 2004.

Bachelard, Gaston. *Air and Dreams*. Translated by Edith Farell and Frederick Farell. Dallas, TX: Dallas Institute Publications, 1988.

———. "The Imaginary Fall." In *Air and Dreams*, translated by Edith Farell and Frederick Farell, 95–110. Dallas, TX: Dallas Institute Publications, 1988.

Bader, Graham. "Honored in the Breach: Graham Bader on Absence as Memorial." *Artforum* 50 (April 2012): 81–82.

Badiou, Alain. *Handbook of Inaesthetics*. Translated by Alberto Toscano. Palo Alto, CA: Stanford University Press, 2005.

Baer, Ulrich. *Spectral Evidence: The Photography of Trauma*. Cambridge, MA: MIT Press, 2002.

Banfield, Ann. "The Imperfect of the Object Glass." *Camera Obscura* 8, no. 3 24 (September 1990): 64–87.

Barthes, Roland. *Camera Lucida: Reflections on Photography.* Translated by Richard Howard. New York: Farrar, Straus and Giroux, 1982.

———. "Diderot, Brecht, Eisenstein." *Screen* 15, no. 2 (1974): 69–78.

———. "The Eiffel Tower." In *The Barthes Reader,* translated by Richard Howard, 236–250. New York: Hill & Wang, 1983.

———. *The Eiffel Tower and Other Mythologies.* Translated by Richard Howard. Berkeley: University of California Press, 1997.

Batchen, Geoffrey. "Requiem." *Afterimage,* January/February 2002.

Bate, David. *Photography: The Key Concepts.* New York: Berg, 2009.

Battersby, Christine. "Terror, Terrorism and the Sublime: Rethinking the Sublime after 1789 and 2001." *Postcolonial Studies* 6, no. 1 (April 2003): 67–89.

Baudrillard, Jean. "The Art of Disappearance." In *Art and Artefact,* edited by Nicholas Zurbrugg, 28–31. London: Sage, 1997.

———. "The Evil Demon of Images." In *The Jean Baudrillard Reader,* edited by Steve Redhead, 83–98. New York: Columbia University Press, 2008.

———. "Photographies." The European Graduate School. Accessed April 9, 2014. http://www.egs.edu/faculty/jean -baudrillard/articles/photographies.

———. *Simulacra and Simulation.* Translated by Sheila Faria Glaser. Ann Arbor: University of Michigan Press, 1995.

———. *The Spirit of Terrorism.* Translated by Chris Turner. London: Verso, 2003.

Bazin, André. "The Ontology of the Photographic Image." In *What is Cinema? Volume 1,* edited and translated by Hugh Gray, 9–16. Berkeley: University of California Press, 1967.

Benjamin, Walter. "Little History of Photography." In *Walter Benjamin: Selected Writings; Volume 2; Part 2, 1931–1934,* edited by Michael W. Jennings, Howard Eiland, and Gary Smith, 507–530. Cambridge, MA: Belknap Press of Harvard University Press, 2005.

———. "A Small History of Photography." In *One-Way Street and Other Writings,* translated by Edmund Jephcott and Kingsley Shorter, 240–257. London: New Left Books, 1979 [1931].

———. "The Work of Art in the Age of Mechanical Reproducibility." In *Illuminations: Essays and Reflections,* edited by Hannah Arendt and translated by Harry Zohn, 217–252. New York: Harcourt Brace & World, 1968.

Bennett, Jill. *Practical Aesthetics: Events, Affects and Art after 9/11.* London: I. B. Tauris, 2012.

Berger, John. "Understanding a Photograph." In *Classic Essays on Photography,* edited by Alan Trachtenberg, 291–294. Stony Creek, CT: Leete's Island Books, 1980.

Bernstein, Fred. "At the Pentagon, Visions of 184 Pieces for the Missing." *New York Times,* December 22, 2002.

Bersani, Leo. "Psychoanalysis and the Aesthetic Subject." *Critical Inquiry* 32, no. 2 (Winter 2006): 161–174.

Bersani, Leo, and Ulysse Dutoit. *Arts of Impoverishment: Beckett, Rothko, Resnais.* Cambridge, MA: Harvard University Press, 1993.

Berten, Hans. *The Idea of the Postmodern: A History.* New York: Routledge, 1994.

Bertrand, Donald. "New Furor Sparked by Falling-Bodies Art." *New York Daily News,* September 21, 2002. http://www .nydailynews.com/archives/news/new -furor-sparked-falling-bodies-art -article-1.512008.

Bishop, Claire. "Antagonism and Relational Aesthetics." *October,* no. 110 (Fall 2004): 51–79.

———. *Artificial Hells: Participatory Art and the Politics of Spectatorship*. London: Verso, 2012.

———, ed. *Participation*. Cambridge, MA: MIT Press, 2006.

Blanchot, Maurice. *The Writing of the Disaster*. Translated by Ann Smock. Lincoln: University of Nebraska Press, 1995.

Blumenthal, Karen. *Six Days in October: The Stock Market Crash of 1929*. New York: Atheneum Books for Young Readers, 2002.

Boccioni, Umberto. "Technical Manifesto of Futurist Sculpture." In *Modern Artists on Art*, edited by Robert L. Herbert, 45–51. Mineola, NY: Dover, 1999.

Boime, Albert. "Perestroika and the Destabilization of the Soviet Monuments." *ARS*, nos. 2–3 (1993): 211–226.

Borges, Jorge Luis. "Funes, His Memory." In *Collected Fictions*, translated by Andrew Hurley, 131–137. New York: Penguin, 1999.

Borradori, Giovanna, and Jacques Derrida. *Philosophy in a Time of Terror: Dialogues with Jürgen Habermas and Jacques Derrida*. Chicago: University of Chicago Press, 2003.

Bourriaud, Nicolas. *Relational Aesthetics*. Translated by Simon Pleasance and Fronza Woods, with Mathieu Copeland. Dijon-Quetigny: Les presses du réel, 2002.

Bray, Patrick M. "Aesthetics in the Shadow of No Towers: Reading Virilio in the Twenty-First Century." *Yale French Studies* 114 (2008): 4–17.

Broughton, John. "The Bomb's-Eye View: Smart Weapons and Military TV." In *Technoscience and Cyberculture*, edited by Stanley Aronowitz, Barbara Martinsons, and Michael Menser, with Jennifer Rich, 139–165. New York: Routledge, 1995.

Brouwer, Joke, and Arjen Mulder, eds. *Interact or Die!* Rotterdam: NAi, 2007.

Büchler, Pavel. "Live View." *Philosophy of Photography* 1, no. 1 (2010): 14–17.

Buck-Morss, Susan. "Visual Empire." *Diacritics* 37, nos. 2–3 (2007): 171–198.

Burgin, Victor. *The Remembered Film*. London: Reaktion Books, 2004.

Calvino, Italo. "The Adventures of a Photographer." In *Difficult Loves*, 220–235. New York: Mariner Books, 1985.

Campany, David. "Safety in Numbness: Some Remarks on Problems of Late Photography." In *The Cinematic*, 185–194. Cambridge, MA: MIT Press, 2007.

Canavan, Gerry. "Terror and Mismemory: Resignifying September 11 in *World Trade Center* and *United 93*." In *Portraying 9/11: Essays on Representations in Comics, Literature, Film and Theatre*, edited by Véronique Bragard, Christophe Dony, and Warren Rosenberg, 118–133. Jefferson, NC: McFarland, 2011.

Cantor, Eddie. *Caught Short! A Saga of Wailing Wall Street*. Whitefish, MT: Kessinger, 2003. First published 1929 by Simon & Schuster.

Cartier-Bresson, Henri. *The Decisive Moment*. New York: Simon & Schuster, 1952.

Cavell, Stanley. *The World Viewed: Reflections on the Ontology of Film*. Cambridge, MA: Harvard University Press, 1979.

Chow, Rey. *The Age of the World Target: Self-Referentiality in War, Theory, and Comparative Work*. Durham, NC: Duke University Press, 2006.

Churchill, Winston S. *The Great Republic: A History of America*. New York: Modern Library, 2000.

Corben, Richard. *Bloodstar*. Paddington: Ariel Books, 1976.

Costello, Diarmuid, and Dawn M. Phillips. "Automatism, Causality, and

Realism: Foundational Problems in the Philosophy of Photography." *Philosophy Compass* 4, no. 1 (January 2009): 1–21.

Crary, Jonathan. "Eclipse of the Spectacle." In *Art after Modernism: Rethinking Representation,* edited by Brian Wallis, 283–294. New York: New Museum of Contemporary Art, 1984.

Crowther, Paul. *The Kantian Sublime: From Morality to Art.* New York: Oxford University Press, 1989.

Cumbow, Robert C. "Survivors: The Day after Doomsday." In *Omni's Screen Flights, Screen Fantasies: The Future According to Science Fiction Cinema,* edited by Danny Peary, 35–42. Garden City, NJ: Doubleday, 1984.

Cumins, Robert. *Running toward Danger: Stories behind the Breaking News of 9/11.* New York: Rowman & Littlefield, 2002.

Darton, Eric. *Divided We Stand: A Biography of New York's World Trade Center.* New York: Basic Books, 1999.

Davis, Whitney. *A General Theory of Visual Culture.* Princeton, NJ: Princeton University Press, 2011.

de Certeau, Michel. " *The Practice of Everyday Life.* Translated by Steven Rendall. Berkeley: University of California Press, 1984.

———. Walking in the City." In *The Practice of Everyday Life,* translated by Steven Rendall, 91–110. Berkeley: University of California Press, 1984.

De Landa, Manuel. *War in the Age of Intelligent Machines.* Cambridge, MA: Zone Books, 1991.

Debord, Guy. *The Society of the Spectacle.* Translated by Fredy Perlman and Jon Supak. Detroit: Black & Red, 1970.

———. *The Society of the Spectacle.* Translated by Donald Nicholson-Smith. New York: Zone Books, 1994.

———. *Society of the Spectacle.* Detroit: Black & Red, 2000.

Deleuze, Gilles. *Cinema 1: The Movement-Image.* Translated by Hugh Tomlinson and Barbara Habberjam. Minneapolis: University of Minnesota Press, 1986.

———. *Francis Bacon: The Logic of Sensation.* Minneapolis: University of Minnesota Press, 2005.

DeLillo, Don. *White Noise.* New York: Penguin, 1999. First published 1985 by Viking.

Der Derian, James. "9.11: Before, After, and In Between." Accessed April 2, 2014. http://essays.ssrc.org/sept11/essays/der_derian.htm.

Derrida, Jacques. "Response to Daniel Libeskind." *Research in Phenomenology* 22 (1992): 88–94.

———. *The Truth in Painting.* Translated by Geoff Bennington and Ian McLeod. Chicago: University of Chicago Press, 1987.

"Design Competition." 9/11 Memorial website. Accessed April 5, 2014. http://www.911memorial.org/design-competition.

Deutsche, Rosalyn. *Evictions.* Cambridge, MA: MIT Press, 1996.

Doss, Erika. *The Emotional Life of Contemporary Public Memorials: Towards a Theory of Temporary Memorials.* Amsterdam: Amsterdam University Press, 2008.

———. *Memorial Mania: Public Feeling in America.* Chicago: University of Chicago Press, 2010.

Douglas, George H. *Skyscrapers: A Social History of the Very Tall Building.* Jefferson, NC: McFarland, 2004.

Dowd, Maureen. "Powell without Picasso." *New York Times,* February 5, 2003.

Drucker, Johanna. "Temporal Photography." *Philosophy of Photography* 1, no. 1 (2010): 22–28.

Durden, Mark. "Documentary Pictorial." In *Picturing Atrocity: Photography in*

Crisis, edited by Geoffrey Batchen, Mick Gidley, Nancy K. Miller, and Jay Prosser, 241–248. London: Reaktion Books, 2012.

Eastlake, Lady. "A Review in the London Quarterly Review: 1857." In *Photography in Print: Writings from 1816 to the Present,* edited by Vicki Goldberg, 88–99. Albuquerque: University of New Mexico Press, 1981.

Edwards, Griffith. "Jack London." *Alcohol and Alcoholism* 2, no. 1 (1965): 27–29.

Elkins, James. *Visual Studies: A Skeptical Introduction.* New York: Routledge, 2003.

Elmer, Greg. "A Diagram of Panoptic Surveillance." *New Media & Society* 5, no. 2 (June 2003): 231–247.

Elsner, Jaś. "Iconoclasm and the Preservation of Memory." In *Monuments and Memory, Made and Unmade,* edited by Robert S. Nelson and Margaret Olin, 209–232. Chicago: University of Chicago Press, 2003.

Flusser, Vilém. *Towards a Philosophy of Photography.* Translated by Anthony Mathews. London: Reaktion Books, 1983.

Foster, Hal. "September 11th." *Art Forum,* January 2012.

Foster, Hal, Iain Boal, T. J. Clark, Joseph Matthews, and Michael Watts. "An Exchange on *Afflicted Powers: Capital and Spectacle in a New Age of War.*" *October,* no. 115 (Winter 2006): 3–12.

Foucault, Michel. *Discipline and Punish: The Birth of the Prison.* New York: Vintage Books, 1995.

———. *The Order of Things: An Archaeology of the Human Sciences.* New York: Vintage Books, 1994.

Frank, Manfred. *What is Neostructuralism?* Translated by Richard Gray and Sabine Wilk. Minneapolis: University of Minnesota Press, 1989.

Freud, Sigmund. *Civilization and Its Discontents.* Oregon: Rough Draft Printing, 2013.

———. *The Interpretation of Dreams.* New York: Basic Books, 2010.

Freund, Charles Paul. "The Art of Terror." *San Francisco Chronicle,* October 6, 2002. http://www.sfgate.com/opinion/article/The-art-of-terror-2764708.php.

Fried, Michael. *Why Photography Matters as Art as Never Before.* New Haven, CT: Yale University Press, 2008.

Friedlander, Paul J. C. "The Traveler's World: New York's New View from the Top." *New York Times,* April 9, 1972.

Friend, David. *Watching the World Change: The Stories behind the Images of 9/11.* New York: Picador, 2011.

Gallop, Jane. *Living with His Camera.* Durham, NC: Duke University Press, 2003.

Gamboni, Dario. *The Destruction of Art: Iconoclasm and Vandalism since the French Revolution.* London: Reaktion Books, 2007.

———. "Image to Destroy, Indestructible Image." In *Iconoclash: Beyond the Image Wars in Science, Religion, and Art,* edited by Bruno Latour and Peter Weibel, 88–135. Cambridge, MA: MIT Press, 2002.

Giedion, Sigfried. *Building in France, Building in Iron, Building in Ferroconcrete.* Translated by J. Duncan Berry. Santa Monica, CA: Getty Center for the History of Art and the Humanities, 1995.

Gillespie, Angus Kress. *Twin Towers: The Life of New York City's World Trade Center.* New Brunswick, NJ: Rutgers University Press, 1999.

Giroux, Henry A. *Beyond the Spectacle of Terrorism: Global Uncertainty and the Challenge of the New Media.* St. Paul, MN: Paradigm, 2006.

Glanz, James, and Eric Lipton. *City in the Sky: The Rise and Fall of the World Trade Center.* New York: Times Books, 2003.

Goldberg, Ariel. "Letters to Robert Gober and Ehren Tool." *Very Small Kitchen Sink,* March 28, 2012. http://verysmallkitchen .com/2012/03/28/vsk-project-ariel-gold berg-letters-to-gober-and-tool/.

Goldstein, Ann. "Portraits of Self-Reflection." In *Thomas Struth: 1977–2002,* by Douglas Eklund, Ann Goldstein, Maria Morris Hambourg, and Charles Wylie, 166–173. New Haven, CT: Yale University Press, 2002.

Green, Tyler. "9/11 Wrap-Up with Paul Schimmel." *Blouin ArtInfo,* September 2007. http://de.blouinartinfo.com/blog /tyler-green-modern-art-notes/911-wrap -up-with-paul-schimmel.

Groensteen, Thierry. *La bande dessinée: Un objet culturel non identifié.* Mouthiers-sur-Boëme: Éditions de l'An 2, 2006.

Grossvogel, David I. *Scenes in the City: Film Visions of Manhattan before 9/11.* New York: Peter Lang, 2003.

Groys, Boris. *Art Power.* Cambridge, MA: MIT Press, 2008.

Gunnell, D., and M. Nowers. "Suicide by Jumping." *Acta Psychiatrica Scandinavica* 96, no. 1 (July 1997): 1–6.

Habermas, Jürgen. "Interpreting the Fall of a Monument." *Constellations* 10, no. 3 (2003): 364–370.

Hambourg, Maria Morris, and Douglas Eklund. "The Space of History." In *Thomas Struth: 1977–2002,* by Douglas Eklund, Ann Goldstein, Maria Morris Hambourg, and Charles Wylie, 156–165. New Haven, CT: Yale University Press, 2002.

Hansen, Mark B. N. *New Philosophy for New Media.* Cambridge, MA: MIT Press, 2009.

Harvey, David. *A Brief History of Neoliberalism.* New York: Oxford University Press, 2007.

Haskell, Kari. "Before & After; Talking of the Towers." *New York Times,* September 16, 2001. http://www.nytimes.com /2001/09/16/weekinreview/before -after-talking-of-the-towers.html.

Hawthorne, Nathaniel. *The Marble Faun; or, The Romance of Monte Beni.* New York: Digireads, 2007. First published 1860 by Ticknor & Fields.

Haxthausen, Charles W. Review of *Thomas Struth: Dallas and Los Angeles. Burlington Magazine* 144, no. 1194 (September 2002): 585–587.

Hegel, Georg. *The Philosophy of Art: Being the Second Part of Hegel's Aesthetik, in which are Unfolded Historically the Three Great Fundamental Phases of the Art-Activity of the World* (New York: Appleton, 1879), 89.

Heidegger, Martin. *The Question concerning Technology and Other Essays.* New York: Harper Torch Books, 1982.

Heller, Dana. *The Selling of 9/11: How a National Tragedy Became a Commodity.* New York: Palgrave Macmillan, 2005.

Hirsch, Marianne. "Collateral Damage." *PMLA* 119, no. 4 (2004): 1209–1215.

"Hollywood Caught in a Quandary." Fox News, September 27, 2001. http://www .foxnews.com/story/2001/09/27 /hollywood-caught-in-quandary/.

Horkheimer, Max, and Theodor W. Adorno. "The Culture Industry: Enlightenment." In *Dialectic of Enlightenment,* 120–167. New York: Continuum, 1998.

Hoskins. Andrew, and Ben O'Loughlin. *War and Media: The Emergence of Diffused War.* London: Polity Books, 2010.

Huxtable, Ada Louise. "Big but Not So Bold: Trade Center Towers Are Tallest, but Architecture Is Smaller Scale." *New York Times,* April 5, 1973.

———. "Who's Afraid of the Big, Bad Buildings?" *New York Times,* May 29, 1966.

———. "World Trade Center: Daintiest Big Buildings in the World." *Telegraph*, April 17, 1973.

Huyssen, Andreas. "Of Mice and Mimesis." *New German Critique* 81 (Autumn 2000): 63–86.

———. *Present Pasts: Urban Palimpsests and the Politics of Memory*. Palo Alto, CA: Stanford University Press, 2003.

Iliadis, Andrew. "Interview with McKenzie Wark." *Figure/Ground*, December 15, 2012. http://figureground.org/interview-with-mckenzie-wark/.

InfoTrends. "Digital Camera Sales Capture 21% of Worldwide Camera Market in 2001." September 25, 2001. http://www.capv.com/public/Content/Press/2001/09.25.2001.html.

Jacobus, Mary. *The Poetics of Psychoanalysis: In the Wake of Klein*. New York: Oxford University Press, 2006.

Jameson, Fredric. "History and the Death Wish: *Zardoz* as Open Form." *Jump Cut* 3 (1974): 5–8.

Johnston, John. "Machinic Vision." *Critical Inquiry* 26 (Autumn 1999): 27–48.

Kaes, Anton. "The Cold Gaze: Notes on Mobilization and Modernity." *New German Critique* 59 (Spring–Summer 1993): 105–117.

Kan, Leslie. "Spectacle." University of Chicago: Theories of Media; Keywords Glossary. Accessed November 13, 2013. http://csmt.uchicago.edu/glossary2004/spectacle.htm.

Kaplan, Brett Ashley. *Unwanted Beauty: Aesthetic Pleasure in Holocaust Representation*. Champaign: University of Illinois Press, 2007.

Kaplan, E. Ann. "A Camera and a Catastrophe: Reflections on Trauma and the Twin Towers." In *Trauma at Home: After 9/11*, edited by Judith Greenberg, 95–106. Lincoln: University of Nebraska Press, 2003.

———. *Trauma Culture: The Politics of Terror and Loss in Media and Literature*. New Brunswick, NJ: Rutgers University Press, 2005.

Kazan, Elia. *America, America*. New York: Popular Library, 1962.

Khalil, Samir al-. *The Monument: Art, Vulgarity and Responsibility in Iraq*. Berkeley: University of California Press, 1991.

Kittler, Friedrich A. *Gramophone, Film, Typewriter*. Translated by Geoffrey Winthrop-Young and Michael Wutz. Palo Alto, CA: Stanford University Press, 1999.

———. *Optical Media*. Translated by Anthony Enns. Cambridge: Polity, 2009.

———. "The World of the Symbolic – A World of the Machine." In *Literature, Media, Information Systems*, edited by John Johnston, 130–146. New York: Routledge, 2012.

Kleinfield, N. R. "A Creeping Horror." *New York Times*, September 12, 2001.

Kogod, Lauren, and Michael Osman. "Girding the Grid: Abstraction and Figuration at Ground Zero." *Grey Room* 13 (Autumn 2003): 108–221.

Latour, Bruno. "What Is Iconoclash? Or Is There a World beyond the Image Wars?" In *Iconoclash: Beyond the Image Wars in Science, Religion, and Art*, edited by Bruno Latour and Peter Weibel, 14–37. Cambridge, MA: MIT Press, 2002.

Lefebvre, Henri. *The Production of Space*. New York: Wiley-Blackwell, 1974.

London, Jack. *Before Adam*. North Hollywood, CA: Aegypan, 1906.

Lott, Tim. "She Killed Herself, I Didn't: Why?" *Times* (London), January 6, 2006.

Lower Manhattan Development Corporation. "About Us." Accessed April 6, 2014. http://www.renewnyc.com/AboutUs/index.asp.

———. "Reflecting Absence." Accessed
April 6, 2014. http://www.wtcsite
memorial.org/fin7.html.

———. "Virtual Exhibit of All 5,201
Submissions from around the World
Opens." Accessed April 6, 2014. http://
www.wtcsitememorial.org/submissions
.html.

———. "WTC Memorial Jury Statement
for Winning Design." January 13, 2004.
http://www.wtcsitememorial.org/about
_jury_txt.html.

Luke, Carmen. "As Seen on TV or Was
That My Phone? 'New' Media Literacy."
In *Media/Cultural Studies: Critical Ap-
proaches,* edited by Rhonda Hammer
and Douglas Kellner, 194–205. Bern:
Peter Lang, 2009.

Manovich, Lev. "Macrocinema: Spatial
Montage." 2001. http://manovich.net
/macrocinema.doc.

———. "The Mapping of Space: Perspective, Radar, and 3-D Computer Graphics." Accessed April 2, 2014. http://
manovich.net/TEXT/mapping.html.

Marks, Laura U. "Getting Things Unfolded." In *Enfoldment and Infinity: An Islamic Genealogy of New Media Art,* 1–35.
Cambridge, MA: MIT Press, 2010.

———. "Invisible Media." In *New Media:
Theories and Practices of Digitextuality,*
edited by Anna Everett and John T.
Caldwell, 3–46. New York: Routledge,
2003.

Martin, Rebecca. "New Mad Men Poster
Sparks 9/11 Controversy: Is the Ad Insensitive?" *Wetpaint,* January 19, 2012.
http://www.wetpaint.com/news
/articles/new-mad-men-poster-sparks
-911-controversy-is-the-ad-insensitive-.

Massumi, Brian. "The Thinking-Feeling of
What Happens: A Semblance of a Con-
versation." In *Interact or Die!,* edited by
Joke Brouwer and Arjen Mulder, 70–97.
Rotterdam: NAi, 2007.

Matthews, Kevin, and B. J. Novitski.
"World Trade Center Destroyed."
Architecture Week, September 12, 2001.
http://www.architectureweek.com
/2001/0912/today.html.

McClanan, Anne, and Jeffrey Johnson.
"Introduction: 'O for a muse of fire . . .'"
In *Negating the Image: Case Studies in
Iconoclasm,* edited by Anne McClanan
and Jeffrey Johnson, 1–12. Aldershot,
UK: Ashgate, 2005.

McKim, Joel. "Agamben at Ground Zero:
A Memorial without Content." *Theory,
Culture & Society* 25, no. 5 (2008):
83–103.

Melnick, Jeffrey. *9/11 Culture: America
under Construction.* New York: Wiley-
Blackwell, 2009.

Miessen, Markus. *The Nightmare of Participation.* Berlin: Sternberg, 2011.

Miller, Greg. "How Our Brains Make
Memories." *Smithsonian,* May 2010.
http://www.smithsonianmag.com
/science-nature/How-Our-Brains
-Make-Memories.html.

Mirzoeff, Nicholas. *An Introduction to
Visual Culture.* New York: Routledge,
2009.

———. *The Right to Look: A Counterhistory of Visuality.* Durham, NC: Duke
University Press, 2011.

———. "The Subject of Visual Culture."
In *The Visual Culture Reader,* edited by
Nicholas Mirzoeff, 3–23. New York:
Routledge, 2012.

———. *Watching Babylon: The War in Iraq
and Global Visual Culture.* New York:
Routledge, 2005.

Misrach, Richard. Interview by Robert
Ayers. *Blouin ArtInfo,* January 30, 2008.
http://www.artinfo.com/news/story
/26514/richard-misrach/.

Mitchell, W. J. T. *Cloning Terror: The War
of Images, 9/11 to the Present.* Chicago:
University of Chicago Press, 2011.

———. "The Pictorial Turn." *Artforum* 30, no. 7 (March 1992): 89–95.

———. "Poetic Justice: 9-11 to Now." *Critical Inquiry* 38, no. 2 (Winter 2012): 241–249.

———. *What Do Pictures Want? The Lives and Loves of Images.* Chicago: University of Chicago Press, 2004.

Mondzain, Marie-José. "Can Images Kill?" *Critical Inquiry* 36, no. 1 (2009): 20–51.

———. "Iconic Space and the Rule of Lands." *Hypatia* 15, no. 4 (Autumn 2000): 58–76.

———. *Image, Icon, Economy: The Byzantine Origins of the Contemporary Imaginary.* Palo Alto, CA: Stanford University Press, 2004.

———. "Remembering the Historical Present." *Critical Inquiry* 33, no. 3 (Spring 2007): 471–494.

Montgomery Schuyler. "The Towers of Manhattan and Notes on the Woolworth Building." *Architectural Record* 33 (February 1913): 98–122.

Morris, Gary. "Crossing the Bridge." *Bright Lights,* August 2005. http://brightlightsfilm.com/49/joy.php.

Morris, Meaghan. "Banality in Cultural Studies." *Discourse: Journal for Theoretical Studies in Media and Culture* 10, no. 2 (1988): 14–43.

Mulvey, Laura. *Death 24x a Second: Stillness and the Moving Image.* London: Reaktion Books, 2006.

———. "Visual Pleasure and Narrative Cinema." In *Visual and Other Pleasures (Theories of Representation and Difference),* 14–26. Bloomington: Indiana University Press, 1989.

Musil, Robert. "Monuments." In *Posthumous Papers of a Living Author,* translated by Peter Wortsman, 61–64. Brooklyn, NY: Archipelago Books, 2006.

Naggar, Carole. "Thomas Struth, 1977–2002." *Aperture* 173 (Fall 2003): 6–8.

Nelson, Robert S., and Margaret Olin, eds. *Monuments and Memory, Made and Unmade.* Chicago: University of Chicago Press, 2003.

Newcomb, John Timberman. "The Footprint of the Twentieth Century: American Skyscrapers and Modernist Poems." *Modernism/Modernity* 10, no. 1 (2003): 97–125.

Newseum, Cathy Trost, and Alicia Shepard. *Running toward Danger: Stories Behind the Breaking News of 9/11.* Lanham, MD: Rowman & Littlefield, 2002.

Nilges, Mathias. "The Aesthetics of Destruction: Contemporary US Cinema and TV Culture." In *Reframing 9/11: Film, Popular Culture and the "War on Terror,"* edited by Jeff Birkenstein, Anna Froula, and Karen Randell, 22–33. New York: Continuum, 2010.

Nobel, Philip. *Sixteen Acres: Architecture and the Outrageous Struggle for the Future of Ground Zero.* New York: Metropolitan Books, 2005.

North, Michael. "Introduction." In *The Final Sculpture: Public Monuments and Modern Poets,* 17–39. Ithaca, NY: Cornell University Press, 1985.

Olin, Margaret. *Touching Photographs.* Chicago: University of Chicago Press, 2012.

Orbán, Katalin. "Trauma and Visuality: Art Spiegelman's *Maus* and *In the Shadow of No Towers.*" *Representations* 97, no. 77 (Winter 2007): 57–89.

Orozco, José Clemente. *José Clemente Orozco: An Autobiography.* Austin: University of Texas Press, 1962.

Page, Max. *The City's End: Two Centuries of Fantasies, Fears, and Premonitions of New York's Destruction.* New Haven, CT: Yale University Press, 2008.

Plato. *Plato's Theaetetus with Introduction & Analysis.* Translated by Benjamin Jowett. Rockville, MD: Serenity, 2008.

Quan, Roy. "Photography and the Creation of Meaning." *Art Education* 32, no. 2 (February 1979): 4–9.

Rancière, Jacques. "Are Some Things Unrepresentable?" In *The Future of the Image,* translated by Gregory Elliott, 109–138. London: Verso, 2007.

Rastogi, Nina. "Wall Street Suicides." *Slate,* September 22, 2008. http://www.slate.com/id/2200633/.

Retort. *Afflicted Powers: Capital and Spectacle in a New Age of War.* London: Verso, 2005.

Rice, Alison. *Time Signatures: Contextualizing Contemporary Francophone Autobiographical Writing from the Maghreb.* New York: Lexington Books, 2006.

Rich, Frank. "Whatever Happened to the America of 9/12?" *New York Times,* September 10, 2006.

Riegl, Alois. "The Modern Cult of Monuments: Its Character and Its Origins." Translated by Kurt Forster and Diane Ghirardo. *Oppositions* 25 (Fall 1982): 21–51. First published as *Der moderne Denkmalkultus: Sein Wesen und seine Entstehung.* Vienna: W. Braumüller, 1903.

Roberts, John. "Photography and the Photograph: Event, Archive and the Non-Symbolic." *Oxford Art Journal* 32, no. 2 (2009): 281–298.

Rogers, Bob. "Photography and the Photographic Image." *Art Journal* 38, no 1 (Autumn 1978): 29–35.

Rogers, Will. "Daily Telegram #1013." October 4, 1929.

Rogoff, Irit. "Studying Visual Culture." In *The Visual Culture Reader,* edited by Nicholas Mirzoeff, 24–36. New York: Routledge, 2012.

Rosenblum, Barbara. *Photographers at Work: A Sociology of Photographic Styles.* Teaneck, NJ: Holmes & Meier, 1978.

Rossi, Aldo. *The Architecture of the City.* Cambridge, MA: MIT Press, 1984.

Sagalyn, Lynne B. "The Politics of Planning the World's Most Visible Urban Redevelopment Project." In *Contentious City: The Politics of Recovery in New York City,* edited by John Mollenkopf, 23–72. New York: Russell Sage, 2005.

Saltzman, Lisa. *Making Memory Matter: Strategies of Remembrance in Contemporary Art.* Chicago: University of Chicago Press, 2006.

Sapir, Michael. "The Impossible Photograph: Hippolyte Bayard's Self-Portrait as a Drowned Man." *Modern Fiction Studies* 40, no. 3 (1994): 619–629.

Sartre, Jean-Paul. *Being and Nothingness.* New York: Washington Square Press, 1993.

Schmidt, John F. "Imaginary History." January 20, 2001. http://www.conservativetruth.org/archives/john-schmidt/01-20-02.shtml.

Shaviro, Steven. *Post-Cinematic Affect.* London: Zero Books, 2010.

Shepherd, William. "Eyewitness at the Triangle." Remembering the 1911 Triangle Factory Fire. Accessed May 14, 2014. http://www.ilr.cornell.edu/trianglefire/primary/testimonials/ootss_williamshepherd.html.

Simpson, David. *9/11: The Culture of Commemoration.* Chicago: University of Chicago Press, 2006.

Sipser, Walter. "It's Me in That 9/11 Photo." *Slate,* September 12, 2006. http://www.slate.com/articles/news_and_politics/culturebox/2006/09/its_me_in_that_911_photo.html.

Smith, Terry. *The Architecture of Aftermath.* Chicago: University of Chicago Press, 2006.

Snyder, Gary. "What Happens by Itself in Photography?" In *Pursuits of Reason: Essays in Honor of Stanley Cavell,* edited by Ted Cohen, Paul Guyer, and Hilary

Putnam, 361–373. Lubbock: Texas Tech University Press, 1993.

Sobchack, Vivian. "Cities on the Edge of Time: The Urban Science-Fiction Film." In *Alien Zone II: The Spaces of Science Fiction Cinema,* edited by Annette Kuhn, 123–143. London: Verso, 1999.

Sontag, Susan. "The Imagination of Disaster." *Commentary,* October 1965.

———. *On Photography.* New York: Farrar, Straus and Giroux, 1977.

Spiegelman, Art. *In the Shadow of No Towers.* New York: Pantheon, 2004.

Spivak, Gayatri Chakrovorty. *In Other Worlds: Essays in Cultural Politics.* New York: Routledge, 2006.

Stallabrass, Julian. "Spectacle and Terror." *New Left Review* 37 (January–February 2006): 87–106.

Steranko, Jim. *Red Tide.* New York: G. P. Putnam's Sons, 1976.

Stiegler, Bernard. *Technics and Time, 3: Cinematic Time and the Question of Malaise.* Translated by Stephen Barker. Palo Alto, CA: Stanford University Press, 2010.

Storr, Robert. *September: A History Painting by Gerhard Richter.* London: Tate, 2011.

Stubblefield, Thomas. "Do Disappearing Monuments Simply Disappear? The Counter-Monument in Revision." *Future Anterior* 8, no. 2 (Winter 2011): 1–11.

"Suicide Leaps from Twenty-First Story." *New York Times,* April 2, 1904.

Sutton, Damian. "Real Photography." In *The State of the Real: Aesthetics in the Digital Age,* edited by Damian Sutton, Susan Brind, and Ray McKenzie, 162–171. London: I. B. Tauris, 2007.

Tafuri, Manfredo, and Francesco Dal Co. *Modern Architecture.* Translated by Robert Erich Wolf. New York: Harry N. Abrams, 1979.

Torres, Alissa. *American Widow.* New York: Villard, 2008.

Versluys, Kristiaan. "Art Spiegelman's *In the Shadow of No Towers:* 9/11 and the Representation of Trauma." *MFS Modern Fiction Studies* 52, no. 4 (2006): 980–1003.

———. *Out of the Blue: September 11 and the Novel.* New York: Columbia University Press, 2009.

Virilio, Paul. *War and Cinema: The Logistics of Perception.* Translated by Patrick Camiller. London: Verso, 1997.

Wark, McKenzie. *The Spectacle of Disintegration: Situationist Passages out of the Twentieth Century.* London: Verso, 2013.

Weber, Samuel. *Targets of Opportunity: On the Militarization of Thinking.* Bronx, NY: Fordham University Press, 2005.

———. "War, Terrorism, and Spectacle: On Towers and Caves." *South Atlantic Quarterly* 101, no. 3 (Summer 2002): 449–458.

Wellbery, David. *Lessing's Laocoon: Semiotics and Aesthetics in the Age of Reason.* Cambridge: Cambridge University Press, 2009.

Wells, Liz. *Photography: A Critical Introduction.* New York: Routledge, 2004.

Wesely, Michael. *Open Shutter.* New York: Museum of Modern Art, 2004.

White, Mimi. "Site Unseen: An Analysis of CNN's War in the Gulf." In *Seeing through the Media: The Persian Gulf War,* edited by Susan Jeffords and Lauren Rabinovitz, 121–141. New Brunswick, NJ: Rutgers University Press, 1994.

Whitehead, Anne. "Trauma and Resistance in Art Spiegelman's *In the Shadow of No Towers.*" In *The Future of Memory,* edited by Richard Crownshaw, Jane Kilby, and Antony Rowland, 233–244. New York: Berghahn Books, 2010.

Wigley, Mark. "Insecurity by Design." In *After the World Trade Center: Rethinking New York City,* edited by Michael Sorkin and Sharon Zukin, 69–85. New York: Routledge, 2002.

Williams, Raymond. "Programming as Sequence or Flow." In *Television: Technology and Cultural Form*, 86–96. London: Fontana, 1974.

Willis, Susan. *Portents of the Real: A Primer for Post-9/11 America*. London: Verso, 2005.

Winnicott, D. W. *The Maturational Processes and the Facilitating Environment: Studies in the Theory of Emotional Development*. London: Hogarth, 1965.

——. *Psycho-Analytic Explorations*. Edited by Clare Winnicott, Ray Sheperd, and Madeleine Davis. Cambridge: Harvard University Press, 1992.

Wolk, Douglas. *Reading Comics: How Graphic Novels Work and What They Mean*. Boston: Da Capo, 2007.

Wollen, Peter. "Fire and Ice." *Photographies* 4 (March 1984): 118–120.

Wright, Terence. *The Photography Handbook*. New York: Routledge, 1999.

Wyatt, David. "*September 11* and Postmodern Memory." *Arizona Quarterly* 65, no. 4 (Winter 2009): 139–161.

Wylie, Charles. "A History of Now: The Art of Thomas Struth." In *Thomas Struth: 1977–2002*, by Douglas Eklund, Ann Goldstein, Maria Morris Hambourg, and Charles Wylie, 147–150. New Haven, CT: Yale University Press, 2002.

Yates, Frances A. *The Art of Memory*. Chicago: University of Chicago Press, 2001.

Young, James E. "The Memorial Process: A Juror's Report from Ground Zero." In *Contentious City: The Politics of Recovery in New York City*, edited by John Mollenkopf, 140–162. New York: Russell Sage, 2005.

——. "Memory/Monument." In *Critical Terms for Art History*, edited by Robert S. Nelson and Richard Schiff, 234–247. Chicago: University of Chicago Press, 2003.

Young, Marilyn B. "Ground Zero: Enduring War." In *September 11 in History: A Watershed Moment?*, edited by Mary L. Dudziak, 10–34. Durham, NC: Duke University Press, 2003.

Zelizer, Barbie. *About to Die: How Images Move the Public*. New York: Oxford University Press, 2010.

——. "Photography, Journalism, and Trauma." In *Journalism after September 11*, edited by Barbie Zelizer and Stuart Allan, 46–68. London: Routledge, 2002.

Žižek, Slavoj. "Censorship Today: Violence, or Ecology as a New Opium for the Masses." 2007. http://www.lacan.com/zizecology1.htm.

——. "On 9/11, New Yorkers Faced the Fire in the Minds of Men." *Guardian*, September 10, 2006.

——. "Reflections on wtc." October 7, 2001. http://www.lacan.com/reflections.htm.

——. *The Sublime Object of Ideology*. London: Verso, 1989.

——. *Welcome to the Desert of the Real*. London: Verso, 2002.

Zurier, Rebecca. "Classy Comics." *Art Journal* 50, no. 3 (1991): 98–103.

Index

THOMAS STUBBLEFIELD is Assistant Professor of Art History at the University of Massachusetts, Dartmouth. His research forges connections between the fields of film and media studies, art history, and critical theory so as to open larger fields of contemporary visual culture to analysis. Recent projects focus on the visual culture of disaster, cultural memory, theory of photography, social media as immaterial labor, and the artistic possibilities of censorship. His work has been featured in numerous academic journals (*Future Anterior, Afterimage,* and the *Canadian Journal of Film Studies*) and anthologies (*Blast, Corrupt, Dismantle, Erase: Contemporary North American Dystopian Literature* and *Theorizing Visual Studies: Writing through the Discipline*).